LIVING BY THE CODE

{

LIVING

BY

THE

CODE

}

**REFLECT, REFACTOR & REFRESH:
TOP DEVELOPERS, LEADERS & INNOVATORS
IN TECH SHARE THE CAREER ADVICE THEY
WISH THEY'D HAD WHEN THEY STARTED**

BY ENRIQUE LÓPEZ MAÑAS

CONTENTS

FOREWORD

Dan Kim
Basecamp

A career in tech is filled with tremendous promise and potential. There are opportunities abound all over the world, in every industry, for every interest. The possibilities of where your choices can lead you are endless, exciting, and insanely intimidating!

If you've ever found yourself wondering if you're on the "right" path, I can assure you that you're not alone. And it's not just a handful of us who've thought the same thing—every single one of us has pondered these important questions, none of which have easy answers.

"What does my career path look like? Where am I going to be in one, five, or even ten years?"

"Is management the right direction for me? If so, how do I develop those new skills? If not, how do I continue to improve as a developer and leader?"

"Why is being part of my developer community important? How can I get involved?"

I can relate because I've lived with that uncertainty, too. I've been in the industry for 20 years, and I had no idea what I was doing when I was starting out. Even today, while I'm more confident in my direction and choices than I have ever been, I'm under no illusion that I have it completely figured out.

That journey from constant doubt to relative confidence takes time and can be a difficult path—one that's made easier by a chorus of wonderful colleagues, friends, and mentors.

Through the course of a career, many people will lift you up, point you in the right direction, and course correct you when you need it.

Cherish these folks.

And while there's no doubt these personal connections will be your deepest, most valuable resources, it takes a bunch of time and energy to develop them. It can take many years, many jobs, and many life experiences to build relationships with the people who will serve as your guiding lights.

Surely there must be a way to learn from a broad base of successful folks more quickly?

There is, and you've found it! Enrique has pulled together a wonderful collection of experiences from a diverse group of people within our industry. He asks unique, personalized questions to each individual, helping us to understand how they got to where they are today—their philosophies on life and work, the resources that help them move forward, and the tactics they apply to be successful. If you've ever wondered how people have handled their fear of public speaking, starting a business, losing a job, work life balance, tough career transitions, toxic work environments, or remote work, you've come to the right place.

What makes these stories truly valuable is that these people are your peers. They are business owners, developer advocates, conference speakers, freelancers, managers, and developers of all levels, just like you. They aren't living in ivory towers, expounding generic self-help advice. I know many of the people in this book, and they're as real as it gets. No glamorized stories. No overnight successes. Just real stories of regular people making their way, building careers, and landing on their feet. I know these stories can help you because many of them have already helped me.

There's really only one guarantee about your career in tech, and it's this: It's going to be full of twists and turns. I never could have guessed that I would end up where I am today. You can't predict or fully control where you'll end up, but you can start laying the foundation for where you want to go.

The diverse experiences of everyone in this book will help you do that.

My advice: Read through all the stories once and make note of the passages that mean the most to you. Consider them and begin integrating these ideas into your life and work. Then come back after a bit and evaluate. What's changed? What worked? What didn't?

Wherever you land, remember that the landscape is constantly shifting. So don't fret. Rather, embrace where you're at. Make adjustments that feel right to you. Keep writing your story. Share what you've learned. Mentor and lift up others. And most of all, keep your head up and take time to appreciate the good stuff.

Good luck on your journey. It's sure going to be challenging, but more than anything, it's going to be a ton of fun!

Dan Kim
🐦@dankim

PROLOGUE

Enrique López Mañas

A few years ago, a copy of *Tools of Titans* by Tim Ferriss fell into my hands. I devoured it. It was different from the books that I usually read; it was neither narrative, nor fiction, nor an essay. Tim had interviewed several reputed folks from different fields, such as the literature, sports, or the film industry. The common denominator among all of them is that they were role models in their fields. They all had a story to contribute about their routines, beliefs or success stories.

When I finished the book (a book that you can get value from reading every few months) I thought: "I would love to have a similar manuscript interviewing people in tech." After making a living developing software professionally for around 12 years, there were a few things I was still struggling to understand—things that were not clearly available to me.

How can we make our daily routine as productive as possible? What do the daily routines of the titans of the tech industry look like?

How does a permanent job compare with contracting? How do we switch from one paradigm to the other? What are the advantages and disadvantages?

How can the transition between technical and management positions be done? Do we strictly need to become managers to make our career progress?

What is good leadership? How can one achieve those traits?

How can we work remotely effectively? Are companies willing to accept this? What do they expect?

It is not easy to get a unique answer to those topics. There might be multiple answers. There is no formal education about it; you need to try by yourself, sometimes fail, and take your lesson. The problem is that we only have a limited number of decades in our professional career. So, in order to be successful, we need to observe what others are doing. We need mentorship. We need to hear the opinions of others that have walked that path.

This project aims to connect all those dots. I have personally failed many times trying to get those answers until I reached a professional status I felt comfortable with. Although the process of learning never ends; there is always the next step you want to reach.

In this book, I wanted to explore a set of core principles that were immutable for developers. Aspects we could research today, and that would still be valid in a few years. That was the motivation behind *Living by the Code*.

I ran this idea among some peers. I probed a few colleagues, asking them their thoughts and feelings about this. The enthusiasm grew slowly but steadily when most of the comments about it were positive. And this project finally kicked off.

I feel extremely proud to have convinced a few of the role models I have to be a part of *Living by the Code*. You will find some of them discussing technical interviews. You will find others discussing soft skills, academia, career or different work paradigms. You might find some of your answers to remote work. Each contribution to the book is brilliant on its own. I wished I could have had this book when I started my career in tech, more than a decade ago.

Our main wish and objective with this book is to deliver value to you, dear reader. We hope this will be a book that you might review from time to time, trying to disentangle some of the questions you have had in your career. If, as a result, your life improves and you're able to be more effective and successful in your job and life, we will have achieved our goal.

ABOUT THE AUTHOR

Enrique López Mañas is a software engineer, mostly focused on Android and backend development with Java/Kotlin. As a contractor, he has filled his hours with an eclectic variety of technologies: TensorFlow, iOS, Swift, NodeJS, RoR, and Python. Before *Living by the Code*, he published the books *Android High Performance*, *100 Android Questions and Answers*, and *100 iOS Questions and Answers*. He has been a member of the Google Developer Expert crew since 2014.

Besides his programming duties, he also runs a few side projects. He is the editor and maintainer of *Kotlin Weekly*, a mailing list that delivers news about the Kotlin universe every Sunday. He is the organizer of Kotlin Users Meetup Group Munich and Droidcon Vietnam. He speaks monthly on the *I/O Investing* podcast about finances and investing.

In his free time, he reads, writes, and runs long distances for extended periods of time. Over time, he has developed an interest in finances, communities, science fiction, and high-performance sports. He tries to practice transparency, and shares as much as he can on his Twitter account (@eenriquelopez).

COMMUNITY

" *I wish someone had told me: You belong here. You'll never have all the answers. Feeling like an imposter is normal and there are many others out there like you who feel the same way. Find them.* **"**

—Sarah Olson

BRITT BARAK

" *Balance vision and execution.* "

🐦 @BrittBarak

Britt is currently a Product Manager at Facebook. In the past, she led the mobile engineering teams of various startup companies in Israel, the "Startup Nation." Britt is a Google Developer Expert, a worldwide public speaker, who is passionate about developers and startup communities, and diversity in tech.

" *The ability to move between the big picture and the details, between vision and execution, between ideal to pragmatic is a great skill for leaders.* "

What is your definition of a good leader?

A good leader demonstrates empathy and humility and finds a balance between vision and execution.

A leader is a visionary who can transform a vision into a plan. A good leader can create a plan that's bigger than what they can do alone, leaving gaps for others to play a role, without dictating. Leading means facilitating the growth of others, toward a shared goal. You have to choose your battles to do that.

You must be able to listen to the team that you're leading, as well as the team that manages you, and then build the intermediate layer. You have to see the bigger picture and the details simultaneously. The details help you understand the bigger picture and help you find the balance between theory and reality.

For example, when I was focusing on mobile development, I also thought about the business and the product to better prioritize my work. I learned about the server and architecture to understand the best options for the client that I was responsible for. Since I became a manager or a leader, the proportion of my focus shifted. Now I focus more on the bigger picture but make sure to be hands-on enough to be able to dive into the details when I need them.

The ability to move between the big picture and the details, between vision and execution, between ideal to pragmatic is a great skill for leaders. As you evolve, I believe that you still need both ends.

The biggest change is in the proportions of how much focus you spend on each.

How would you recommend a fellow software engineer transition from Software Engineering to Developer Relations? What are the relevant skills in each field?

Developer Relations, or Developer Experience, which is my focus, is an intersection of many different roles. At least for me, I experience my day-to-day as somewhere between engineering, user experience, product management, support, marketing, community management, and entrepreneurship. And if that's not enough, you need great people skills! At the heart of it, though, is being a great developer. You have to deeply understand the work process, the way of thinking, and developers' preferences. The other skills are wrappers on top of your engineering heart.

If being an advocate is something that you want to do, I believe that in one way or another, you'll find yourself drawn into it. You'll find yourself conference speaking, blog writing, building libraries, contributing to open source, or otherwise involved in the community. After contributing for a while and enjoying it, many engineers are tempted to get into advocacy despite having little development experience.

My recommendation is to acquire a strong foundation as a developer before taking an advocacy role. All your experiences will reflect in a DevX or DevRel position. There's endless room for improvement and evolution. However, your perspective shifts when you move from being a developer to thinking about developers and representing them within your company. You'll be writing smaller educational code rather than a core, complex system. Often this kind of role limits the growth you can achieve as a developer. I'd highly recommend obtaining a strong technical and engineering base, before stepping to the other side as an advocate.

While you're a developer, try stepping into DevRel tasks before you leap. Explore which types of tasks you enjoy more than others, and work on improving your skills. It will also be helpful for you to start getting involved in the community and start building your professional network. DevRel work is often individual by nature, making its activities harder to learn. The set of tools and skills you bring to the role is essential, as well as your network and having professionals to advise with.

I'd suggest starting as a developer who's doing DevRel activities, and when you're ready, flip the ratio and become an advocate who does development activities.

Describe your work-life balance. How do you stay productive?

It took me time to realize that the secret to productivity is to take a break when you need it. I used to fight with myself to soldier through things. But we're human beings, and we have physical limitations.

For an instant refresh, I take a walk or do a handstand—if you need a boost of energy, a handstand, even against the wall, is magical! It gives you an adrenaline boost and increases circulation. If you do that with friends at the office, smiles are guaranteed.

The idea is to have healthy habits in general so that you can be more productive as a routine. Doing enough things that you love and that make you happy are essential as a base for everything. The entire package of your well-being, as a pattern, will yield positive results over time.

I'm a yoga enthusiast, and I mean yoga as a lifestyle, not just a physical workout. It teaches you many things about life. For example, in yoga, you practice being aware of the resources, either physical or mental, you put into something. Then, you practice relaxing unnecessary effort. It's a more subtle aspect of being focused.

Many times I've found myself diving into a task that I didn't anticipate will take that long, or trying to over-perfect my work, or taking too many commitments, or being overly concerned about one thing while doing another. The return on investment for these tasks might not be worth it. Yoga is one tool that has helped me learn to be aware of demands on my resources, to direct them consciously.

In terms of time management, I strictly keep an elaborated updated calendar. I block time for all of my personal and professional tasks. Even exercising, meeting friends, preparing for meetings, thinking, anything gets a slot. It helps with having a more concrete sense of time, focusing on what I should do when, and balancing personal and professional events.

What are the three tools you cannot live without as a developer?

First, the online, worldwide Android community. It has been life-changing for me in many senses. I'm not even sure I would love being an engineer as much without that amazing community, culture, and support. Second, Android Studio, our beloved IDE. It's not perfect but makes programming much more enjoyable compared to other IDEs. There is a handful of the more obvious things, too, like Google search, Stack Overflow, crash reporting, and YouTube.

Which three books have had a lasting impact on how you do your work?

I love reading, although I haven't done it enough in recent years. Three books that have been impactful on my life and therefore on my work are *The Power of Now* by Eckhart Tolle, *Wishes Fulfilled* by Dr. Wayne W. Dyer, and *Conversations with God* by Neale Donald Walsch. I write this in my head to see all the people who expected a more technical answer and are raising an eyebrow. In the context and timing with which they came into my life, they opened the door to transforming my life. Work is just one aspect of life. Having a healthy, happy and mindful life and soul will reflect in any other aspect of your life, including work.

What resources do you rely on to keep yourself current in your industry?

I got into tech communities to keep my knowledge current while making new friends and creating a professional support network. Not long after the first meetup I attended, I joined to lead the Android community in Israel and later started a Women Techmakers community. Now, I'm fortunate enough to speak around the world, to be a part of Google Developer Experts, and the worldwide wonderful Android community. Most of how I stay current comes from there and from conferences, listening to other people's talks, and conversations we're having. I pick up interesting topics and read about them and learn and explore more. Now I'm lucky to have many connections to people in the community and to the devs who are working on features and libraries, so I have enough people to ask questions if I have any.

What is something you wish someone had told you back when you started software development, that you had to learn the hard way instead?

Some things we have to learn the hard way, or rather, we have to learn them by experience. Even if someone had told me what I wish I'd known, it wouldn't be helpful. One of the challenges I've been facing is that you can't know everything, and you can't keep up with everything constantly. The world of technology and development is faster and broader than you can grasp at a time, and that's perfectly fine.

What negative trends do you see on the rise in our industry?

Once in a while, there's a new architecture that becomes trendy, and everyone's talking about it and thinking about using it to rewrite an existing project. A recent example is the single Activity navigation in Android, with multiple fragments. Once in a while, there's a recurring effort to advocate for using that pattern. There are many different reasons it's not always the right solution. Often Google listens to community trends like supporting Kotlin. However, this is an example where it's the other way around. There's an attempt to advocate for this particular trend because it was the initial idea, but the community has been voting differently. The way trends find a foothold in the industry is an interesting process.

An alternative would be to use whichever architecture makes sense to the team. Rewriting is often more painful than expected. Think hard before breaking things that work. Good architecture is very important! You should plan it with an eye toward the future. However, don't overcomplicate things for the sake of an idea or a trend.

What do you think is one core concept that most software developers don't pay enough attention to when growing their careers?

I can only share my specific experience. I'm from Tel Aviv, where we have a thriving startup-dominant ecosystem. In that industry, the teams are small, the resources are relatively sparse, the pace is very fast, the focus is more on innovation in a volatile atmosphere. Many devs who grow up in that environment are mostly self-taught and are educated to be confident and run fast. That's great in many senses, but sometimes the price of confidence is a lack of humility. I've often felt that the startup culture seems to cultivate this lack of humility in some way. I don't criticize it, I understand its relative benefits. However, it's also important to learn from others and to listen. When you move to bigger companies and face bigger systems and projects, you suddenly understand that there are different rules and motivations.

I think it goes both ways. There are many things that devs in big companies can learn from an experience in a small startup. It's incredibly beneficial for a dev to experience and learn from both worlds and build a more complete picture for themselves.

The importance of continued learning and a commitment to good interpersonal communication skills is emerging as a theme here. How can a developer implementing these principles move up the leadership ladder?

First, decide that you want it. Some people think they are interested in leading only because it sounds good to them. This is never a good reason to do anything, except for maybe music.

Then, start practicing being a leader in your daily tasks. Later, initiate a small project. It could be a partnership with someone from the company or another team. Most importantly, I believe, is to be present. More than anything, be there, listen, observe, and experience. After a while, the stakeholders expect your presence, and they've experienced you as a daily leader, it will be natural to move you into a leadership role. If you listen and observe and experience enough, your perspective, skills, and experiences will be richer and will help you be a better leader.

BRITT'S RECOMMENDATIONS

The Power of Now: A Guide to Spiritual Enlightenment |
Eckhart Tolle

Wishes Fulfilled: Mastering the Art of Manifesting |
Dr. Wayne W. Dyer

Conversations with God: An Uncommon Dialogue |
Neale Donald Walsch

ELLEN SHAPIRO

" *Work with other people and build something cool.* "

𝕏 @DesignatedNerd   designatednerd.com

E llen is a mobile developer who has been building iOS and Android apps since 2010. She worked for years in Chicago, where she eventually became Director of iOS Development for a small agency called Vokal, then Lead Mobile Developer for the parking app SpotHero. She moved to the Netherlands in 2017 and joined Bakken & Bæck's Amsterdam office. She's recently joined Apollo GraphQL to work on their iOS SDK, and now lives in Madison, WI.

You are one of those individuals who are extremely talented in both iOS and Android mobile platforms. What's your secret, and how do you stay at the top of both development communities?

Part of my secret is that I started learning both around the same time, with the idea that I'd specialize in one when I felt like it—and that sort of happened. I've always been fascinated by the two different approaches to what is essentially the same problem. Here is a device, for example, that fits in your palm. It's got a somewhat weaker processor than a normal computer. It's definitely got less RAM, and it's got a terrible battery. How do you take all of that and make an experience for users that's good, consistent and interesting? And iOS and Android have long had different approaches to that problem. I find it interesting to see, both from a developer-tools standpoint and from a UX and hardware standpoint, how each platform approaches it.

I'm better at iOS than at Android. You might try to stay completely up on both, but there are only 24 hours in a day, so you tend to have more expertise in one area or the other. But I try to cultivate working with Android teams and then also continuing to follow Android news and Android development trends because I do feel like I learn a lot from how both platforms attack the same problem.

It's definitely something that I feel like I accidentally stumbled into. But it's something that I do feel like I keep purposefully continuing with because I think it is something that has provided me some valuable insights over the years.

You're the founder of your own company, Designated Nerd Software. What's the focus of your company, and what motivated you to start it?

At this point, Designated Nerd Software is mostly the umbrella name for all the random stuff that I do. I actually get paid by Apollo GraphQL at this point. When I first started Designated Nerd, it was called Designated Nerd Technical Support. I used to work in television production, and I always joke that I'm in technology because I knew how to set up a Mac with a networked printer in 2003—because I knew how to do that, people kept asking me more and more complicated questions, and I got better and better at Googling the answers.

There came a point at which I was working at a couple of different television shows; when you're a peon at these TV shows, you always have more time than money, but there's a fairly large number of people who have more money than time. If people needed their home network set up, I would go to their homes and set it up or help them troubleshoot their computers—and I got paid for it. That was the birth of Designated Nerd Technical Support. Then, once I actually learned how to develop, I turned it into Designated Nerd Software and Technical Support. That was how I put out my first few apps when I first started programming. Then, over the years, I dropped the technical support side because I don't have time to go to people's houses and set up their routers anymore.

Then you started developing apps for other clients?

When I first started developing apps, it was mostly trying to build a portfolio. I wanted to have something to show, primarily because I didn't have a computer science degree. I had a certificate in application development from UCLA Extension. I wanted to try to be taken at least somewhat seriously, so I started building apps. Then, I tried to make things better app over app, trying to show that I could grow an idea over time—roughly at the end of 2011 when I finally got a job.

I knew I was not the world's best developer, particularly when I got hired. I got thrown into the deep end on my first job, but I don't think anything that I've ever worked on for software on my own has ever even threatened to pay the bills, so I've always had more traditional jobs. That's actually been really useful for me because I spent most of my career working at agencies or consultancies.

But, essentially, I get contacted by a company that I work with and they say, "Hey, we want you to build a thing." And I build it. So I wind up working with all kinds of different industries, solving all kinds of different problems, working with technologies that maybe I haven't worked with before. It is something that was helpful, particularly at the beginning of my career, because it gave me a lot of chances to work—and to try and fail and try again in an environment wherein I had people who were there to help; they were there to be able to answer questions that, normally, I would have been going to Stack Overflow over. And that was hugely helpful for me; it's a big piece of why I like working on teams.

Mentoring, can it help you leom stuff
→ by passing knowledge on?

66 *The best way to learn is to teach. The way that you walk through the knowledge is by watching somebody else do something, then you try something yourself, and then you show other people how to do it.* 99

In addition to doing this, your developing career, you work full-time as a speaker and creator of educational content for developers. What have you learned from working on all of these diverse projects?

How to operate on very little sleep. No, that's a bit of a joke. But I think it's all tied together. One of the things that I've learned from preparing for talks is that, the more that you dive into any subject, you realize how much deeper that subject is than you thought it was when you first decided to dive into it. You start to see a lot of the nuance that you might miss trying to work with it just once.

When I was at my first job, the thirteen-ish-year-old son of a guy I used to work with was interested in doing iOS development, and I wound up tutoring him remotely over Skype. One of the things that I thought was interesting was that I realized that, in order to explain a concept to someone else, I had to understand it way better than I felt like I already did. Even trying to explain something like delegation, when I first started doing that tutoring, was an eye-opener. It's a critical, core principle of iOS development—especially at that time because this was in 2013. In 2013, if you couldn't explain delegation, you were going to have a hard time explaining a lot of other stuff. I found it to be interesting how mentoring is not just beneficial to the mentee but to the person who's mentoring, forcing them to understand something before they try to explain it to other people.

The best way to learn is to teach. The way that you walk through the knowledge is by watching somebody else do something, then you try something yourself, and then you show other people how to do it. That's obviously a fairly long process going from one end to the other, but I think it is a useful way of learning in a way that sticks.

What is your daily motivation and inspiration to work on software engineering?

Being able to work on a team is the most important thing for me. I enjoy working with other people and building something cool. I have always been someone who enjoys making things—I was a songwriter when I was younger; I went to film school; I worked in TV for a long time. One of the biggest things that I enjoy about doing iOS and Android development is the opportunity to create something from nothing. Being able to work on a team of developers and designers, and other people who are involved in trying to make something awesome that works for a lot of people is super fun. It's something that keeps me going, even when I'm working on something that makes me want to throw my computer out the window.

In setting yourself up for success, how do you start your day off with a bang? Do you have any secret morning routines that set you up for success?

Oh, god, no. My morning routine is such a mess. Particularly when I was at Bakken & Bæck working in Amsterdam three days a week, which is about an hour-and-a-half train ride from where I live. If I was working in Amsterdam, my mornings were usually spent desperately attempting to get to the train. Then, if I wasn't working in Amsterdam, I was usually arguing with myself about when to get up. I am so not a morning person in any way, shape, or form. Early on, when I had finished the schoolwork that I had done, and before I was working a job, I basically wound up working from 8:00 in the evening until 4:00 AM, sleeping from 4:00 in the morning until noon, and then going out during normal human hours from noon to 8:00 PM.

I have a weird internal clock, and so I think one thing that is very helpful for me in terms of getting started in the morning is having a routine. It's one of the things that's been hard about having something that I'm not doing five days a week; I have a routine for the days that I'm scrambling to get out the door, but I don't have quite as much of a routine for days I'm working from home. If you're not a morning person, having a routine is really helpful because you can sort of zombie your way through that and get to the point where you're like, "Okay. I made it to my desk. I have whatever caffeinated beverage will actually get my brain working right now." And then you can proceed from there.

There is no single recipe for success. It seems that it's very up to the individual.

I've certainly found that to be the case. I think any work-structure that tries to overly enforce schedules—everybody has to be here from this time to this time—winds up being so counterproductive because you're not accounting for the things that some people are better at or some people prefer. For example, Bakken & Bæck, where I used to work, has offices in Amsterdam, and headquarters are in Oslo. There's also an office in Bonn. But the Oslo office has this reputation that everybody is at their desks by 8:00 AM, and everybody is gone by 4:00. And the Amsterdam office is like, "Oh yeah. If the whole office is actually there before 10:00 AM, there must have been a meeting." And people there work later. For a strict schedule, for people that are better workers early in the morning, that's great. For people who aren't, that sounds like torture. Allowing people to have the schedule that allows them to be the most productive is best. You need core hours when you can have meetings and do business, but allowing people to set their own schedules makes everybody a lot happier and a lot more productive.

What else would you recommend to an aspiring developer who is starting their career? Which first steps should this individual take in order to have a successful career as a software developer?

One of the things that I feel like a lot of people experience, including me when I first started learning development, was feeling like there was a point at which I would learn everything. That's not possible. One of the things to remember is that, particularly as these platforms grow and evolve, things are going to change a lot. The thing that's much more useful in the long term than learning any particular API or particular way to do things is learning how to learn new stuff. There are always going to be new tools and techniques to try. There are always going to be people saying, "This is the one true way to do things," and then other people saying, "No it's not. This is the one true way to do things." Being able to look at those claims dispassionately and figure out what actually works for you is the bigger thing to focus on in terms of learning.

I'm a hyper-competitive grade grubber, which helped me early on. I was always good at school, and I was one of those obnoxious kids who'd said, "Yeah. I got an A in everything," and then, "Oh, my god. I got a B+. I'm gonna die now." So I had this paralyzing fear of failure. When I first started developing, it was hard if something didn't work when I first tried it; it felt like a failure. I had to sit back and realize—and it took me a long time to do this—that if something doesn't work, it's trying to tell me something through the way in which it doesn't work. Either I have a compiler error, or I have a crash, or something doesn't show up on the screen. Why didn't I get the result that I wanted?

People joke about debugging being like trying to solve a murder mystery in which you are the murderer. I started slowing down, just throwing stuff at the wall to see what worked, and asking myself, "Why didn't that work?" I was able to come to an answer. That kind of thing also helps you the next time you come back.

If you try to do something, and, the first time you try to do it, it takes 100 tries to get it right, the next time you go back, it'll take you maybe 25 tries to get it right. All of that time that you spent having it not work was actually useful because you basically know what not to do the next time. Over time, as you continue to build more and more, you learn patterns, you learn what to look for over time, and you start to see why things aren't working the way that you think they should. And that's a big thing in terms of being able to hunt down a problem, learn new things, and try to figure it out.

Are there any trendsetters or leaders that have been helpful for you through your career—people that you follow and like to learn from?

Peter Steinberger is one. I first heard of him when I was trying to work on something that involved a bunch of weird nonsense with PDFs. He's the guy behind PSPDFKit. He is someone who, even when his company was basically just him and a couple of other people, has been doing tons of programming for years. He's able to find all kinds of crazy bugs and workarounds in PDFs. One of the things that I enjoy about him is that he gets just as exasperated as everybody else, and I think, particularly as a younger developer, there were often times when I would feel dumb because I couldn't get something to work. Then I would see more advanced developers like him also couldn't get it to work, and it was a lot more comforting. Having someone like Peter at a community level, who is able to work through some of the more difficult problems and who is a leader in reporting those problems to Apple, has been helpful in that.

In terms of other leaders, I often also wind up following my peers, the people that are working on similar things that I do or people whose talks I found interesting. Finding other people who you feel provide helpful advice or commiseration is helpful.

What are the traits of a good leader from your point of view?

Who is a good leader often comes down to what they are trying to lead. Are you trying to lead a small development team? Are you trying to lead a huge development team? Are you trying to lead an entire company? A good leader of a small development team means being able to personally interact with the people on your team and understand what they are trying to accomplish, what is hard for them, and how you can help them work around those issues. That's a great trait for the leader of a small team. But when you get to a certain size of team, you can't have the CEO worrying about what every single person does because then they don't have time to actually deal with the consequences of everything that's happening in a company of that size.

A lot of people don't necessarily realize that leading increasingly large groups of people leads to completely different challenges. Some people recognize this and do a great job of trying to prepare themselves for the new levels, but then there are some people who think, "I want to lead a bunch of people because that's the obvious next step in my career," without thinking about the challenges. Leadership isn't only being in charge of people. It's figuring out how best to support them, not just given what those people are doing, but given what you're doing, given what your actual job is.

Is there something you wish that someone had told you when you started in software development that you had to learn the hard way?

When I first started, testing on iOS was not really a thing. We would find out something was wrong, and it was several months later after the app went through QA that I'd have to figure out what I was working on three months ago – what was I even trying to do? I wish I had understood that tests take more time up front, but they save you so much more time both in debugging later on, and they ensure that the app actually does what you want it to do.

Testing also helps whoever comes and looks at the app next because they know what the previous developer expected it to do, especially if there's an app in which you don't have a lot of documentation about what it's supposed to do. Having tests is helpful in terms of being able to figure it out. Testing is never going to have you shipping bug-free software, but at least you can understand what it's supposed to be doing when it's working right and potentially some of the cases in which it could go wrong. The emphasis on testing has shifted pretty dramatically over the last few years. We see what a huge difference it makes in terms of the quality of the product that you're making and your ability to make changes without screwing everything up.

In drawing insight from other sources, what do you read or listen to?

One podcast that I have enjoyed for the last twelve years is a podcast called Planet Money from NPR. I don't have any background in economics, but it basically looks at how economics and money shape the world that we live in. It started as a sort of a response to some of the financial crisis in 2007 and 2008, trying to explain what was going on. But over the last few years, it's been something that's evolved to explain how hidden economics affect things or your own life in ways you might not expect.

Particularly for software developers, we always have to be on the lookout for these confounding factors. When people say, "Okay.

I want to do this and that and the other thing." But have you considered this aspect that is also affecting all these things that you're doing? I think it's a useful podcast to show that you have to look deeper where you aren't necessarily expecting to find something. You have to think about the things you aren't taking into account.

ELLEN'S RECOMMENDATION

Planet Money podcast | National Public Radio (NPR)

ANTONIO LEIVA

❝ *Try to do what you think you can't.* ❞

🐦 @lime_cl ▶️ /c/antoniolg28 📷 antonioleivag contact@antonioleiva.com

Antonio has been working as a software developer for more than 10 years. A few years ago, he specialized in Android development and he currently helps other Android developers boost their careers as a freelance Kotlin and Android trainer. He's the writer of the book *Kotlin for Android Developers*, and is also a trainer, speaker and mentor. He is also currently a Kotlin Trainer Certified by JetBrains.

A few years ago, you started working on your book *Kotlin for Android Developers* when Kotlin was not yet well-known. Kotlin has since been announced as a first-class language for Android development. How did you know all those years ago that Kotlin would be so important?

I didn't, but I think I just felt the same frustration other Android developers had at that point, working with an ancient language. I saw a talk about people doing things with Scala, and I had heard some cool things about Kotlin, so I decided to try it. It was so fascinating that I decided I had to tell the world about it. If you suspect you are at the forefront of a new trend or industry innovation, talk about it in the best way you can: articles, talks, books, or even online courses. It will never be a waste of time as you'll get a lot of skills in the process. Then, if it finally takes off, you'll be very well positioned.

You recently quit your work at Plex and started working full-time on your own projects. What led you to make that decision?

I had a great time working at Plex, and the work-life balance was pretty good because it's a remote company. But I also had my projects, and, after our baby was born, my time was dramatically reduced. So I had to make a decision: keep working for a company and forget about my projects, or run my own business. I decided to do the second for two main reasons. First, I've put a lot of effort into my projects for the last few years, and I couldn't just throw everything away. Second, because working for myself would provide me with even more flexibility, and since my top priority is my family, flexibility is important to me.

But one question I usually ask myself in these situations is, "What would my future self regret most not having done?" And that was clear to me. I've always had in my mind the idea of running my own business, and I would regret not having tried. I can always get back to work for a company, but I could not be in the same position to build a profitable project ever again.

How does working on your own projects compare to guaranteed employment?

Well, the uncertainty is probably the biggest challenge. You don't know the amount of money that you're getting at the end of the month; that can be pretty scary, especially if you don't have a financial cushion, which I always recommend doing if you can. But, on the other hand, growth has no limits. If you're working for a company, you know there's determined salary limits that are pretty difficult to overcome. If you run a business, that issue doesn't exist.

If you are working for yourself, you can also balance your work and life as you want. If you do it wrong, you'll end up working more than in a regular company for less money. If you learn to delegate, your company could ideally continue working without you. I always try to keep that in mind: I'm building up a business, not a self-employed job.

A common fear of many indie developers, or people working on their own, seems to be the fear of not earning enough income. How do you manage to have enough projects on your plate to ensure a decent living?

This is still something I haven't accomplished entirely, but there are some rules that I try to apply in my projects. There's something called a "sales funnel" that can lead your followers from simple readers to customers, and from cheap products to high-priced services. The trick is to have one product or two at the beginning of the funnel that many people can get at a low cost. Then, based on your historical sales, you can predict how much income you'll have for the following month. Then you know you can count on that to pay your regular expenses and your collaborators if you have them. The trick is to find automated ways to sell these products so that you can spend more time in the premium products and services, which will bring you a significant income. These are more difficult to find—and you may find some months in which you have nothing—but are the most profitable.

You have been producing a lot of work on your own—mentorship courses for developers, instructional courses, as well as self-publishing a book through different platforms. What led you to self-produce this content, instead of relying on a third-party company, such as a publisher?

If I had produced the same work, but by using publishers, I couldn't be living off of it now. Publishers are usually, though not always, a good amplifier of your work. But you'll often get a very minimal income for your work. If your only plan is to use the content that you create as branding to earn a reputation, a publisher can help. But if you want to make it profitable, then you need to go on your own. The journey is long because you need to be positioned somehow in your field so that people trust you and get your products. But, once it's done, it's much more worthwhile.

What are the most important tools or resources for someone interested in self-publishing or self-producing? Any that you'd wish you'd had for your own work?

The first thing is a blog—a place where people can reach and read your free stuff. WordPress is the most flexible and extensive solution for this, so I wouldn't reinvent the wheel. Then, you need a community, and email marketing is what continues to work. This means giving something for free to someone to get their email in exchange. Once you have that, you can keep giving them free content and start making some sales from time to time.

To start selling, the simplest option is to use a cart solution like SendOwl, which allows you to sell and serve the content files of your digital product. For books, this is more than enough. For online courses, I'd look for a sound learning management system. You can do this on WordPress, too, or use software as a solution (SaaS). Both have their pros and cons to discover.

To write the book, using Leanpub helped me a lot, not just as a sales platform—I sell the book in many other places—but also for the book editing. With them, you need to write the book in markdown, and, with a few settings, Leanpub creates the book for you. This translates to tons of hours saved. Then you can export it for printing, and use print-on-demand resources like Amazon's Kindle Direct Publishing, or KDP, to sell printed books. This is by far the cheapest and easiest way to sell physical books.

In general, that's it. I use several other tools for business logistics, invoicing, etc. But that will come later when you start generating some income.

Are there any instances in which you think self-producing would not be the best option for someone in your position?

For the book specifically, if you find a good publisher that can deliver your book to all major shops and make it reach many potential customers, it can really help. You won't get as much income from the book as self-producing, but your reputation can help sell other products or services. There are other things to consider, too.

You are a non-native English speaker who writes books in English. There are many developers like you who are shy to start developing publicly, writing or teaching. What advice would you give them? How can they overcome their linguistic fears and improve?

That is my major fear. I've struggled a lot to learn to live with it. My only suggestion is to try to do what you think you can't do and see what happens. I've been rejected in some places because of the language barrier. I've had some bad reviews of my book because of it. I've had several uncomfortable moments when talking to native-English speakers, but these have been very few examples when compared to the gratitude received for doing all that I've done and for helping them achieve their goals. I keep working hard to improve my English and to push my limits forward. For instance, now I'm starting to interview other Android developers in English, and I'm creating a powerful teaching program that requires a lot of my own interaction; I know my English won't be perfect, but if it can help other people, it'll be good enough.

Working on your own projects, how do you start your day off with a bang? Do you have any secret morning routines that set you up for success?

I'm terrible with routines. I've tried many different things, but I haven't found any routines that make me feel more productive or successful. I try to sleep enough—around seven hours—and have everything well-planned so that I don't have to think once I sit in the chair.

How do you stay highly productive for long stretches of time?

For me, proper planning makes it all. I have a big picture of the whole current quarter, what goals I want to achieve, and a way to measure them to let me know whether I succeeded or not. These goals are more of a personal challenge rather than an inflexible rule, because things happen. I like to have room for improvisation. I organize all these quarterly projects in a tool called Plutio—though there are several similar ones—and divide each project into smaller tasks. Those tasks are usually no longer than a few hours, up to one or two days.

Then, by using a productivity tool called time blocking, I block some time for those tasks in Google Calendar, and leave some free space for possible unexpected tasks, and also for some recurring tasks like checking emails, social networks, monthly accounting tasks, etc. Once I have my week organized, I need to check the calendar in the morning and start doing. This is, by far, what makes me productive, reduce stress, and lets me be realistic about the goals that I want to achieve.

What resources have helped you? What are three resources that have had a lasting impact on your work?

The most impactful books in my career are not related at all to the career itself. Based on my experience, the people who make you change your paradigms and the way you understand the world or your life are the most valuable ones.

First, *The 4-Hour Workweek* by Tim Ferriss is a classic one, I know! But thanks to this book, I realized that you don't need to follow the traditionally established path; you can shape your life however you want. After reading the book, that was the first time I started thinking about passive income, which led to my book. I also saw the possibility of running my own business, which ultimately made me leave my life as an employee and start as a freelance trainer.

I'd also recommend *The Money Code: Free, Wise and Rich* by Raimon Samsó. The book is like the Spanish version of *Rich Dad Poor Dad: What The Rich Teach Their Kids About Money—That The Poor And Middle Class Do Not!* by Robert Kiyosaki, but way better, in my opinion. Depending on the education we receive, we can have many mental blocks regarding our relationship with money, and this book helps unlock them all.

Finally, a Spanish podcast and radio show about self-improvement called Pensamiento Positivo, hosted by Sergio Fernández. It explores that the better you know yourself, the more you can impact other people with your acts and your work. I got many life-changing ideas from this podcast.

For instance, the ideas brought here helped me realize that, even by being a very shy person, I could put myself in front of an audience and say what I have to say. And this only comes when you realize that the worst thing that can happen is so insignificant in the whole progress of your life, that the outcome doesn't matter. Just do what you think is right and forget about the people that might not like it.

Or that only when you have helped yourself, you will be able to help others. But it's really important to be selfish, because it's only when you feel at peace with who you are, and only when what you're doing is aligned with your values, is when you can start doing great things and leave a footprint in the lives of others.

> 66 *The community, events, and networking are the most powerful tools to become a great developer—more than reading tons of books or working hard on your own every day.* 99

What is something else you wish someone had told you back when you started software development that you had to learn the hard way?

That the community, events, and networking are the most powerful tools to become a great developer—more than reading tons of books or working hard on your own every day: The inspiration you get from other people, those ideas that you overlooked but were necessary, those connections that open doors to new opportunities. I owe most of my success to the Android community, but it took me several years until I realized this.

What is a current community or industry trend that you think is wrong?

I think that one of the most exciting aspects of our industry is also one of the most dangerous: everything evolves very fast—too fast for a developer to stay up to date. So I see many developers worried about being left behind because they don't have time to learn this new library or that new framework. And that's dangerous because it creates a global feeling of impostor syndrome. This, together with the crazy hiring processes, makes developers feel that they are not good enough for any good positions.

What would you suggest is a better alternative to this trend?

It's not easy, but the most visible faces of the software industry in each field could help a great way by showing their limits and how they don't know everything, either.

ANTONIO'S RECOMMENDATION

"Achieving Your Childhood Dreams" lecture | Randy Pausch

LARA MARTIN

“ *Our work is not only coding.* ”

🐦 @lariki   lara.martin.carretero@gmail.com   https://laramartin.dev/

Lara is a Mobile Developer based in Berlin. Her passion for programming made her transition from her background in science to software development. She's currently working as an Android Developer and is a Google Developer Expert for Flutter and Dart. She has spoken in conferences like App Builders, DevFest Florida and Droidcon Berlin, and in many other meetups. Her dream is to make apps more accessible for everyone. When she's not attending a tech meetup, you will find her playing video games, with her dog Lily for doing arts and crafts.

You've made interesting transitions in your career. You were first a biologist; how does a biologist become a software tester?

After my studies in biology, I tried basic programming, and I found it very fun. I wanted to learn a little bit more, but I didn't know how. I enrolled in a master's degree program in biotechnology so I could use my biology knowledge, more or less, hoping that it would be my thing, but sadly, it wasn't. After earning my Master's degree, I decided to look for something else.

I found out about quality assurance, this QA role in IT, and I started working as QA online to try it out and see if it was something I could do professionally. I found that I liked it. After getting some experience in the field, I started looking for a full-time job. It took several months to find a job, but I finally got a job as a QA in a big company here in Berlin, and I ended up working with a Mobile team.

66 *I don't think it's possible to know everything. There's a tremendous amount of information we get every day because the technology is evolving so fast.* 99

That's very interesting. You went from biologist to tester and then from tester to software developer. I'm assuming maybe the second transition was probably easier, since it's there in the same domain.

I can't say it was easy, to be honest. The very same week I started working in QA, I started attending a study group in my city. We met every two weeks for four months to learn basic Android development. I spent four months learning just a tiny bit of the basics of Android to try it out. It turned out I loved it, so I kept learning for a year and a half while I was working in QA. I had a full-time job in QA, and then I spent my evenings and weekends learning Android. The transition from QA to Android development was tough because there aren't many open job positions for juniors without experience. It took some time, but I managed to switch.

You've been open about what it took to make these career moves. Imagine a person in your situation, who either wants to get a start in IT, or who's working in QA and thinking about going into development. What advice would you give them?

One thing that helped me grow as a professional was connecting to the community. I started going to local meetups, and also, I started to go to conferences and meet people from my field. I also found people like me, with similar, non-technical backgrounds, trying to get into development. We grew together.

Having these connections with the community is important at all levels. I've seen friends that were doing development professionally but without any connection to the community. The moment they started going to meetups, reading blog posts, and the like, they changed. They started to learn faster. Also, it's important to give back to the community. You can give back to the community by hosting meetups, organizing, and volunteering. You can write blog posts or give talks or lead workshops. That's something I find important.

What advice would you give to people that are already in programming if they want to strengthen their skills and become better?

Get better at communication. Communication is a hard skill to master, and it's almost 50 percent of our work. Our work is not only coding. Some ways to improve communication skills include going to trainings, reading books, and also teaching junior developers.

That's an interesting approach. The teacher is also learning, then?

Yes. I like to say that in order to master something, you have to teach it.

Let's talk about other ways to learn. What resources have helped you on your journey as a developer?

I don't usually listen to technical podcasts or read technical books because I find it difficult to focus for a long period of time. I personally engage with shorter resources, for instance, blog posts or tech talks. Summaries of books can provide the main ideas and key points. I also like the type of content where I can watch a video of a topic, pause, and then try something myself. That's how I learned Android development.

You're a Flutter GDE. Do you see Flutter as a trend for the future? What are your thoughts on this multi-platform development?

That's very difficult to say. There have been many attempts to create a good cross-platform framework, but in the end, developers have chosen to stick to native solutions. Some of these frameworks were not easy for everyone to learn. For example, I tried to learn React Native, and I found it very difficult because I don't have a background in JavaScript and React. However, I found Flutter easy to understand. I think that's one of its biggest strengths.

It looks like Flutter has a future because Google is developing Fuchsia OS, which runs native Flutter apps. Everything is pointing towards Flutter being the framework of the future and replacing Android.

What's something you wish you'd known earlier in your career?

In the beginning, I didn't understand the importance of being able to communicate with people with different backgrounds, different cultures—different everything. That's very difficult. I learned this the hard way.

Is there something or someone you can think of who has influenced your success and your career?

I cannot point to one person. I'm inspired by other women in the community. The Android community, for example, is relatively small, so we know each other, more or less, and we support each other. I especially appreciate and get inspired by successful women developers who help to push beginners. Stacy Devino and Chiu-Ki Chan inspire me. They promote beginners and elevate the work of others. They show us that what we're doing isn't a competition and that everyone is benefiting from it. I find that inspiring.

The cake can be very big and everybody can have a big piece.

Exactly. This is not a competition. We learn from each other.

What is your leadership philosophy?

As I've been growing as a developer from level zero, I find that a good leader is one who helps other people grow. For me, a good leader is one that helps their peers become better.

Is a good leader made or born that way?

I think that we all can learn to be leaders.

Are there any trends in software development that you'd like to change?

Yes. There are not enough junior positions in the industry. When I started looking for an Android development position, I could only find a few in my city for juniors, but without experience, there were almost none. This is something I still see. After two years of doing professional Android development, I still see that this is true.

For this reason, I recently created and gave a talk about the importance of hiring juniors and helping them grow. Ideally, companies won't be afraid of hiring juniors and will see the benefits of bringing juniors to their teams. Ideally, there would be open positions for juniors as well as seniors.

One of the problems in our industry seems to be the lack of developers. We need more developers, but we want them to come to a company with experience.

Exactly. There's a huge demand for developers, and there are not enough developers, but it seems like all companies want to have seniors. Companies may see junior developers as students who need a lot of training and teaching. But seniors were juniors once.

What do you think about the trend toward remote work?

I hope it's a trend that is here to stay because I like remote work. I have a job in the city where I live, but I still commute for an hour and a half every day. If I work from home, I have one hour and a half more every day to take care of my family, the house, do errands or self-care. I hope that remote work is here to stay so everyone is able to enjoy life. Not everything is work.

How do you keep yourself up to date with the latest trends?

I don't think it's possible to know everything. There's a tremendous amount of information we get every day because the technology is evolving so fast, but there are several ways to keep up. I attend conferences, watch talks, and consume a lot of information. I attend local meetups for the same reason, so I get to know what the local community likes or is doing. This way, I also connect with local people in the field.

Finally, I subscribe to newsletters, read blogs, follow development-related YouTube channels, and use Google and Twitter. I'm a heavy user of Twitter. I follow a lot of people that are creating blog posts and content. I keep up, more or less, with what people like and what people are doing.

LARA'S RECOMMENDATIONS

Women Tech Makers organization | womentechmakers.com

Women Who Code organization | womenwhocode.com

SARAH OLSON

> " *Find people who have your back.* "

🐦 @saraheolson in/saraheolson

Sarah is a Senior Engineer working on the Trello iOS and Android apps at Atlassian. She has over eighteen years of development experience in a variety of technologies, including Java, WordPress, iOS and Android development.

As a fully remote worker without a commute, do you use podcasts or books, and do you have a preference for either?

I tend to prefer books over podcasts. I'm also much more of a visual learner, so the words stick better to my eyeballs than my ears. A book that comes to mind that's had an impact on my work is the "Gang of Four"—also known as GoF—book for Java development, where I started. The full title is *Design Patterns: Elements of Reusable Object-Oriented Software*. The insights from the four authors, Erich Gamma, Richard Helm, Ralph Johnson, and John Vlissides, are still patterns I refer to to this day.

In addition to the insights from this book, what is something you wish someone had told you at the start of your software development career that you had to learn the hard way instead?

I wish someone had told me: You belong here. You'll never have all the answers. Feeling like an imposter is normal and there are many others out there like you who feel the same way. Find them.

66 *I have spent the past few years building up my network of peers who can help me with my career, and, as a person who has faced barriers and discrimination, that has made all the difference.* 99

Do you have any role models, either technical or non-technical, that helped you become a better developer? How did they shape your thinking or daily practice?

I've had coworkers who've helped me ramp up in new technologies, but no, I've never really had a role model or a mentor. I've tried to become that person for others, since I never had it. I have spent the past few years building up my network of peers who can help me with my career, and, as a person who has faced barriers and discrimination, that has made all the difference. Find people who have your back and can help you through the weeds.

As you navigate the industry, do you find any current industry trends to be wrong?

Honestly, the implication that any tech or trend is "wrong" is problematic. Any trend is probably still a choice you could make under the right conditions. Over the years, I've heard developers debate about which technology is best and they belittle the ones they didn't like. I began to notice that tech that was typically undervalued were the entry points in which underestimated developers would come in from other fields. For example, I've heard a lot of developers belittling PHP/WordPress developers, and then I'd look around the room and see that's where the women were. So I don't trust trends, and I especially don't trust people who like to point out everyone else who is doing things "wrong."

But, one trend I particularly don't like is open office spaces. I'm an introvert who gets overstimulated by too much sound, harsh lighting, etc., and I need my personal space. But it works for some! So I don't think it's necessarily wrong, but that it's ill-suited to people like me. What we need is to be willing to offer other options.

The more we embrace the fact that we're all different—that we make different choices based on our own preferences or the information we have at any given time—the better off we'll all be. And the more diverse and welcoming we'll be as well.

Although it's not an easy problem to solve, how can people start making a difference in tackling these issues with welcoming diversity—specifically gender bias that seems to be an ever-present issue in this industry?

First, I'd say start asking white men this question! But, really, progress is slow on this front in the software industry because leadership doesn't care, doesn't want to change, and/or doesn't want to give up their power. Research has proven that diverse companies perform better, and yet companies fail to put any incentives behind diversifying their workforce. Diversity starts at the top. If leadership isn't demanding change, it won't happen. Underestimated individuals don't have all the answers. You can't expect them to do the work for you—they're already overburdened as it is. But there are people out there who specialize in diversity and can help you and/or your company make progress. Pay them.

Your own career has been very diverse. You have worked with many different technologies, starting with DB management, then backend development, and currently iOS development. What led you through this interesting career path? What challenges have you encountered while transitioning between these very different platforms?

I took a full-time job while still in college, working with a database and programming language called Progress. From there, I was hired to work at Cargill after graduating because I was already familiar with those technologies, and they had a Center of Expertise built around it. I then moved into Perl, working with content management software consulting, traveling all over the world. That led me to middleware, and eventually to Java. I spent over a decade as a Java developer, mostly focused on backend work but doing some middleware and frontend as well. I ended up at a custom dev shop that was technology-agnostic, and I expressed my desire to learn iOS. We ran out of Java work shortly after joining, so they threw me right into an iOS project. I ended up bouncing around between Java, Android, iOS and WordPress projects for a few years, until I realized I couldn't keep up in all those technologies at the same time, so I decided to focus specifically on iOS. I've been a full-time iOS developer since then.

One of the biggest challenges I faced in transitioning technologies was not knowing the right terminology to use. I knew what I wanted to accomplish, but couldn't find the correct Google terms to get me what I needed. I remember a specific instance in which I needed to have an app read text aloud, and I had a difficult time finding the name of the class to use! It was AVSpeechSynthesizer... not terribly intuitive. Having a mentor around to help "translate" for me was incredibly helpful.

Another challenge, as a mostly self-taught developer, was not knowing generic language terms for talking about programming languages in general. As an example: knowing what a closure means and how that concept is applied in various languages. Learning multiple programming languages allowed me to compare and contrast different languages and the benefits and drawbacks of each, thereby better understanding the one I was currently working in.

For your daily work, how do you start your day off with a bang? Do you have any secret morning routines that set you up for success?

As a fully remote employee, I've found that having a morning routine is really helpful to establish my day. I make myself a latte in the morning, eat a small breakfast, and then work out in my home studio. Afterwards, I go upstairs to my office and start my work day. Having a dedicated room or area for work is also really helpful for me.

How do you stay highly productive in your own work, for long stretches of time?

I'm one of those people who works in bursts. There are times where my progress will be slow, because I need time to think things through in my head, or my mind is too busy to process. But then it'll all come out in a huge burst of productivity. Even though we don't do time tracking, I personally keep track of everything I accomplish in Trello so I can prove my productivity. It also helps me remember all the awesome stuff I've done when it comes time for reviews.

SARAH'S RECOMMENDATION

Design Patterns: Elements of Reusable Object-Oriented Software | Erich Gamma, Richard Helm, Ralph Johnson and John Vlissides

PACO ESTÉVEZ GARCÍA

" Stay open and help others. "

🐦 @pacoworks   github.com/pakoito

D uring his career, Paco has experimented with early prototypes and bleeding edge software, at-scale video services, and a bit of video game development. These days, the challenges he faces revolve around applying functional concepts to improve development experience workflows, learning and efficiency.

> 66 *Code is not always the hardest part of the job... The primary challenges are still interpersonal relationships, communicating with stakeholders, and gathering information.* 99

What are the three books that have positively influenced you?

As a kid, I was influenced by Terry Pratchett's books. My favorite is *Night Watch*, and you need to have read some of the previous books to get all the references. Generally, Pratchett presents a way of living that was completely different from my life in Spain. A couple of decades later I'm living in London and I have a *raison de vivre* that is completely different from people in my home country.

A technical book I recommend is *Functional Reactive Domain Modeling* by Debasish Ghosh. When I was starting doing functional programming I was working in isolation. Reading this book helped validate my approach.

Another book I really like is *How to Make Friends and Influence People*. This book describes how people's behavior hasn't changed much despite the technological revolution. People are still people at the core, and they tend to click in the same ways. That book gave me good ideas about how to interact with other people and how to be the best version of myself.

Writing code is not always the hardest part of the job, and the hardest problems haven't changed. The primary challenges are still interpersonal relationships, communicating with stakeholders, and gathering information. Those kinds of problems are still front and center.

You have a great reputation in the functional programming community. For those on the outside, the functional programming world seems like a magical universe. How would you explain functional programming to a developer that doesn't have any experience with this world?

Functional programming can be thought of in terms of constraints. It's an approach to programming that is very structured. When learning programming you were told you could do anything you wanted. On the other hand, what functional environments offer is a limited set of approaches to solving a problem, that you have to compose together into a larger solution. Those limitations are actually liberating. Instead of potentially endless options for how to create a program, functional programming, or FP, defines a set of tools that work in combination. Think of FP as more like putting a puzzle together rather than sketching or inventing a world from scratch.

How would you explain the relevance of functional programming to someone developing software to manage a database or an interface? How can they benefit from functional programming?

The books that I read and the processes that I follow are the same across multiple languages, and they've been consistent for many years. When I approach a corporate codebase, I find that there are twenty different ways of doing twenty things. On the other hand when I'm working in a functional codebase, or when I'm approaching a functional language, I know what the available constructs are as well as which ones I'm going to use. That means I can move fast in a codebase that uses Java, JavaScript or Lisp, or F#. All of them have a set of commonalities. These restrictions are the pieces that you're building your program from.

If you're a corporate developer, you're more worried about frameworks, which are specific to each company. Those skills may not be transferable and may make it difficult for other engineers coming into your team to be proactive.

This is one of the biggest advantages of this paradigm, and at the same time it's the largest adoption barrier. It seems counterintuitive that you need to spend time unlearning dogmas that are widespread through the industry in order to unlock your productivity. Still, since you can apply functional programming in so many environments you start seeing the job of coding differently. Many people think of functional programmers as programmers with special knowledge of big or abstract concepts. The concepts aren't big or abstract, instead these programmers have reshaped the way they think about code. Functional vocabulary makes it possible to communicate in a consistent way with any programmer who understands those concepts. On the other hand, if you're a Java developer talking to a JavaScript developer the differences may seem insurmountable.

Having a single set of abstractions that are consistent and common across every platform would be very beneficial to many companies. For one thing, it would make hiring easier. You would need fewer instructors, fewer evangelists, and fewer people thinking about this because everybody would be writing pretty much the same code across different languages. Sometimes you want fast languages and sometimes you want expressive languages, and for both you'd still have the same core set of constructs.

Programming languages today are evolving, all of them, in the direction of unification. Java is getting pattern matching and structs. Rust is a huge success in the C++ community, and it is mostly ML (meta language) which is the base of OCaml and F#. We are coalescing. Even JavaScript is adding new features based on those languages!

Standardization may evolve slowly, but it's what's coming in the next ten to twenty years.

What's the best way for inexperienced developers to learn functional programming?

There are multiple approaches to this question. Some people like to take a class or follow a book. Others prefer to be thrown to the wolves and figure it out. An approach I would recommend starting today is to stop using re-assignment so that the only place where you can assign things is on creation and initialization. Impose the restriction on yourself that you can't assign anything to a variable afterward. With that simple restriction you're going to start finding necessary patterns.

For example, you're going to iterate through a list and aggregate the results. Because you can't assign a variable to the new list of values outside of that loop you'll be forced to find a way to write the pattern. Next, you'll discover abstractions like folding a list. To do that, you'll apply a function in order to change all the values in a list. That function is called mapping.

By avoiding reassigning, you'll start thinking about these functions. That's pretty much at the core of it. Everything else is just how you compose those at scale. When you get to composing for a larger scale, books can be helpful because people have experimented with this for many years. We already know the most efficient ways of combining simple functions to prevent assignment. If you have the time, avoiding re-assignment is a great place to start learning functional programming.

In doing this, you could keep using your previous language, right? This is possible in any platform, technology or language—to work without an FP library or any language similar to FP.

Correct. The only difficulty might be with original C. The language used has to have a feature called closures. Closures mean that your lambda, an anonymous class, or any similar construct can capture variables from an external context. That's the only requirement. If you have that you have an entry point for FP.

Aside from being a software engineer at Facebook, you're also a contributor to Arrow, which is the FP library for Kotlin that is being developed by you, Raul Raja, and others. The consulting and development firm 47 Degrees is actively supporting this work. What is this library contributing to the world of Kotlin? How will people working in that world benefit from this library?

We're thinking of the ways the library will benefit people coming from both directions. As learners start needing composable functions they'll start writing them themselves. They'll be able to check the library and reuse it. In other words, for beginners it's a way to move up the learning stack. Learners will get these abstractions and be able to read and understand them from their mechanical implementation.

For experienced users, we've opened up the Kotlin language to people who have historically used Scala, F# or OCaml, or even Clojure. These developers didn't even have access to mobile phones.

You can't develop an application in Scala for any scale due to hardware limitations. However, you still want the same toolset that you had in Scala. Because this is not a language-specific approach, we put everything you're expecting in your day-to-day toolbox in Kotlin. For people who know what they want they only have to search in which package to find it. Where is my optics library? Oh, it's here. Even if you feel that you don't need it, there it is just in case for when you do. People are happily telling us that the functionality is the same as the best parts of Scala. That's it. The syntax is somewhat different, and the expectations are exactly the same.

You're an active contributor to open source code. What are the main difficulties you find in contributing to open source projects?

First, there are people who lack the confidence to contribute. They need encouragement and a guide. This is something you have to care about. I've learned many of the things that I know about programming, engineering, and computer science from collaborating with other people in open source. Through their code and their interactions with the community they showed me how I could improve myself. I pay that forward by teaching other people and getting them into this ecosystem. Some companies don't like it, and we should continue getting people into that open source sharing mindset.

Other common barriers of entry is snobbism and community gate keeping. This is somewhat common, where people believe that only a few big companies with huge backing, money, and rockstar engineering should be doing the important things. These people advocate for only using things built at scale for solving big problems, or those built by the best engineers. This is obviously a fallacy, usually pushed by internal incentive models that force employees to compete for attention. The best you can do is ignore them and focus on providing the best experience to your users and contributor colleagues.

It's on each of us to be the ones taking that first step to make sure that your specific community is welcoming, that you're getting people from every avenue of life, that you're teaching them. Don't think of it in terms of what you're doing for them. Think instead that you're building something together. You're not better than others just because you are working on this massive big project within a mega corporation, neither as an engineer or a person.

For those people who are not contributing yet to open source, how would you recommend they get started? How can we spark their interest in being effective contributors?

There are two ways for people to start programming. There's the university path, where you show up to class one day and now you're a programmer because you have written some code. That's going to be your new work life. Others feel motivated to learn programming by themselves and sit down with a book or with online resources and start developing.

That same drive that you have to learn programming is the one that you can apply to open source. You just have to show up and find the project that you can contribute to.

Now, not every project is right for every developer. Some long-running projects may not welcome contributions from day one. One case would be, for example, the Linux kernel or the Android OpenSource Project. If you try to contribute there and it's less than pristine, there's a good chance somebody's going to take issue with it. That's a bad experience, and it makes people afraid to try.

What you want is a nurturing community focused on something you care about or something that you know you can contribute to. Don't be afraid to ask whether a group is willing to take contributions and don't feel discouraged if they don't. You can also use conferences, meetups, and your day job to find people interested in starting a new project together.

Once you find a group of people you're happy collaborating with, or a project that takes contributions, you write the code, and make a pull request. You're an open source contributor now!

How are you so productive and able to contribute to so many projects? Do you have any sort of routine?

I'm awake when everybody else is asleep. I've been lucky that most of the companies that I've worked with allow for a flexible schedule. Most people wake up early, get the day started, show up in the office, and work until they're done. I come to the office around noon, work, and then take a three- or four-hour break to have dinner and catch up with friends. And then, after midnight, I have another three hours of uninterrupted productivity.

Sometimes in those three hours I can solve one open-source problem. Or maybe I take a look at the documentation, read through it, and find an improvement. Or I can review a couple of pull requests. There are no notifications. There's no WhatsApp, no Messenger chats or anything happening at that time. That's my approach to productivity: by shifting my schedule by several hours I have uninterrupted time every single day, at the expense of some daytime activities.

How do you keep up to date on all the new trends and developments in our field. How do you keep learning?

Several years ago I drank from the fountain of social media, followed papers, watched all the talks, went to all the conferences, read all the books and everything you could think of. At some point your brain gives up. You can't keep up with everything that is going on. You have to be selective to the things that are important to you. For some people that means mobile development. Maybe for you, it just means following a single framework, and whether it has some deprecations in the next release. You don't have to follow everything. Once you're selective with your time, you can enjoy the things you're actually catching up to.

I prefer to watch talks that are about general concepts. I'm very rarely going to watch a talk about version 2.0 of the framework. I will have plenty of time to read through the documentation, go through the examples, and write the code myself for that once I start working with it.

What I do need is somebody telling me about their experience. What approach did they take to a problem? Why did it work or not? I feel less affinity to frameworks and monolithic approaches than to general suggestions or explanations of how people tackle problems. And this also applies to my own projects. In the case of Arrow we've tried not to be prescriptive about architecture, or which parts of the library or patterns are required to be "pure functional programming."

I also try to give the same type of talks that I like to watch. I prefer not to be dogmatic about architecture or approaches. My talks have a lot of information about how I am tackling specific problems. I tend to address the steps that I took, my thought process, and implications of time and scale. You're free to take that information and apply it to your own frameworks. I think that's helpful for many people because sometimes you don't have the benefit of having a breadth of approaches in your codebase.

What do people underestimate in this industry?

The importance of empathy. I know it's a bit of an overused word, yet still, I've found that some of the biggest problems in our industry center around communication, especially with regard to mismatched needs. Say somebody is working on their own product's code and they find a big conceptual problem at the core of it. Maybe it's the theming, the UX, or a piece of the logic that's incomplete. They complain about it, and they get very angry and passionate about why this is a problem that has to be fixed by somebody else. At that point a very confused team fails to see the value, which creates a loop of bad feedback. It's easy to contribute negativity and detract from the general value, both for the reporter and the person receiving the reports.

It's the same for people working in new libraries or frameworks. I see a lot of condescension directed toward users, that they're dumb or just not as good as engineers and get easily confused and will not learn further than what's taught in university. That lack of empathy shows often in internal meetings between maintainers, especially at large tech companies. This is something that our industry could definitely work on.

How can we encourage folks to develop more empathy?

One proactive way would be calling out bad behavior. Be argumentative but not confrontational with the people that are not being empathic, in a way that is empathic itself. Don't return aggression with aggression. Kill them with kindness.

I like the idea of killing them with kindness. Is there something that you didn't know when you started in this business and you had to learn the hard way instead?

Yes. What I learned over time and what we are trying to teach people when mentoring them is that it's not always about the code. The code is a really important part, and it's a really fun part, but if you get lost in the code sometimes you lose that connection to your users and the needs of your company. You have to balance mentoring, interviewing, reviewing code from other users and gathering information. All of these are necessary parts of being a great engineer.

Also, it's not always the best coders whose careers advance the most. That's a paradox. There's the archetype of the isolated technical genius who nobody wants to work with. They're assigned to specific projects that keep them separated from the rest of the company. They're prevented from progressing because the moment that they interact with all people, they detract from the global productivity. People like that are a net negative contributor to the outcome of the company. That happens sometimes, and you have to try not to be that guy.

You may be asking yourself why. How is this guy who is so productive on his own contributing negatively to the productivity of everybody else? And it's simple math. You want to be the person that is actually doing 90% for yourself and lifting the rest of the team to 120% for each one of them. As your team grows the overall output would be great, and those other people will go and help others. If you're the guy that is putting in 120% but you're the only person on the team who is growing, that doesn't correlate with progress, success, or getting the best projects in the company. Instead people start to resent you, to the point where you may even be driven out of the job.

What would you recommend to a junior software developer who is currently starting their career?

There's no single correct path. Everybody whom I've spoken to comes from a different avenue of life. The commonality between most of them is hard work. You have to sit down and do the work. The work is not writing code. The work is everything that is required without burning yourself out. I can't emphasize it enough—how important just doing the work is.

It sounds very abstract. It's important that others perceive you as being a good worker and an honest, capable and open person.

It's not so much about your coding output. Many people are going to be better than you at that. There's always going to be somebody that is better than you. It is about showing that you can do the work, and showing that you take pride in what you do. For me, that's what's most valuable.

Any final words of advice?

Keep mentorship in mind as you're progressing through your career. Check yourself for elitist attitudes and beliefs. Share information. Don't alienate anyone. Be nice to everyone as you don't know what they're going through or who they're going to become. They may impact your long-term trajectory more than you can do just by yourself! Stay open and help others.

PACO'S RECOMMENDATIONS

Structure and Interpretation of Computer Programs | Harold Abelson and Gerald Jay Sussman

Domain Modeling Made Functional: Tackle Software Complexity with Domain-Driven Design | Scott Wlaschin

Functional and Reactive Domain Modeling | Debasish Ghosh

"Simple Made Easy" presentation | Rich Hickey | infoq.com/presentations/Simple-Made-Easy/

COREY LEIGH LATISLAW

" Bring people along with you. "

🐦 @corey_latislaw   CoreyLatislaw.com

C orey is an international keynoter, an avid sketchnoter, and the Head of Engineering at Kin + Carta | Create Europe. She has developed high profile Android applications over the years, including Capital One, XfinityTV, and Pinterest and ran teams large and small. She's a former Google Developer Expert (GDE) in Android and Google Developer Group (GDG) organizer.

You spend a lot of time volunteering. What drives you to do this? Can you talk a bit about the specific causes and groups that are important to you?

I want to have an impact on our world and I want my work to mean something and to benefit millions, if not billions, of people. I've worked in many organizations that are operating at different scales and I get excited by the ones that are solving real, human-scale problems.

One of the places I found to have a meaningful mission and a solid plan for implementation was installing solar power in rural Tanzania. They are connecting people to the world. I also worked with a nonprofit, installing computer labs in emerging markets. That was about connecting children with computers and technology and changing the course of their lives. That's the sort of thing I'm interested in.

In my daily work, I make space for individual mentoring, especially with women. The tech world can be a hostile environment, and I want to foster the opposite. I'm frustrated by the slow pace of change in the tech culture—there's been a lot of money invested in diversity and inclusion, but we haven't gotten anywhere—but this makes me feel that I'm making an actual difference.

Do you think we could do better than we're doing now?

Yes, absolutely—though I don't know exactly what that answer is. I've been doing a lot of thinking about how to embed diversity and inclusion into competency frameworks so that it becomes part of the fabric of the business culture and shows up on performance reviews. If we say that it's important we should be measuring it and we should be accountable for moving our companies and the industry forward.

In London last year, you were giving the keynote at a conference. How do you prepare for something like that?

I'm terrified of public speaking, believe it or not. I failed my first public speaking course back in college and slowly got to the point where I am now. Luckily, public speaking is a learnable skill.

In the beginning, I tried to look smart on stage. I overcomplicated the talks with technical details and spent loads of time preparing—for example, for my first keynote I wrote a 30-page research paper with citations for the script! I read more or less from the script on stage, but it felt too wooden. That was a lot of work and a whole lot of stress.

Recently, I've shifted to talking about my own experience, which is much easier to talk about. I've also shifted to a more fluid preparation style. For my "The Creative Technologist" keynote, I came up with the idea and wrote that talk in two weeks using improvisational techniques. I would record myself talking about my topic off the cuff, play it back, and keep the parts I liked.

To come up with a topic, I do a mind map to generate talk ideas. Then I find themes and write up an outline or abstract—either in Google docs or in a rough sketchnote, which is a visual note with a mix of drawings and words. I ask other speakers for feedback on which topics might be the most compelling.

Once I have settled on a topic, I do a sketchnote. This helps me outline the ideas and major takeaways. The next step is to make thumbnail sketches for the slides. I make myself practice aloud instead of just editing the script. I always do dry runs in front of people to refine the talk and mentally prepare.

The keynote I gave in London was called "The Art of Intentionality," and it was about how to be more intentional with your time and energy. At some point, I decided that I'd draw live on stage, and I ended up creating a ten-page worksheet for everyone.

I prepare intensively, which is probably why I don't do several talks in a short period. I usually like to give a talk at least seven to ten times. That gives me time to refine my presentation style and material. I try to choose topics that are going to be relevant for a long period.

Sample sketchnote, an image with a mix of drawings and words.

Your keynote speech, "The Art of Intentionality," will be relevant for years to come.

It's about figuring out your guiding light and setting goals and tracking success, as well as cutting things that are a drain on your time. It should be relevant forever.

Should all software engineers be involved in public speaking?

It's certainly accelerated my career and helped me develop better communication and research skills. I don't think that everyone needs to necessarily speak at a conference, but I do think that public speaking and storytelling are skills that everyone is going to need.

We all engage in public speaking at some point in our careers. If you're in a meeting, it's a smaller audience, but you still need to prepare for that so that you can contribute your best work. Meetups are a great place to share your unique view with the community.

The only people who shouldn't speak are the ones who can't keep sexual jokes out of their talks or people who are actively working against diversity and inclusion. Those people create a hostile environment.

> **❝** *Once you know you're building the right thing, it's important to make something that both technical and non-technical audiences will understand.* **❞**

What skills are the most underrated or under-appreciated for software engineers?

I don't like the term "soft skills," but our industry is seriously lacking them. If you look at senior engineering job specs, about half of those skills are related to communication, leadership, influencing, and growing those around you. These skills are really important, but I think that a lot of people focus on deep technical knowledge instead of growing the full toolbox of skills. It's going to limit your growth if you don't focus on them, so you might as well start now!

The ability to zoom out and see the big picture is very important to understand what we're doing and why. As engineers, we should be empowered to push back and ask questions to ensure we are building what's needed. It also helps to take a step back when solving a problem. Take a walk, take a nap, talk to someone else. You might find that the answer jumps out at you when you are "doing nothing."

Once you know you're building the right thing, it's important to make something that both technical and non-technical audiences will understand. That brings it back to thinking about the audience and to speaking and storytelling skills. Being able to bring people along with you and making your products understandable by everyone is a really important skill.

How can we improve our soft skills?

Books are my favorite resource. There's a business book I like called *Crucial Conversations: Tools for Talking When Stakes Are High* by Kerry Patterson, Joseph Grenny, Ron McMillan and Al Switzler. It's about non-violent communication. The whole concept is that we make up stories for why people act the way they do, but, in reality, it's rarely about us. For example, if I walk by you in the morning, and you say hello, and I don't respond, you might think I'm snubbing you or are angry with you. In reality, I might have a lot on my mind or not even have realized that you had said hello.

In these stories, we often place ourselves into the category of victim, and we label others as villains. This book helps illuminate that mindset and offers curiosity as a solution. The phrase that best illustrates a curious mindset is "tell me more." When we default to a "tell me more" reaction, we avoid creating these stories. I tell everyone to read this book.

What other books can you recommend?

One of my favorite books is *Drawing on the Right Side of the Brain* by Betty Edwards because it changed the way I think. It talks about left brain and right brain research, tells you how to tap into your creative side, and describes the five components to drawing. It focuses on drawing as a teachable skill, and I have seen a difference. I didn't know how to draw when I started to read this book. I first picked it up in 2005 (and twice more since), and now I can draw fairly well.

This book also really helps you to find flow. With coding, you build a picture of the architecture or code structure in your head. It's fragile. Being able to maintain it is important, but it's also important to get back into it quickly if you lose it. This book teaches you how to quickly tap into your intuitive side and see things holistically.

One of the more interesting things it discusses is how to bore your inner critic and make it drop out. For example, you would turn a photo upside down and then draw it, and your brain is thinking, "What are you doing? That doesn't look like anything real! Why are you doing this? What is happening?" Eventually, it gets bored and disappears and then you are just drawing. Different tricks like that are really helpful.

Another creativity book I love is called *The Artist's Way*, by Julia Cameron. It's a 12-week program to recover your lost creativity. The basic idea is that creativity is a teachable skill and we all can tap into it. Its central practice is writing three pages every morning and taking yourself on an "artist date" once per week. In the morning, you get all the heavy stuff out of your head and onto paper, and then during the artist date, you're refilling the well of your creativity. Both of these books were influential to me.

Finally, I read *The First Ninety Days* by Michael Watkins just before starting this new job. Its overarching theme is how to be valuable as quickly as possible in a new organization. An organization invests in a new employee, and then it takes a while for that employee to start giving back—which can take about six months to break even. This book is all about front-loading and trying to get to value more quickly, which helps both the business and your career. Something I took away from it is the importance not only of building vertical relationships with your boss and her boss, but also horizontal relationships across the entire organization.

When I started with this company, I set a goal for myself to meet twenty people in the first week. I met thirty. I set up coffee and lunch dates with people and asked them who they thought I should meet. I kept branching out based on their recommendations. That helped me when, in the first three months, I launched an internal program for the company to get people into conference speaking and participating in meetups. I don't think I would have been able to get that off the ground without the support of the people inside the organization.

I've integrated key takeaways from each of these books into my life. You don't have to adopt everything, but there might be one or two key concepts in there that you'll find utterly invaluable.

What's something you wish you'd known at the beginning of your career?

How to understand people and their motivations. It's important to figure out how to work with and how to influence your colleagues, especially when you don't have formal authority. I think that those are all hard-earned lessons. I guess at the core of this is politics, which is seen as a dirty word in tech, but it's about building effective relationships. Learning how to work with different people, even if they are jerks or make you sad. It's important to figure out how to forge a productive working relationship with everyone.

What do you see trending in the industry?

Machine learning will be transformative, but it's hard for people to get up and running with it right now as it requires a base of theoretical and mathematical knowledge. Commoditizing it and making it easier to use will allow anyone to leverage machine learning to inform their decisions.

I'm also excited about the potential for 3D printing to solve medical and other real-world problems.

Finally, the usage of technology in art is really interesting and I have been seeing more installations and works recently. There will be a marriage of tech and art, which will redefine what art and technology itself means. These are the things I'm excited about right now.

Do you have any morning routine that sets you up for success, or in the evening if you work in the evenings?

I have a morning and evening routine. In the morning, I wake up at 6:00 AM and do my morning pages for 30 minutes and then meditate. Then I go to the gym or run in a nearby park for at least 45 minutes three to five times a week. After that, it is breakfast and coffee, and that's when I start creative time.

Usually, I will try and do at least two hours of creative work before I go into the office. That way, I get to work on my passion projects because I found that if I tried to do that in the evening, I was too tired, which made me feel like I was just a work machine. Now, I honor my values and make space for creativity.

In the evening, when I leave the office, I'm done. I don't look at emails or Slack or whatever. At home, I meditate or create, and then I make dinner and stop using electronic devices at 8:30 PM. I go to my bedroom around 9:00 PM and read—often falling asleep to the light of my backlit Kindle.

Does meditation play an important role in your creativity or concentration?

Yes. I started doing meditation in 2016. In general, it's made me more grateful, less stressed and anxious, and more tuned into what I'm thinking and feeling. I'm generally calmer. It's been a great addition to my life, so I've been doing it nonstop since then. I enjoy it.

What makes a good leader?

Empathy and the ability to create psychological safety are super important. If you're afraid of making mistakes, or if your employees are afraid of making mistakes, they're not going to tell you the truth when things are going badly, and they're not going to make the best decisions. It's better to have happy, motivated teams who believe in honesty and transparency. As much as they can, leaders should eliminate barriers that create a culture of blame, and they should create and reinforce transparency.

I also really value creativity in a leader. You can be creative in how you resource a project and build people's careers. The whole idea around creativity is you are taking what you know and somehow creating something new from that, and that can change the course of an entire business or a career.

The skill I want to develop is storytelling. I want to get people excited and bring them on a journey. I want to be able to explain what my mission is and have them be excited about it. I think I can do that in a keynote now, but I'd like to get better at doing it off the cuff and in person.

Have you had any useful experiences with failure?

I have only ever been fired once. I knew it was going to happen because I was protecting my team. I chose to do what I thought was right, and it led where I thought it would lead. Still, it was a shock because I am an overachiever and I like to excel. There was just no winning in this situation at all. I was afraid for a while about finances and whether I would be let back into tech. All these anxious thoughts were running through my head.

I was able to calm down and found out that failure wasn't so bad and scary. I took the opportunity that this unexpected time off offered me and started my own business. That shocking failure pushed me into trying something new, and it's been successful, so I'm really happy with it. Right now I have a salaried job, but I have the ability at any point to consult instead, which is a nice comfort.

COREY'S RECOMMENDATIONS

Crucial Conversations: Tools for Talking When Stakes Are High | Kerry Patterson, Joseph Grenny, Ron McMillan and Al Switzler

The Artist's Way: A Spiritual Path to Higher Creativity | Julia Cameron

The Bullet Journal Method: Track the Past, Order the Present, Design the Future | Ryder Carroll

WORKING MANAGERS

On Balancing Production and Leadership

COREY LEIGH LATISLAW

I've been a mixed individual contributor (IC++) and manager for several years. Even when I was supposedly a full-time IC, I found myself doing tasks outside of my job responsibilities like mentoring, teaching, architecting, defining process, project managing, managing clients, managing engineers, writing specs, influencing strategy, interviewing candidates, and recruiting.

Although I enjoyed the problem-solving side and the satisfaction of shipping features to millions of users, I enjoy the mentoring and managing side more. I love teaching, sharing my experience, removing roadblocks for others, and helping people grow in the ways they want to. When I wasn't getting enough fulfillment out of my day job, I would seek leadership opportunities externally. I served on several nonprofit boards when the leadership opportunities were especially lacking internally.

The hardest professional challenge has been context switching between delivering something (which necessitates unbroken sessions of focus) and doing the mentoring and organizational stuff that management requires (interruption-driven). I used to revel in my ability to multi-task, but as I've started focusing on one item at a time I find that I do a much better job and enjoy my work more (many studies back up these findings like Alina Tugend's article, "Multitasking Can Make You Lose ... Um ... Focus").

Context switching became especially pronounced at Capital One when I ended up leading the QA automation team in addition to my sprint team. I was in tons of meetings and "interrupted" by my direct reports and higher-ups all day for a multitude of reasons. If you were an IC, this would be frustrating beyond measure. I wrote very little code during this period.

The most baffling part for me was performance feedback from my managers. Although my role breakdowns usually reflected some portion of management-y work, I still found myself often judged by IC expectations. I got excellent marks, but the feedback always contained a line to the effect of "it would be great if we got more code out of you too." In short, the goalposts should have changed, but they didn't.

Management output is hard to quantify and features being shipped is a somewhat straightforward measure of business value provided. However, when you are measured against the code output of the ICs on your team, it makes it look like you're not particularly productive. You're doing two (or more) roles so trade-offs need to be made, unless, of course, you're planning to work double the hours.

CREDIT

A version of this article was first published on Corey Leigh Latislaw's personal website (October 18, 2016). The original article can be found here: http://coreylatislaw.com/working-managers/#more-2863

ZARAH DOMINGUEZ

❝ Be the best without stepping on others. ❞

🐦 @zarahjutz   zarah.dev

Z arah is an Android developer based in Sydney, Australia. She started doing mobile development work in 2007, and has been on a constant rollercoaster of emotions with the Android platform since the days of Donut.

Recognized as a Google Developer Expert for Android, she helps organise GDG Sydney and the Android User Group Sydney. She loves board games, books, and dessert, and has a knack for eating breakfast food for dinner.

AN INTERVIEW WITH ZARAH DOMINGUEZ

What is the most significant mistake you see junior developers making over and over again in their work?

They sometimes make things a lot more complex than they usually need to be. There seems to be an assumption that they need to know everything all the time right now—that's one mistake that I tended to make when I was starting, and I see it a lot now when I work with more junior developers. It's a hard skill to learn; it takes years of experience and writing to actually recognize that something you're doing can be done in a much simpler way. But I think the mistake is mainly rooted in trying to do everything all at once.

What suggestions can you give for overcoming this problem?

A lot of it is practice. Also coming back to something you've written in the past, because sometimes—especially when we're on a project— we ship something and then it's done, right? But I find that if I go back to something that I did even a few months ago, usually there are new ideas that come to me like, "Oh, I could have done it this way rather than that way." Or the project is actually more simple than I thought. It's kind of like reviewing past work for a future exam. If you go back and review your code, I think that really helps a lot.

For your learning or growth, do you draw from podcasts or books?

For technical information, usually podcasts. There are a couple that I would recommend to any fellow software developer. The first is the *Android Developers Backstage* podcast, which is hosted by members of the Android development team. They talk to a lot of Android engineers and people who drive changes and developments in the Android community, so it's a really good reference as some of the episodes are very highly specific to a topic.

I'd also recommend another Android-focused podcast called *Fragmented*, hosted by Donn Felker and Kaushik Gopal. They talk to a lot of Android developers in the community about relevant topics that those people are working on. It's a good first-hand account if you want to start navigating anything Android, but they also cover nontechnical topics like how to be a better developer, so it's a really good resource.

Finally, I'd suggest *Android Dialogs*, which is a conversation-based video series on YouTube. It's really good because the episodes are short so you don't have to invest in a full 30-minute chunk of time to watch. It's a really good overview to get on topics that are interesting, and then you can do more research on what interests you.

In addition to these community resources, what about social media? Who are people or groups that you follow on Twitter who are role models for you?

I follow one called Feminati (@AndroidFeminati). It's a collection of female developers in the Android community. I really like this group because, personally, for the longest time, well even now, I've been the only female developer on my team. It can be pretty lonely. But having this group of women supporting you, seeing how they interact with each other and how they bring everyone up, it's really inspiring. They're from all over the world, so it's a really interesting collection of really awesome women.

The other Twitter resource to follow are the publications like *Android Weekly* or *Kotlin Weekly*. They are a good collection of community-driven content. If you were looking for technical content or what's hot and new in the community, it might give you an idea for something you're doing.

I also like to follow members of the DevRel team in Android. One area of development that truly interests me is the UI, so I follow them for tips, especially when I was doing a lot of vectors and animations.

But my most consistent resources are the newsletters. If there is a big conference happening and the organizers release their playlists, I go through them and see what people are talking about—especially in conferences that announce new things, like I/O or KotlinConf. That's when new tools and new libraries and all those announcements go up. You don't have to watch everything, so I usually just pick and choose which ones I want to watch and spend time with.

What are three other resources—tools or apps—that you are using?

I use Trello a lot. One of my teams uses it, but I also use it for personal stuff. I actually have a Trello board for TV shows I watch! So, like to see which season I'm on or if they're on hiatus or something. So I use Trello very heavily. I'm an Android developer, so I use Android Studio. But one tool I use a lot within Studio is the ADB Idea plugin. It's a small plugin, but I feel like all the mundane tasks of reinstalling your app or resetting your app, all those things like, it's very useful for. It's a useful shortcut basically. Finally, I use Hierarchy Viewer a lot. It's just because I work with UI a lot. I'm not sure, I think it's really an under-appreciated tool. And it was gone for a little while, but now it's back and more powerful; I think it's really useful, and it could be beefed up more. But yeah, just debugging UI stuff makes it so much easier, using the Hierarchy Viewer. I think it's called Layout Inspector now.

Is there something that you learned the hard way in your career that you wish you had known when you started?

Coding is not a thing that you do by yourself. You can be the best technical developer ever in the whole wide world, but you still need people. You still need to get along with people on your team. It's something that I try to help my team with—if you think you know something better than another person on your team, you don't have to be braggy or snarky about it. It's important to be kind and to help others. You need social skills, is my main point, here. So, it helps if you are a good developer, but skills can be taught. You can learn new things, you can read books or listen to podcasts, and do all kinds of things to learn the technical side of things. But it always helps to be kind.

And training people in these "soft skills" of team management is, I think, one of the biggest challenges of our industry. Having been in the software industry for more than 10 years now, I do think we're taking steps as a community to get there. Conferences I attend, for example, are not purely technical now. I think a lot of people are more aware of the social aspect of software development.

How do we learn that? Don't discard those talks that don't seem technical. It's important to go to those talks in conferences because, in the long run, those talks actually help you be a better person and not just a better developer.

Meeting new people is important, too. Following people on Twitter is mainly how I expand my network. On Twitter, you find people from different countries and different cultures, and they may present you with different points of view as well; just talking to these people would help these skills.

What's the biggest obstacle, it could be either technical or personal, that you have had to overcome to get where you are today?

I don't think I've really overcome my biggest obstacle. For me, it's a constant work in progress, learning to trust myself. We usually set, well I personally set, the highest bar for myself sometimes, and if I don't meet that bar I get extremely disappointed. Sometimes I don't trust myself that I will be able to do something, or that I don't deserve to actually be where I am now. So I'm still working on it.

What would you suggest for a person that needs to acquire this trust in oneself? Is there any way to offer training for these skills?

If you feel like you can't do it, just give it a go. Take that jump. It's scary and it's risky, but sometimes it's super worth it, especially with trying new things. One example I gave was I used to hate working with the Android build system. But it came to a point in which no one else will do it; it's just me. So even if it's scary, just give it a go. I'm pretty sure you'll learn something.

In this industry, do you think what you describe above is a trend that is easily resolved?

Yes. I think one of the main things that is very misleading in the industry is that you always have to know everything. Especially now, Android specifically, there are so many new things that are new all of the time. And, now, I/O is happening, so there's probably a hundred more new things that are coming out. When I started, I felt that the Android community dictated that I had to go and try everything that was new. Knowing everything about everything is not scalable. There's only one of you, and there are a thousand different things. And it's not possible to know everything all at once. So it's fine if you haven't tried the latest, newest thing that is out there.

How do we fix it? Helping each other as a community. There are a lot of people who share their knowledge about all these new things. And I see many times when someone writes something about learning a new thing, some people just want their opinions heard and leave negative comments and criticisms. So maybe instead of spending our energy criticizing people, we should spend more of our energy building others up.

Gaining new and positive experiences seems like a priority for you. You're a person who has lived in different countries; what is most difficult for you about initally working in a new country?

The biggest challenge is adjusting to the culture—especially the work culture. Australia, in general, is very laid back. And I came from the Philippines where in general our work ethic is closer to the stereotypical Western way of thinking–long hours, sacrifice your time with your family, and kill yourself doing the work. But here it's more relaxed. One of the things that my first manager here taught me was that not everything needs to be fixed now. Not everything is priority one. And that's something that I really struggled with my first few months, here.

What would you recommend to an aspiring, fellow developer who is thinking of switching countries? Would you have a recommendation for this first experience?

The first priority would be to really find someone whom you can relate to. In that sense, I was lucky when I joined the first company I was with in Australia because there were a couple of us who were new to the country and new to the company. We need to find that support system, because, usually when you move to different countries, chances are that you don't have any family there; that's one of the hardest things to adjust to. You're basically alone, like moving out of your parents' house, but a thousand miles away. Find that support system first as a good first step. How to do that? Go to a local meetup. My second week here, I went to an Android meetup and that's how I got to know the people who are in the local Android community. Then they became my friends. So that's certainly a good first step.

ZARAH'S RECOMMENDATIONS

Android Weekly newsletter | androidweekly.net

Kotlin Weekly newsletter | kotlinweekly.net

Patrick Rothfuss books | patrickrothfuss.com/content/books.asp

JUHANI
LEHTIMÄKI

❝ Everywhere, create connections. ❞

🐦 @lehtimaeki   juhani@snappmobile.io

Juhani is an Android Lead, Founder, and Partner at Snapp Mobile, based in Germany. He is an Android developer, design fanboy and Android GDE. He blogs, talks and raves about the need for engineers to appreciate, design and preach about a way multi-discipline teams can to work together to create great real-world products. He had 10 years backend developer experience in Java before jumping on Android, which he's been doing for almost 10 years. His true passion is to build amazing and helpful, easy-to-use user interfaces for Android apps. He believes that the core of all this is to create a fluent and tight integration between the designer and developer disciplines. He self-identifies as a nerd.

Tell us a little about how your career in development started. How has it evolved since then?

I got into my first programming job after completing my first year of university studies. That was around 2000, and getting a programming job was very easy. I fairly quickly moved into working full time and studying part-time. The first 10 years, I mostly worked as a Java backend developer with some notable exceptions as an Eclipse plugin writer for a couple of years. I've had three big milestones in my career.

In 2008, I moved from my home country, Finland, to Germany. While my job stayed pretty much the same, working in an international environment with the English language was something new. To this day, I think the best thing I ever did was the move. Not because I dislike Finland but because the international and new environment of Munich provided a lot of new things to learn. I'd recommend everyone to move into a foreign country for at least a couple of years.

Around 2010, I moved into Android development. This happened by accident by being in the right place at the right time. My company, at that time, was looking for Android developers; while I was already dabbling into Android, I hadn't gotten off the ground with it. So I offered myself for the role, explaining that I already knew Java—how hard could it be? Over the next couple of years, I spent pretty much all my available time learning the new system. This is an example of taking control of your future. When an opportunity presents itself, jump on it! You can always change your mind later, but you might never get that opportunity again.

Then, a couple of years later, I joined forces with my previous colleagues to run our own company. Initially, I was external but, in later incarnations of our company, I was a founding partner. I'm currently running our company, Snapp Mobile, together with four other partners. Running your own company is a challenge, but worth it if you're that kind of a person. I don't think it's very likely that I'd join a multinational corporation as an employee in the future.

Throughout my career, I've worked in many, many different types of companies—large to small, design lead to tech-only, and local companies to multinational. I sometimes wish I would have started my company earlier. However, I believe that the experiences I gathered on the way were needed to establish the success of our current company. In any company, you can learn lessons of what to do and what not to do. In every workplace, you create connections either with friends or future colleagues and partners. In the end, I'm very happy that I took the time to explore my options before settling in.

> **"** *If you're shy like me, talking at conferences is a great way to meet people. As a speaker, people want to come talk to you instead of you having to approach them.* **"**

What did you wish someone had told you back when you started software development that you had to learn the hard way instead?

Software engineering is people business. We might be staring at our screens and talking more to computers than we are to people during a normal work day, but in the end becoming successful is all about your connections to people. Expand your circles and create connections. Learn to know people who think differently, have different ambitions and skillsets. These connections are what will later bring you opportunities in forms of customers, possibilities, and even potential business partners. I regret not actively putting effort in creating people connections outside my immediate circle for the first 10 years of my career.

I've always been shy and hated the so-called "networking." I believed that if I just sit down and write the best code possible, I will be fine throughout my career. Unfortunately, that's not the case. You need other people. I shifted my approach to work around 10 years ago—but I wish I had done it earlier—and forced myself in front of crowds and started organizing local meetups. It resulted in talking at conferences. This shifted my career to a new gear. If you're shy like me, talking at conferences is a great way to meet people. As a speaker, people want to come talk to you instead of you having to approach them.

You are a senior developer who managed to stick with coding, despite founding a company and executing all of the management that comes along with that. Even though many developers seem to move into management or CTO positions as they advance in their careers, how can developers stay hands-on as they take on more management responsibilities?

I'm in a lucky position where I get to influence and choose my own role as long as I'm willing to put in the time and investment to make sure that I carry my weight in our company. I don't like this de facto idea that if you're a developer with a lot of experience, the way forward is to become a manager or a CTO of a company.

For a small company, like ours, the multiplication factor is important financially. Each one of the senior partners must bring in more than just their own salary to the company. The easy path seems to be to take over management of a team and increase your contribution that way. While for some people that can be a valid option, for me, that is not what I want to do.

I'm an Android expert, meaning that I've chosen to go deep in a single tech instead of learning a bit about everything, though I'm not saying that the other approach is wrong. My belief has long been that deep expertise can help with a company's marketing and, in some cases, like ours, completely replace the need for marketing. When customers see what we can do, they want more. The people we have worked with contact us again after they change companies. Being good, technically, creates tons and tons of business opportunities.

Naturally, I have to sit on many seats including many management tasks. However, our company runs everything decentralized and nearly all communication is done asynchronously via our Slack channels. This means that I can participate in the company leadership discussions even when working in customer projects or other coding tasks whenever I have time.

You have written a book for Android UI: *Smashing Android UI: Responsive User Interfaces and Design Patterns for Android Phones and Tablets*. Can you tell us a little about your opinion on mobile UI? Do people take UI design seriously enough?

This is an area where we have seen a lot of improvement in the past years. Nearly 10 years ago when I first started blogging about UI and Android, there was very little guidance on what constituted a good UI on Android. iOS has been way ahead for years. The situation has greatly improved since Google introduced the Material Design guidelines.

The role of the guidelines was initially, and sometimes still, misunderstood. Especially technically minded people often took the guidelines as requirements, and apps not following some parts were seen as automatically bad. On the other hand, the long iOS dominance made the Google guidelines slow to be adopted by designers. Still, today, there are some designers willing to shoehorn iOS design into an Android platform causing damages to project development and UX.

The biggest issue plaguing the industry, now that Material Design guidelines are available, is understanding the processes for creating great software. There are still companies who fail to understand the importance of different disciplines collaborating in creating new products and apps. I've seen both sides of the failure from tech companies not understanding what designers can bring to the table to complete design-first companies promising impossible solutions based on Powerpoint presentations. We still see attempts in some companies to ignore design or drift towards old waterfall-style processes in which design is seen as a specification for development. This approach simply doesn't work.

What are the biggest gaps or challenges between the UX design team and the implementation or programming team? How do you close those gaps?

We have already failed if we separate design team from development team. The only way to succeed is to unify the disciplines under one team, a product development team. Communication is key here as in many other places. It doesn't matter how amazing the design is if it doesn't get implemented correctly.

To ensure great communication between the disciplines there are a few key points. First: respect. Respect needs to be earned but both sides have to leave room for that to happen. Designers and developers have often been seen as opposite contributors. One side is artistic and utilizes more soft skills, driven by opinions; the other side is seen as very detail-oriented with work based on hard rules. This can cause disagreements. However, when both sides are open to discussion and open to understanding that each discipline contributes towards the same goal—a great product— the cooperation is greatly rewarding and provides great results. Bidirectional communication of possibilities, opportunities and effort guarantees the right work prioritization.

Next, handover tooling is important. Design-developer tooling has been improving greatly, and tools like Zeplin are creating remote-ready environments wherein handover can be done painlessly and in a format where both sides have exactly the information they need. Any team still using tools like Photoshop for design need to update their working toolchain to support modern methods.

And, finally, iterations. Initial design is an initial guess. Implemented design is not a series of screens but a functional system with user flow throughout the app. All combinations of states, transitions, micro animations, unexpected situations, etc. are not something that designers should spend time specifying ahead of time. These are things that are built into the system during design iterations and experimentation. Android is a hugely powerful prototyping environment in the hands of capable developers. That capability should be used. Developers must support their designer counterparts in experimentation. When deciding transitions, animations and user delight the designer especially must have room to try out different things. The developer's role is to bring these experiments to life so they can be evaluated on real devices, and in some cases with real users. The designer-developer pair can, in good circumstances, put together 10–15 iterations of the same feature during a single working day, ending up with something that is not just good but great. The iteration workflow is based on the solid communication and respect discussed above.

What is another current industry trend that you think is just plain wrong?

For some reason, in many cases, software engineers tend to gravitate towards overly complex solutions to problems that don't need that complex approach. It might come from the way we think about issues in general, but I feel that we're setting ourselves up, and the ones we work with having to maintain our code, for failure. Whether the excuse for the overly complex approach is testability, maintainability or abstraction, developers often do not think if the particular aspect is needed.

We, as developers, also tend to worship vocal figures in our community—especially those who write a lot or present in many conferences. The community is rarely critical enough about the provided solutions from blogs and talks, and they skip the part in which they think for themselves if the provided solution is needed. This has lately become an issue in the Android community when selecting architecture models or frameworks—especially when discussing asynchronous code—where de facto popular frameworks like Rx crept into many projects without there being a need for such heavy tools. We also tend to believe that systems that took a long time to learn are good.

With this kind of complexity worshiping, we cause negative side effects. An example is when a more senior developer who subscribes to this way of thinking talks to a new developer. New developers and others who have not chosen to invest their time to dig into these overly complex approaches are talked down to and might even get ignored in job interviews or slammed in code reviews, causing toxicity and negative atmosphere for learning.

What would you suggest is a better alternative to this trend?

I want the industry to be more pragmatic in our approach to technology. We should place usability requirements to our tools and frameworks the same way we must as our user-facing work. We should demand easy-to-learn and easy-to-use framework documentation and tools and reject systems with complexity for complexity's sake. I want people to be more critical and more open to ideas. Specifically, people who are part of software projects but not directly involved in the engineering phase should not dictate architectural solutions that they have read from a blog post but have never tried. And I want to see friendlier code review practices to welcome new developers. Nitpicking or strange and meaningless demands need to be moved aside when bringing new people on board. Systems with high learning curves should be prioritized because of their learning curve and alternatives proposed.

One trend you have advocated against is predatory practices in mobile game development. How can gaming companies find a balance between profit and "fair" gameplay for all?

I'm no longer really a gamer; however, I follow a lot of e-sports and other gaming content on YouTube. I love gaming, but I just don't have time to sit down and play games anymore. Mobile gaming is something I would love to do. A few minutes at the time doing something fun and potentially light is something I'd be more than happy to pay for.

Unfortunately, mobile gaming started well, but ended up in the gutter. It turns out that traditional pay-up-front business models didn't work well in the mobile app stores where apps averaged around 2–5 EUR each. In-app purchases (IAP) seemed to work well, however. I remember being in multiple Google I/O talks wherein Google pushed IAPs as the recommended way to monetize games. The idea initially seemed good: give a part of your game for free and ask for money from people to get more content.

But, again, publishers soon found out that, if the crowd was big enough, there was a better way to make money: make the game addictive by using gambling mechanisms, abusing the sunk cost fallacy, and so on. They created ways to get only a very small portion of customers to pay for the game, but to get these few customers to pay huge amounts—so-called "whales." Gaming on mobile was no longer about gaming but about finding out how to make the game last as long as possible and adding as many paid shortcuts or time blockers as possible. This way, most people didn't have to pay, and the masses cannot vote with their wallets as the few are still hooked and provide enough income.

As a developer, I see this doubly as sad as just a gamer. I see huge amounts of talent in gaming developers. Many games include amazing graphics and run really well on a large variety of mobile devices—this is not easy to code. But then the games are not actually games, but clicking simulators with cash stores for pixel money. I feel bad for these talented developers in the rotten industry.

I want to see gaming companies create games we want to pay to play more and not to pay to skip. I'm happy to pay to get more of something I like and enjoy, and I believe others are as well. I feel that Google is in a place to lift up games with fair business practices in their storefront, but I'm concerned that it might not be in their business interest not to do so. Google is, after all, making 30% of the ill-earned money themselves from these bad game publishers.

In keeping up with industry trends, which do you prefer: podcasts or books?

I prefer podcasts but end up reading more books than listening to podcasts for some reason. I suspect it is mostly due to my relatively short commute. In general, I try to keep my eyes open for both.

What are the three books or podcasts that have had a lasting impact on how you do your work?

First, *About Face: The Essentials of Interaction Design* by Alan Cooper, Robert Reimann, David Cronin and Christopher Noessel. This book was part of a university course about usability. The course and the instructors probably shaped my career more than any other book. It's a book about a way of thinking about user interfaces and how users see them. It describes user goals, personae and mental models, all of which are very central tools for me when creating products or talking about usability. I wish everyone in the industry would read this book.

Second, the *Java Posse Podcast*, made up of Tor Norbye, Carl Quinn and Dick Wall. The podcast is now, sadly, already dead, but it shaped my thinking about engineering the most. I listened to these guys all the way from the very first episodes for about 10 years they kept making the podcast. I learned a lot about new technologies, new platforms, etc. But the most important lessons were about the attitude towards software engineering in general and the passion for learning new things.

Finally, *The Design of Everyday Things* by Don Norman. This is another book that pushed me towards championing the importance of design to my engineering colleagues and community. It's an entertaining read about design failures and importance of design thinking.

In terms of starting your own work, how do you start your day off with a bang? Do you have any secret morning routines that set you up for success?

Coffee and Twitter.

I'm a stereotypical developer: I love coffee. I usually don't drink coffee at home but wait to drink my first cup at work. Drinking coffee is a great way to relax after a commute and get your bearings. Even when working onsite with customers, it's perfectly fine to sit and relax if you have a coffee cup in your hands.

I use Twitter as my primary source of tech news—I miss Google+. I use my commute for reading Twitter most of my days. This helps me to keep in the know for new developments and new ideas. I also gather a list of blog posts, mostly written by one of the amazing Android GDEs, to read later. During my commute Twitter sessions I usually try to find posts and comments that relate to the current customer or project work I'm engaged with. This helps me to get motivated and excited about the coming day. There are so many cool and interesting things happening in the tech world every day that you can usually bring something new to the table most days.

So Twitter helps me to get to the headspace of bleeding edge tech and coffee—or a coffee break—helps me to get to the project mood.

How do you stay highly productive for long stretches of time?

When we talk about staying productive during a day, nobody should ever underestimate the power of a nap. If you feel tired, sleep for a bit. No developer is productive when tired. I also tend to show up later at work if I had a sleepless night or went to bed late. I don't believe I can deliver much value to my customer or to our company if I'm sleepy. Being at work only physically doesn't serve anyone.

Now, about staying productive on a long project is a much more difficult question. I believe that you can't stay excited about a project for more than 6–12 months. After the initially exciting project starts to feel boring, no matter what. As developers do their best work when excited and motivated, this difference can be huge and very noticeable.

I think there are two solutions to project fatigue. First, side projects. Take time to work on something exciting and new on your own. If possible, drop to a four-day work week and spend the rest for something you really enjoy. This separation of work and fun can quickly make you overcome the project fatigue in your work project as well, and you can get the initial excitement and motivation back. Secondly, change projects. If you're part of a consultant company, this should be relatively easy. Talk to your managers and express your desire to change scenery. Sometimes it's enough to agree on an end date to gain your motivation back. When a slightly boring project is finite, you know you can get through it.

JUHANI'S RECOMMENDATIONS

About Face: The Essentials of Interaction Design | Alan Cooper, Robert Reimann, David Cronin and Christopher Noessel

Java Posse podcast | Tor Norbye, Carl Quinn and Dick Wall

The Design of Everyday Things | Don Norman

ERIK HELLMAN

" Better but more complicated. "

🐦 @ErikHellman

E rik is a software engineer with more than 20 years of professional experience. He is currently working as a contractor through his company Hellsoft. Besides writing code for everything from smartphone apps, websites, backend and IoT systems, he is also writing about software engineering on his blog (www.hellsoft.se). Erik has written two books on Android development and can often be found at various tech conferences where he talks about some tricky topics that he has come across in the past. Besides programming, he likes to talk about coffee, gardening and books.

You are one of the most senior and seasoned developers I have met. What is the most significant change you've noticed in the development community since you started your career?

Automation on every level. When I started writing software, there was no such thing as automated tests, IDEs with code-completion, or build tools that optimized your code. Even simple things, such as automatic code formatting, were unknown. Even experienced developers with as much or more experience than me would have trouble writing software in the "good ol' way." I think most of us don't appreciate the advancement made on the tools we work on. Even compilers have gotten so smart today that there is little reason to think about the optimizations we needed to remember only 10 years ago.

We often speak about automation and AI taking over other people's jobs, but already the roles that are highly repetitive in our field, like testers or IT-support, are disappearing because of this automation. It is naive to think that the traditional role of writing code won't suffer the same fate, especially since a lot of the code that we do write today is very similar to the one we've written before.

Is there anything you miss from your beginning days as a developer?

Not really. Everything is better, just more complicated. Sometimes I might miss the times when I learned or discovered something new, as that happens less frequently these days, but that has more to do with me having less free time and also being old and learning things slower.

What do you think is one core concept that most software developers don't pay enough attention to, when they are trying to grow their careers?

Automation. Most of the things we do as developers today will be automated to some degree. Most developers will spend less and less time writing actual code and more time thinking about composition and design of systems. The tools will get smarter. Much, much smarter.

What is the single best investment you have made to help advance yourself as a professional developer?

Starting my own company and working as a contract developer. While this is not for everyone and probably not something you should do at the beginning of your career, it has led me to interact with a very wide variety of businesses that I would probably not have been in contact with if I worked as an employee for a company.

Which other resources do you rely on heavily to keep yourself up-to-date in your industry?

I mostly stay updated through my network of professional developers. Nothing beats hearing someone talk about the latest stuff they worked on and the lessons they learned. Reading about it or hearing about it in a tech talk is great, but the personal touch beats everything.

I'm also all about books. Although I've tried podcasts and videos a couple of times, I've realized I'm better at collecting information reading than listening. I do appreciate that other people have different preferences, so I'm glad that there are skilled people doing blogs and videos.

What are the three books that have had a lasting impact on how you do your work?

The list of good books that I've read that relates to my work is quite long, but there are a few that stand out for different reasons.

First, *Game Engine Black Book: Wolfenstein 3D* by Fabien Sanglard. This is a piece of software history captured in a great way, while at the same time presenting much of the stuff we are taught in computer science classes but rarely get to work with professionally. I enjoyed it tremendously, both from a personal perspective—the amount of time I spent playing Wolfenstein 3D is quite ridiculous— as well as the details about CPU architecture and the smart software solutions that they used.

Next, *Effective Java* by Joshua Bloch. This is probably a popular option. For me, it serves both as a great guide for how to write efficient code, but also as a testament to the fact that we as developers shouldn't try to solve things that are probably already solved in the platform. Understanding best practices and how to apply them, but also understanding when and why to deviate is an important part of being a developer. We still tend to deviate from best practices a lot, so books like this help us to stay on the right path.

Finally, *Against the Gods: The Remarkable Story of Risk* by Peter L. Bernstein. This book is not about computer science, but it is probably the book that has had the most impact on how I work. It describes the history of risk assessment and probability. While the theory of statistics and probability was something we've all studied, we usually don't get equipped with the skill of how to apply it properly and how to recognize our own biases and faults when predicting risks. This book gave me better tools to deal with that.

What three tools can you absolutely not live without as a developer?

First, a solid and ergonomic office setup. Includes everything from desk and chair, to keyboard and screen. Next, a smart IDE. This goes back to automation and smarter tools. We should stop fooling ourselves that a "clean and simple" editor is the best. Code completion, real-time lint warnings, and in-line documentation make us better. Finally: coffee.

How do you start your day off with a bang? Do you have any secret morning routines that set you up for success?

I wish there was some magic I could apply to start things off with a bang. In truth, my days vary from starting with a bang to being a long drudge depending on lots of factors such as travel, meetings, or other boring tasks. I just try to stay as focused as possible, complete meetings and other non-creative tasks that cannot wait as fast as possible and hope that I have enough energy to make something amazing. Having the freedom to pick my projects myself and also leave them when I want helps.

How do you stay highly productive for long stretches of time?

I've learned that it is okay to abandon things that are bad for me, in whatever way that might mean, or that I no longer feel engaged with. This has made me much better at picking the right project, so my focus tends to stay fairly high for the duration of my assignments these days.

What is something you wish someone had told you back when you started software development that you had to learn the hard way?

Social skills are something you gain from experience, which are crucial in any situation. I wished I would have understood the concerns from my parents when I spent a large part of my early teenage years sitting in front of a computer instead of hanging out with friends. While I'm not anti-social, I definitely have issues dealing with more complex social situations today. I still see lots of young developers struggling with finding friends and having a healthy social life.

> **66** *We need to acknowledge the lack of discussions about the ethics in the work we do... It is easy to ignore the effects of your work if it is only software, but people are already suffering from software that has an unethical or questionable intent.* **99**

Are there any current industry trends that you think are just plain wrong?

We need to acknowledge the lack of discussions about the ethics in the work we do as software developers. It is easy to ignore the effects of your work if it is only software, but people are already suffering from software that has an unethical or questionable intent. Social media without any regulations, gambling and betting sites, advertisement, and violent content on YouTube are just a few things we've helped to create.

What would you suggest is a better alternative to this trend?

While I'm not pro-censorship, there needs to be a better middle ground where free exchange of ideas can occur but where we limit the damages of the new systems we have created. This starts with us, the developers writing the software for this, to recognize our role and responsibility.

ERIK'S RECOMMENDATIONS

Game Engine Black Book: Wolfenstein 3D | Fabien Sanglard

Against the Gods: The Remarkable Story of Risk | Peter L. Bernstein

THE RISE OF THE FULL-STACK NATIVE MOBILE APP DEVELOPER

Have You Future-Proofed Your Career?

ERIK HELLMAN

At the end of the 90s, I was still (sort of) studying at the university. I did some small gigs as a web developer (before the terms front- and back-end existed) and was also teaching this topic at the university. These were happy days for anyone with basic knowledge of HTML and CSS. Everybody needed a web site (or homepage, as we called it back then), so there was plenty of work. Lots of people dropped out of university to join one of the many web bureaus that popped up.

Things quickly changed with the dot-com crash at the end of the millennium. Most of the companies that were doing basic web design disappeared as just a basic web site was no longer enough. Just knowing the web technologies for the browser was not enough anymore. The need for back-end developers skyrocketed instead and we still see an increasing need of this skill today.

Today we speak of backend, frontend and full-stack developers, but in this, we usually don't include the native mobile app developers (iOS and Android). We're not seeing a decrease in the need for native apps and there is no sign that web technologies will replace native apps any day soon. Even if we would only have Android smartphones with Chrome as the standard browser, we would probably never see web technologies replace native apps completely. In any case, while we have three (not counting desktop native apps) frontend stacks today (web, Android and iOS), we still only think about the web when talking about full-stack or front-end. I believe this will change soon. Probably sooner than you expect.

Common outsourcing services today are the mobile agencies. These are companies that more or less focus entirely on mobile app development, leaving the back-end development to their client. Lots of apps are developed like this. Here in Sweden, many of the most common apps are basically outsourced to a mobile agency. While it still works, I believe it is not sustainable for long. Like the demise of the web design (i.e., frontend only) agencies of the late 90s, the mobile agencies we see today will have to adapt and become full-stack or become obsolete. If you're only doing native mobile app development today, it is time to learn some back-end technologies.

There is a really great presentation by Duana Stanley from SoundCloud on how they started doing micro-services for their clients. One of the key take-aways is that each client should own their own endpoints. Simply speaking, the team doing the Android development is responsible for the micro-services exposing the endpoints they consume. This proved hugely successful for SoundCloud, as well as for many other companies that provide clients using different technologies (e.g., web, embedded, iOS, Android, etc.). While some people might argue for a common, shared API for all clients, it tends to impede the development pace of the different clients as it creates a bottleneck in that team. Also, each client is different with different requirements, and eventually you will end up with two or more conflicting requirements in your API, requiring you to create a client-specific endpoint.

A micro-services architecture is very suitable for handling these kinds of challenges. The endpoints owned by the respective client-team don't need to be very complicated. In fact, in the beginning, they will probably be identical in many cases across different clients. However, by ensuring that each client has its own endpoint (e.g.,

/api/iOS/v1/articles/search and /api/android/v1/articles/search),
the teams can freely adapt the input and output according to what
works best for their platform.

Another reason why mobile developers would need skills in back-
end development is to gain an understanding of the challenges in
that layer of the system. I'm surprised how many of the app developers I meet today lack an understanding of the performance implications involved when exposing a REST API. For example; traditional
SQL databases on the backend won't disappear any time soon, but
clients are expecting an ever more complicated response from the
API they call (e.g, complex JSON hierarchies and GraphQL). Mobile
app developers who understand the challenges here are more likely
to "survive" a shift in the industry.

It also makes sense from a business perspective. Why do you
outsource the app development, completely disconnecting the con-
sumer-facing part of your system from your core business development? Outsourcing is something you should do with stuff that is
stable and in maintenance. Not with the constantly evolving things
like client-side applications. It is interesting to see that companies
outsource mobile app development but still keep the web-devel-
opment in-house. This will likely change very soon, as the product
owners in these companies realize that they lack the control they
need to make the best return of investment.

Will this mean that every iOS and Android developer will have to
learn how to write back-end code? Probably not. There is still a need
for pure front-end developers for the web, but a full-stack developer
is getting paid better and has a wider selection of jobs. The same will
go for a full-stack developer with Android/iOS AND backend. Even
better, combine two (or three) front-end technologies with a backend
stack. You can always specialize in one, but the important thing is to
be proficient enough vertically to be able to pitch in where needed.

So as an iOS or Android developer, what do you need to learn?
What back-end technologies are most in-demand and future-proof?

As always, it depends. However, the obvious and perhaps boring
answer is to learn Java and/or .NET. These are still the most common

back-end technologies in use and it won't change in the near future. Other technologies, like NodeJS, Python, Ruby, Go and Scala, are also popular, but not remotely as common as Java or .NET. Sounds boring? Don't worry, you can still use Rx and Dependency Injection on the back-end as well. :)

What is going to happen with all these mobile agencies? Well, I might be completely wrong: maybe they will survive and companies will keep outsourcing the native mobile app development. However, the trend to move the app development back in-house is already happening. The obvious change will be that these agencies will transform into traditional consultancy firms. That's what happened to the web development companies that survived the dot-com crash in the 90s, and it will happen again with every specialized skill set that eventually becomes main-stream.

My tip to the (native) mobile app developer at one of these agencies is to start learning a useful backend stack (not the one that seems more fun). Think about what you want to do when your current employer can no longer sustain their business once their clients start bringing the app development in-house. Do you want to work as a regular consultant, do freelancing or join a product team as an employee?

CREDIT

A version of this article was first published on *Medium* (March 14, 2017). The original article can be found here: hellsoft.se/the-rise-of-the-full-stack-native-mobile-app-developer-a0757388bc1b

EDUARDO CASTELLÓ FERRER

66 You are as valuable as your network. 99

ecstll@mit.edu

Eduardo received his Bsc. (Hons) Intelligent Systems from University of Portsmouth (UK) in 2007, and his M. Eng and Ph.D. degrees in robotics engineering from Osaka University (Japan) under the guidance of Prof. Hiroshi Ishiguro. During his graduate studies, Eduardo's research focused on swarm robotic systems and how to achieve collective, cooperative, and collaborative groups of robots. Eduardo is currently a postdoctoral fellow (Marie Curie) at the MIT Media Lab (Human Dynamics Group), where he conducts research on the synergy of swarm robotics systems and blockchain technology. In his previous post-doc position at MIT, Eduardo designed, implemented, and tested a whole range of new robotic agriculture systems (Food Computer) at the OpenAg initiative. His research interests include swarm and multi-agent robotics systems, decentralized and distributed control, bio-inspired robotic systems and technology transfer procedures.

You are one of the most involved individuals in robotics and artificial intelligence (AI) I have had the pleasure to know. There's a lot of confusion between the terms AI and ML, or machine learning. Could you provide clarification?

Artificial intelligence is basically the term we give to the field of computer science in which we design algorithms that do something that can be named as "smart." However, AI is a really big field these days.

For instance, AI could involve algorithms that produce "smart" decisions like: "If you see a pedestrian in front of you please brake," but also could involve techniques that require large amounts of data to achieve this "smartness." That is the case of ML, or machine learning. ML is a subfield of AI in which algorithms learn from processing large quantities of data in order to discover "hidden patterns" and extract knowledge from them. So, for example, all machine learning is artificial intelligence, but not all artificial intelligence is machine learning.

What do you think are going to be the most immediate consequences for the average user of AI?

We now have the ability to combine algorithms that we invented 40 or 50 years ago (e.g., reinforcement learning) with the largest amount of data about human behavior in history. We now have a ton of data about ordinary activities such as where do we go when we are walking around the city, what do we search online, what is our behavior when we want to buy something, how we behave when we are sick, etc.

This important knowledge combined with these smart algorithms can give us a lot of prediction and analysis power of our behavior, not only as a society but also as individuals. In the immediate future, we're going to have a set of new tools that will allow us to surf this immense amount of data that we are creating. On the one hand, this will be good because it will extend us; imagine a doctor who now can see 10x more patients and can have 10x more accuracy in diagnosis. On the other hand, we are going to create a world in which everything will have a score—a score for you as a citizen, as a user, as a consumer, etc. This reputation-based society will impact the average user the most.

Does this raise concerns about the ethics regarding how the data will be employed?

You have to think that ML algorithms are as good as the data that you feed into them. So the data you use in order to train and make these systems "smart" is key. What we currently don't understand is that when we provide this data or when we design these apparently smart algorithms, we are also projecting our biases into them. For example, if you code a very complex deep neural network that predicts the credit score of people (another way to code reputation), but you only train this neural network with a certain population data (e.g., high-income white males), other profiles that might use your product in the future might not be well represented or might be mistreated (e.g., single black mothers). So we need a new social contract about AI, in order to make sure that these systems are deployed in the right way and as diverse as possible. So they are not mistreating certain people just because these people were not there when these technologies were pioneered. Actually, my biggest fear about AI and ML is not super-intelligent machines but dumb ones.

What would you recommend to individuals who'd like to start in the AI domain, which many see as more academic?

A good foundational book, course, or tutorial definitely helps. However, I totally recommend reading the academic literature (i.e., papers) associated with these technologies. It might seem too academic at the beginning but it's very interesting to read these works and then tweak and play with the code researchers provide (e.g., GitHub repos), but it's also very helpful to read how researchers describe this code and explain why they made this or that decision. Once you get into the world of papers and academic literature, you start to get a grasp of how to explain and document something very complex, such as an AI model or a machine learning function. After you read a couple of these papers, you start to realize you have a lot of information in order to start building your own projects. At that point in time, you'd be able to collaborate with these researchers. In my experience, it is a very good way to bridge the gap between the corporate and academic—you discover that you are working on similar things, and then you can collaborate and contribute to each other.

Can software engineers contribute with academic peers and share new knowledge in papers?

Definitely. As software engineers, we are very used to contributing to the open-source world: open GitHub repos, uploading some code that adds some functionality we thought useful, writing documentation, etc. Indeed, this is valuable to the academic community, per se, and we will see a richer set of inputs included into papers in the near future (e.g., testing frameworks, virtual machine images, etc.). Along those lines, we are heading to a world where the idea behind version control systems (e.g., git, Mercurial, SVN) is moving away from just code into something beyond code.

What happens when these open-source repos are not just about code but incremental dissemination of knowledge? What happens when your commit also provides a parameter trade-off analysis for someone else's code? Or you open a branch about the ethical implications of an AI algorithm within the paper repo itself? What happens when Nature or Science become something more like a YouTube playlist than strict venues for academic reputation.

That sounds like a new ecosystem where software engineers can have a significant role.

Through your career, you've worked in diverse environments. In Japan, you did your Ph.D. in robotics and AI. In the United States, you're currently working at MIT with interdisciplinary and international teams. What is the secret to working efficiently in these very heterogeneous environments? Are there any challenges you can think of and how do you solve them?

The key is understanding the culture behind the system; startup, corporate company, public institution, academic lab, it doesn't matter. It's important that you understand the culture of the country and how people operate in these places. For example, in Japan, corporations and academic institutions have very strong team-oriented processes that are very hierarchical; hierarchy is respected a lot. So you need to find a way in which you can do the things that you are passionate about, but, at the same time, respect the hierarchy. On the contrary, in the U.S., while there's some hierarchy (like in any other part of the world), taking chances and assuming risks is valued and appreciated. To summarize this in simple terms, Japan is more about why you do things, and the U.S. is more about how you do things. This is just something you learn from the culture and from the interactions you have with your peers. So it's good once you move to a place, whether it's Japan, U.S., Europe, or wherever, to understand what the connections are, and the networks that assist and sustain the operations there. Then, understand where you can position yourself, make the most difference, and how to play that in your favor.

Is there any approach you follow for solving conflicts, which is something that can happen in diverse space or in any software development team?

Having negotiation skills is a must; you need to develop these because, in the end, everything that you are doing, from agreeing on a salary you are comfortable with to solving an issue in a complex project, is about negotiating. One of the things that I found useful is the fact that, at some point in time, when we have a conflict, we tend to frame the situation as "I am good; you are bad, and therefore we are fighting." But if we elevate ourselves from the process of demonizing each other and start thinking that we might agree on something behind the front line, we might reach a solution beneficial to both parts. If you find what really drives the other side behind just winning that argument, you might find it very easy to come to an agreement that will eventually solve what you are fighting for.

> 66 *People tend to align with people who have a lot of initiative and are passionate about what they do, and they are very self-confident about what they do.* 99

You're exploring the idea of so-called "soft skills." We engineers, know how to grasp the technical skills; these are generally acquired at university or wherever we are acquiring our education. But softer skills are not taught in these environments. How can we acquire or train on them?

It's true that, in the world of engineering, things tend to be binary. Processes are efficient or not efficient, optimal or not optimal, black or white. However, when you have a group of people working on something complex, issues won't become black or white; most likely, there will be infinite shades of grey in the situation. Two of the things that I found useful to move beyond this binary approach are negotiation and leadership skills. Reading books is a good way to start acquiring knowledge about how and when to negotiate, for instance, learning about the experiences of other people.

However, in my opinion, knowing people better and understanding what drives them beyond what they are fighting about is a way better option. Complementarily, leadership is highly regarded in the

Western world. Leadership is all about initiative and moving things forward. People tend to align and follow people who have a lot of initiative and are passionate and self-confident about what they do and why they do it. One of the possible paths towards developing leadership is trying to become the hub of your network.

When I say "hub," what I really mean is to become the central node or player of a process: the router of your network. If you become a hub in your team, for instance, channeling all your co-workers' ideas about the next product upgrade through you, that will put you in the place where you will have to understand a lot of viewpoints. That will force you to develop your soft skills a lot and will also increase your value in the team. From a pragmatic point of view, at some point in time, your superiors will have to face the potential problem that if you go away, the hub that sustains that network will also go away and the network might face the risk of becoming sparsely connected, which is a really bad thing for a team. In summary, move out from your comfort zone and try to move from the periphery of the network to the core of the network and see what happens.

Which skill do you think is undervalued in the IT world that you don't see enough of and that you would like to see more?

Empathy. I don't think we have it and I'd like to see more of it.

Are there any other industry trends that you feel are broken, and how can these be fixed?

If we talk about academia, I can say there are many broken things there. For example, academics are not only valued by the number of publications that they produce but also the number of citations that those publications collect. So we can say that academics are at the forefront of this new phenomenon of being immersed in a digital reputation-based system. As academics, we all have a reputation score (number of publications, citations collected, etc.)

but because this score is not aligned to our main goal, which is to create and disseminate knowledge, there's a big problem ahead of us: an academic might have a lot of reputation but actually their work might mean nothing. Along these lines, many academics end up writing papers that are meaningless or even fraudulent in a certain sense by cherry picking their results (i.e., p-hacking) just to keep publishing and gain more and more reputation. Your reputation as a researcher is very much correlated with the money that you get through grants, with the positions you get, and how you get promoted. This is also known as the rich get richer effect. Publishing a new paper is very easy; however, validating or even replicating the results included in that same paper is extremely hard. Modern academia in combination with the new digital technologies just created a crazy one-way function. In my opinion, the first thing that we need to change in academia in order to be successful and reorient ourselves to our main goal is to change how we measure ourselves. Maybe we should pass from a reputation system in which we measure how many works we publish to a metric based on the impact that those papers created in society—for example, how many projects we launched, how big the communities are that we created around these projects, how many people we helped, how much knowledge we basically transferred to industry and how this knowledge was used. I think that's one of the main things we'll need to solve in academia in the next 25 years.

In this technological world, changes happen extremely rapidly—not only technically but new languages, new libraries, etc. that we'll have to learn. So it's very difficult to predict what's going to be relevant in five or 10 years from now. How do you prepare for this and stay up-to-date with new developments?

Besides reading the common sources that we all read, I think that it's very important to take a look at the academic work. If you are interested in certain technologies or certain fields, you can just basically ask Google Scholar to notify you whenever there's a new article in that field. Maybe you can't read the full 10-page article, but you can definitely read the abstract and the conclusions. So, as you start searching different keywords, you will get notified of new articles every week or every month. When you do this for a while, you'll see very different people from different parts of the world talking about the same things, or pointing out the same problems; at that point in time you can guess from this emergence of topics that those topics are going to be hot in the future. Usually, these academics will end up working in companies, or the students will graduate, and they will start talking about these things in non-academic environments. Eventually, these people will take some positions in relevant research teams or corporate teams and the topics will be pushed forward.

In terms of staying up-to-date, there are a lot of ways to do this. If you live in a place that has some kind of innovation ecosystem—like Boston and San Francisco, Zurich or Munich—or near universities, it's worth going to talks, demos, and workshops. In case of the more academic approach, you can always attend the first lecture of courses that you find interesting at universities. Normally, universities are open systems. You will not be able to register and follow the course for credit, but you can always show up, at least for the introductory lectures in which these lecturers give a general scope about a field of research.

What books influence you or have had a lasting impact on your work?

For technical books, I have a few. *Pattern Recognition and Machine Learning* by Christopher Bishop is a must-read for anybody who really wants to get deep into machine learning with no foundation whatsoever of the field. Another is *Clean Code: A Handbook of Agile Software Craftsmanship* by Robert Martin. The third that really had a lot of impact on me was *Dynamics Of Complex Systems* by Yaneer Bar-yam. Nontechnical books include *Liquid Modernity* by Zygmunt Bauman, *The Iliad* by Homer, and *The Politician and the Scientist* by Max Weber.

What is the cheapest investment you have made that has provided the highest return on investment in your career?

Books are definitely very cheap investments. I recommend, for example, getting books on negotiation as part of that very cheap return on investment. I will say that *Getting to Yes: How to Negotiate Agreement Without Giving In* by Roger Fisher is a very good book that everybody should read, and it will give a lot of good insights. Books are the cheapest thing, and you always get new ideas and wisdom through books. Also, being a little bit more social. Try to be the hub of the network that I talked about previously. Becoming the hub of any social network is a good investment which is very cheap; at the same time, it gets you a lot of return.

How do you start your day, get to your computer and start solving problems? How do you stay productive?

Maybe I'm not the right person to give advice in this case, because I am a creative person. Even though I have a number of technical skills, I'm driven by creativity and creativity cannot be planned. So I will say that I try to finish my to do list. I tried to follow Getting Things Done (GTD) for a while. However, I am not relying on that so much these days. But I will say that I'm very driven by creativity. One of the good things about being in academia is that you have a lot of flexibility. Your working hours are long but also flexible and you are completely objective-driven. Basically, I try to get through one idea and don't stop until I find that idea fulfilled. I'm very unstructured in that sense.

How do you spark your own creativity? Do you have any secret that helps you boost your creative thinking and how you are able to find proper and creative solutions for problems?

That's a very tough question. I realized a couple of years ago that the big innovations that occurred in the last 200 years tend to be the combination of two things that apparently don't have much to do with each other but, together, they do something new and novel. I always bring the same example. In the 1960s, there were researchers like T.H. Maiman that discovered the laser. Then they said, "Oh, well, it's super cool to have this very powerful light but I really don't know what to use it for. It's a completely useless thing." At some point in time, a guy named James T. Russels said, "I can carve a binary pattern in a surface, maybe this could be read with that kind of light." Carving surfaces in plastic and lasers don't have to do much with each other but together they created the CD. Therefore, I believe that, in order to be creative, you need to think out of the box. Thinking out of the box is understanding that there are a lot of connections that apparently are not obvious, but, if you think appropriately, they could be groundbreaking. My secret, I would say, is trying to think out of the box and trying to marry things that have a lot of potential, but apparently don't do much with each other.

What could you recommend to an aspiring software developer to start their career?

There is a very clear way to start in academia: You start a master's degree and then if you like what you studied, you get involved with a lab or research group. If you like what you do, it is very likely that you will try to do some research on your own, normally guided by a supervisor. And if you still like what you are doing, most likely you will get into a Ph.D. degree. That being said, what I would tell this aspiring young person is that academia is very tough, it's very hard, you make a lot of sacrifices. It is definitely a vocational job, that for instance doesn't get paid as much as in the industry. You basically work long hours sometimes in very "abrasive" environments for really low pay. Of course, you have the flexibility and somehow the freedom to explore and explain something that you like, but I would definitely recommend this person first not to lie to themselves.

So please be in academia because you have a vocation to your field of research, not because you don't know anything else; this seems trivial but is a very important statement.

Many people tend to remain in academia just because they don't know anything else and they are used to following that lifestyle. However, something more important than the sacrifice per se is that at some point you will need to justify it. In other words, in my opinion, you shouldn't do something that will make your job hunting (wherever that might be) an extremely hard thing to do. If you think that the topic you are going to tackle in your Ph.D. is going to be very important in the near future, or you will be able to become one of the few world experts, you might be able to capitalize on that sacrifice. Then, my advice is: not only look at the tremendous amount of work you have ahead of you but also think what's going to happen when you finish. You are going to be really tired after that time, and you need it to pay it off. You need to understand that you made a sacrifice for something that is good, and you can capitalize on it in the future somehow. Maybe even emotionally. But it's good that you need to see the light in the tunnel and the fact that the light in the tunnel is a better world.

EDUARDO'S RECOMMENDATIONS

The Odyssey | Homer

Clean Code: A Handbook of Agile Software Craftsmanship | Robert C. Martin

Dynamics Of Complex Systems (Studies in Nonlinearity) | Yaneer Bar-yam

ASH FURROW

🐦 @ashfurrow   ashfurrow.com   github.com/ashfurrow

Ash is a compassionate software developer from Canada. After working at Artsy for seven years, he now works for Shopify. His background is originally in native iOS apps but nowadays he builds a lot of software in React Native. He has published a number of books, built many apps, and is a prolific contributor to open source software. On his blog, he writes about a range of topics, from interesting programming to explorations of music and the humanities.

You're a renaissance man. You've become an expert in many different technologies, defying the traditionally held idea that a developer should master a single technology. Was this an intentional strategy on your part?

I wanted to increase the scale of my impact at Artsy, and iOS is only a small part of Artsy's technology stack. To have a bigger impact on that stack, I had to learn new technologies. This was the motivating factor. My desire was very intentional, but how I went about it was very organic. I happened to be working on a team that was building something with Scala, so I learned Scala. And then the team happened to be building something in JavaScript, so I learned JavaScript and React.

Would you recommend that beginning developers plan to cultivate multi-focal expertise?

For beginners, I recommend focusing on a single technology. The problem is that people continue to focus on one thing for a very long time. Once they have achieved a certain level of depth, developers should start to branch out. There's no right answer about when it's best to branch out, but I think most developers wait too long. The longer you wait to branch out, the more difficult it is to learn new technologies. For beginners, learning how to program is already so overwhelming that focusing on a specific language or a specific framework is a good idea. Once they're feeling confident, I like to encourage them to branch out into related technologies. For example, if they've learned a lot of Swift, they could learn Objective-C. It doesn't need to be something entirely different. They don't need to jump from Swift to some unrelated language, like Scala, or Ruby even. Start with something related to what they already know.

Is there any factor developers seeking to branch out should consider when they're trying to choose a new technology to learn? How might the answer be different or similar for junior and senior developers?

It depends on what their motivation is. If they want to learn something purely because they enjoy learning and it's a hobby, then they should pick whatever is the most appealing to them. If they're working in a team, then they should ask themselves, "What does the team need me to learn?" Ideally, you'd list what the team needs and what you want, and then find out where they overlap. That's where you should focus your attention.

❝ *Not everyone is a skilled writer, but that's okay. The writing isn't the important part. It's the sharing knowledge that's important.* **❞**

You're also a prolific writer and have published several books. What's the biggest lesson you learned from writing your books? Would you recommend other developers follow in your footsteps?

Writing books is something I eventually did, but writing is something that I did from the very beginning. When I started learning how to write iOS apps, called iPhone apps at the time, I started a blog. I would write about the things that I learned like how to use NSArray. Through the process of writing about them and teaching others, I learned so much more about those technologies. That's something I encourage everyone to do. Not everyone is a skilled writer, but that's okay. The writing isn't the important part. It's the sharing knowledge that's important.

To get started, organize a weekly lunch and learn where people share the things that they've learned over the past week with each other. Get in the habit of teaching others something new. I think that's a great way to start building your presentation skills. Maybe you want to write a blog, or maybe you want to present to a meetup or at a conference. I think that sharing knowledge is important, and writing is the way I happen to do that. Everyone can contribute to knowledge sharing. You don't have to be a skilled writer.

For instance, some developers might prefer to make open-source contributions or YouTube tutorials. Right?

Exactly. For instance, I held weekly office hours at Artsy where I invited people to come and work on knowledge sharing. If they want ed to write a blog post, I helped them write a blog post. If they wanted to present at a meetup, I helped them do their outline and their slide designs. If they wanted to start a podcast, I helped them learn how to edit audio. There are several ways to share knowledge, and I encouraged people to try something new and keep at it. Initial failure is to be expected. That's okay.

What resources have had a lasting impact on how you work?

The first book I would recommend is Buckminster Fuller's *Operating Manual for Spaceship Earth*. This was written decades ago, so it's not about computer programming specifically, but it's about thinking in terms of systems that interact with each other and thinking about large scale ideas and concepts. That framework for thinking about things at a high level has helped me as a software developer to think about software architecture and to build software on a team. I don't work as an individual, I work as a team member, so thinking about the team as a system has helped me not just to be productive personally, but to help my colleagues be productive, which I think is more important.

The second resource I'd recommend is a podcast called *Pessimists Archive* with Jason Feifer. It looks throughout history at newspaper articles and other artifacts. It focuses on new technologies that seemed scary at the time, but that now we take for granted. One example is the introduction of the bicycle, which society initially feared. Another example is the subway. In the U.S., people were afraid of being underground, and so it took a long time to get subway construction started. There's such a variety of technologies throughout history that we've been afraid of. Sometimes, those fears are valid. Looking at how people have historically reacted to technology has influenced how I look at the technology I'm building today.

The third resource I'd recommend is a book called *Awakening Compassion at Work: The Quiet Power That Elevates People and Organizations* by Monica C. Worline and Jane E. Dutton. Again, this is not a programming book, but it's a book about how to foster compassion in teams. This has been important for me as an engineer because, again, I work on a team with other people, and the product of the team is influenced directly by the quality of our team and how we work together. A book about compassion and how to be compassionate in the workplace is a great resource for software engineers.

What concerns you about the industry?

The way software developers categorize ourselves is unhealthy. People who call themselves iOS developers or Android developers or JavaScript developers are putting themselves in a box with a label on it. I would prefer that engineers look at themselves as people who solve problems, and they just happen to solve problems with iOS, for example. We shouldn't define ourselves based on the technology that we use to solve problems, because then if we see a problem that can't be solved with our technology, we won't try to solve it.

How would you recommend junior or beginning developers boost their careers?

When you're starting, it's very difficult to stay motivated because there's so much to learn. I recommend people find others who are learning and learn together. This can help you stay motivated and also help you answer questions. More importantly, when you're learning how to build software, pick something that you want to build yourself. I'll speak from my personal experience.

My first iOS app was a very basic app that helped you make coffee. I wanted an app to help me make coffee, and through building my own, I learned the discipline of app building. That intrinsic motivation kept me focused on the difficulties of learning how to write iPhone apps.

What is something you wish someone had told you when you started working as a software developer that you had to learn the hard way?

I wish someone had told me to be more assertive with my bosses. The first two jobs I had after university weren't great, and I stayed at both of them longer than I should have because I was afraid of disappointing my bosses. Eventually, I did leave, and I felt better because I didn't want to work at a place that didn't respect me. It was also better for them because they no longer had an employee who was unhappy and unmotivated, and they could hire someone else who was a better fit.

You've also contributed to a lot of open-source code. How do developers get started doing that?

There are a lot of ways to contribute to open source. I encourage people to open issues on projects they use. If they find a bug or have a feature request or suggestion, they should open an issue about it.

That's a good way to start contributing—to let the project maintainers know that you're using the project, you like the project, and what you'd like to see out of the project.

Other ways to contribute include updating READMEs or documentation and fixing typos. These are all valuable things that help other people use and contribute to a project. I tell people not to focus on the code aspect of contributing to open source, but to focus on a project itself. How is it organized? How is it documented?

There's also the idea of building something yourself. I'd like to see more engineers open source their side projects. If they have an app on the app store, open source it, because it's a great way to get feedback from other developers about how you've implemented things. It's also a great way to give back to the community as other people can learn from your experience.

As junior and senior software developers, how do we keep improving? What should we do to avoid career paralysis?

Many engineers focus on the depth of their technical experience rather than focusing on the impact that they can have on their teams and on the business they work for. I'd encourage people to look at where they like to work in the technology stack that they work in. If they prefer front-end or back-end or somewhere in the middle, find that spot and then look for opportunities to increase your impact at that level.

If you're a front-end engineer, you might look for better ways to write user interface code, or you might look for ways to help your colleagues write better interface code. Focusing on advancement in your existing work environment prevents the disappointment that comes from learning a complicated technical skill and then not having anywhere to apply it.

Besides all your community contributions such as articles, books, and open source, you've been contributing to the offline community in New York and doing some volunteering. Do developers have an obligation to volunteer?

Volunteering has benefits, but I don't think it's an obligation. Not everyone can contribute outside of work. There are people with families and other time commitments that leave them unable to contribute in this way. I think it's something that should be encouraged and celebrated, but I don't think it's something that should be required.

How do you stay highly productive in your work for long periods?

I find it difficult to find long stretches of time to be productive because I have a lot of meetings and responsibilities outside of coding. Some people will block off long periods on their calendar to work, and I find that unhelpful because it sort of divides my time, and I find it difficult to switch between tasks. Instead, I've tried to get better at being productive in short bursts of time. It's difficult to do, but it's worthwhile. If I have ten minutes before a meeting, being able to contribute a request that helps out a colleague or fixes a bug in a very short amount of time is more valuable to me than finding four hours in the afternoon to be productive alone.

There's a theory that developers should work for one or two hours uninterrupted because it takes at least thirty minutes to get into the flow of work. Do you think that this is true?

I think working for long periods is fun, but it's not always the most productive. If you're working on a problem for four hours and it turns out that the problem isn't what you thought, or you weren't solving the correct problem, then you run the risk of having wasted those four hours. On the other hand, if you take 15 minutes to build a quick prototype and then ask for input from others, or if you take five minutes to talk to your designer and your product manager about what exactly you're building, you can spend more time focusing on building the right thing. I encourage people to explore how they work best and how their minds work best and to set up habits and routines to support that.

How does remote work fit into your workflow?

In the past, I found remote work isolating, but I may be in a better position to work remotely now. I have some fully remote colleagues, and they enjoy it. They take steps to make sure that they have opportunities for socialization with other members of the team and that they're able to get outside and get some fresh air. They set up habits to help them be happy and productive as remote workers. Remote work takes effort. It's not just working outside of the office.

ASH'S RECOMMENDATIONS

Operating Manual for Spaceship Earth | Buckminster Fuller

The Pessimists Archive podcast | Jason Feifer

Awakening Compassion at Work | Jane E. Dutton and Monica C. Worline

HADI HARIRI

❝ *Think beyond*
the technology. **❞**

🐦 @hhariri

D eveloper and creator of many things OSS, he has been programming in one way, shape or form since the age of 12. Author of various publications and courses, Hadi has been speaking at industry events for nearly two decades. Host to Talking Kotlin, he works at JetBrains leading the Developer Advocacy team, and spends as much time as he can writing code.

You are an authority in the world when it comes to public speaking and you have blogged extensively about it. What moved you to begin sharing your experiences and ideas through public speaking, as opposed to just publishing them online?

I have to admit that part of my motivation to give a talk was that I really wanted to attend a conference and I couldn't afford to; but after giving the talk, I realized I enjoyed it very much and wanted to repeat it again, despite being very nervous and feeling as though I had failed badly. The more I gave talks, the more I enjoyed sharing my thoughts and experiences. What really made it for me, though, was seeing how what I was sharing impacted people. To think that I could contribute positively to other people's lives—albeit in a very minor way—brings me a great sense of fulfillment.

What advice or tips would you give to a developer who is interested in getting started in public speaking?

Don't believe that you have nothing to share. We all do. User groups and meetups are a very good way to start. You don't have to give your first talk at a conference.

In addition to public speaking, through Twitter, you've raised awareness of certain social issues, including inclusivity in the tech industry, which is notorious for its gender imbalance and lack of opportunities for minorities and women. What steps should we be taking as an industry as a whole to address these issues?

Twitter is good way to connect with your peers and use as a professional platform. Regarding social advocacy, I'm still trying to learn how I can help more. What I would say though is to listen carefully to those who have more knowledge and be a platform for underrepresented groups. Help them share their message by amplifying their voice, not replacing it. As an individual, be conscious. Be aware that these issues exist and don't ignore the problems. Don't fall into the trap that "because it hasn't happened to me or anyone I know, it doesn't exist."

> **"** *We should definitely be more conscious and aware of the unintended consequences of the technology we're developing.* **"**

Are there any other aspects of the current tech industry that you would like to see improved?

I'd like to see more ethics involved in the things that we're doing. I'd like us to question more whether some things just shouldn't be done, and we should definitely be more conscious and aware of the unintended consequences of the technology we're developing. I'm sure we're all aware of the dark side of AI, for instance.

An additional industry trend I generally don't agree with is the constant hype train.

What steps can we take to make these improvements in the short term?

In terms of our ethics, step outside of the technology bubble. Think beyond the technology. Think beyond the excitement of working on cool stuff. Look at the human side of things and the consequences it may have. Raise awareness.

For the hype train? We should be thinking before adopting. Thinking before copying.

With everything else you have going on, do you still have time to write code?

Yes, although I'd like to often have more time. But I do still code. Besides enjoying it, I also think it's very important to do so; otherwise, I'd not be very much of a good developer advocate!

For those developers transitioning to become developer advocates, but who want to also keep coding and developing, what would you advise?

Find a project—be it OSS, be it internal to your company—that keeps you coding. Also, understand that developer advocacy is not a 9–5 job, and personally I think it's much harder than just development. Not only do you need to be on top of new technology, but you have to also test it, work with it, to remain knowledgeable and credible.

In settling in to do your own work, how do you start your day off with a bang? Do you have any secret morning routines that set you up for success?

I wish I could tell you I get up and work out to have a wonderful fresh start. But, usually, it involves waking up at around 5:00–5:30 a.m., making coffee and getting to work. Whether I'm traveling or at home, that's mostly my routine.

How do you stay highly productive for long stretches of time?

That would assume I'm highly productive! To be honest, I've never thought about it. I do know that I'm probably not as productive as I'd like to be, and I'm looking at ways to try and improve. But one thing I've found that really helps me feel more productive, and can be seen somewhat by the results, is waking up early in the morning. Those four hours or so of uninterrupted work can really help accomplish results.

You are currently a Kotlin Developer Advocate at JetBrains. What argument would you make to a person unfamiliar with Kotlin for why they should take up Kotlin or why they should not?

I've always advocated for people to try things for themselves and see if they enjoy it. Often, people ask me, "What killer feature will make me switch to Kotlin?" My response is that it's not about features, but the overall experience. The same holds true for IntelliJ IDEA and our other tools. It's about everything put together. But like everything, people will only try things when they see there's value in it for them. So I look at the issues that we face as developers using other languages and how Kotlin addresses these. If you see enough value, then you should try it.

What is something you wish someone had told you when you started software development that you had to learn the hard way instead?

That I should have paid more attention to Haskell in University. The more I've gotten into functional programming, the more I'm interested in the ways how solving problems are approached. I've now gone back to learning Haskell but it's very hard to "disconnect" from the way in which I've been programming for so long, which is why I wish I'd have paid more attention early on!

In gaining insight from other sources, are there any that stand out as having an impact on your work?

Thinking, Fast and Slow by Daniel Kahneman. *Badass: Making Users Awesome* by Kathy Sierra is another. And *Radical Candor: Be a Kick-Ass Boss Without Losing Your Humanity* by Kim Scott really reaffirmed some of the things I was doing.

HADI'S RECOMMENDATIONS

Thinking, Fast and Slow | Daniel Kahneman

Badass: Making Users Awesome | Kathy Sierra

Radical Candor: Be a Kick-Ass Boss Without Losing Your Humanity|
| Kim Scott

ON PUBLIC SPEAKING AND A SPEAKER'S TECHNICAL MERIT ONLY

Getting Started as a Public Speaker

HADI HARIRI

Should I speak?

One question people often ask themselves is whether they should actually give a talk and if so, on what. I'll address these topics as a series of FAQs.

Should I give a talk?

If it's part of your job, yes. If it's not, only if you enjoy it. However, given you really don't know whether you enjoy something until you've experienced it a few times, then yes. Give a talk.

What if I'm nervous?

It's okay. We're all nervous.

What if I don't enjoy it?

Then stop. Don't even need a FAQ entry, right? It's amusing however the number of times I encounter people that aren't even forced to give talks as part of their job, and yet despite not enjoying it, they continue to do so.

Where should I start?

Generally, I'd recommend starting with smaller crowds, be these inside your own company, a user group, etc. My first public talk wasn't, however, at a small event, but a proper conference. Lesson learned.

What should I talk about?

Whatever you feel strongly about. Whether it's something you've learned and want to share with others, or a topic you're deeply passionate about. I think one of the most important things is to be passionate about a topic. That really does impact a talk.

What should I not talk about?

Anything that you're not passionate about... obviously. Jokes aside, this also is something I've made the mistake of myself and seen others make. Don't pick a topic just because you want to get to speak at a conference on it (whatever your reasons may be). If the topic is not of interest to you, it, again, shows in the talk.

What if I'm not an expert?

It's absolutely fine. You don't need to be an expert to give a talk on a topic. Just make sure you set expectations. If you're a beginner, say you are. In the other series of posts, I touch on this topic a few times.

What if others more experienced are talking about this same topic?

That's like saying, "I'm not going to write a book because there's already a book on this topic." Okay, maybe not entirely the case, because writing a book is a big investment you don't take lightly. But the point is that every talk, much like every article, every blog post, has more value than just the topic it touches on. It should bring insight and personal experience. And that is unique to each of us.

What are the key things I should make sure my talk has?

Generally I'd say a talk should have the following:

Provide value. You have an audience that is dedicating their time to come and see you give a talk. Make sure they walk away with something, beyond you and your ego.

Be inspirational. A talk should be a catalyst for people to want to learn more. It should pique their interest to want to dive deeper into a topic.

Be engaging. Nobody likes a boring talk. The most interesting topic in the world can be projected in the worst way if you're boring as a speaker. The reverse however usually doesn't hold—even a boring topic can be made interesting by a good speaker. Make sure your talk is engaging.

Be thought-provoking. There's nothing better than a thought-provoking talk, something that challenges our beliefs and under-standings. A talk in which everything the speaker says we agree with and nod, well while it will reaffirm our knowledge, it doesn't really challenge us mentally.

I'd say these are the basic four ingredients. Depending on the type of talk, you maybe want to vary the dosage of each one.

What's more important? Contents or Speaker?

Both are just as important. A good topic and great content with a bad speaker will provide a bad overall experience. A good speaker with a very bad topic or no content (note: different from boring content), will also provide a bad experience.

And note the keyword there: experience. Kathy Sierra summarized very well when she talks about what the most important aspect a talk should provide.

"It's About the Experience"

So now you know what you need to know to get started. It's now time to talk about another important part of public speaking:

Who gets to speak? The answer? Everyone.

A post by my colleague Trisha Gee on attracting more female speakers to conferences raised yet another debate on Twitter. One of the aspects people were discussing could generally be summed up in the following statement:

"If a speaker that identifies as male, and one that identifies as female, have the exact same knowledge, why should we discard the first in favor of the latter?"

Makes sense right? If two people have the exact same knowledge, and assuming the first one has submitted a talk, why should we go out of our way to try and find another person of a different gender to cover the topic or potentially discriminate against the first one in favor of the second? Many would consider that to fall under positive discrimination (see poll results).

The Speaker's Experience

If we were to invite people to conferences to give talks exclusively based on their knowledge, then the above could potentially constitute positive discrimination. The reality, however, is that many conferences aren't inviting individuals just because they are knowledgeable about a specific topic. Many speakers get invites because of their line of work, their background, how they use technology, how they interact with it; in essence, their experience in addition to their expertise.

This is an aspect that time and time again I've seen people openly talk about when selecting speakers, and nobody has ever considered it inappropriate. In fact, as someone that dedicates much of their time to Developer Advocacy, this is an aspect we have to always take into account. Having experience on the topics we speak on is fundamentally important, otherwise, we'd be pundits and nothing more.

The Diversity Experience

If we accept that the experience a speaker brings not only adds value to a talk but is also a key factor, and we also accept that different people have different experiences, then why, when it comes to diversity in terms of gender, race, sexual orientation, and other aspects, do we play the "positive discrimination" card? Or do we truly believe that everyone has the exact same experience in the world independently of their background and social environment?

When we have two people that, on technical merit, are 100% equal (which again, is usually not the case), and one of them is from an under-represented group, then it not only provides this person an opportunity that, in itself, can enrich their lives, but it also enriches other people's lives in hearing about their knowledge in the context of their experiences.

The Repeat Speaker

Finally, I'd also like to point out another issue that takes place in the conference world. If you look at every other conference, you often see the same speakers over and over again, talking about the same topics, over and over again. While it is understandable that conferences want to attract certain speakers, because after all, that's one of the main selling points of an event, this also tends to lead to a "boy's club," which is especially even more present in some conferences that do not have an open call for papers but are invite-only.

I know that I myself am part of the problem and that is why for the past several years I have tried to avoid going to the same conferences year after year. And this is something that those of us that speak frequently at conferences should keep in mind. Every time we speak at a conference, we're taking the place from someone else. To be clear, I'm not saying that we should stop speaking, but I find alternating is one way to try and work towards improving the situation.

As I said recently, as developers and professionals in IT, we have a role in shaping the future. Let's make sure that this future is inclusive of everyone and give people a platform to express this.

CREDIT

Versions of these two articles—"Public Speaking: Should I Speak" (September 4, 2018) and "On a Speaker's Technical Merit Only' (April 30, 2018)—were first published on Hadi Hariri's website. The original articles can be found here: hadihariri.com/2018/04/30/a-speakers-technical-merit-only/ and hadihariri.com/2018/09/04/public-speaking-should-i-speak/.

ROMAN ELIZAROV

❝ Be open, not just open-source. ❞

🐦 @relizarov

Roman works at JetBrains as Team Lead for the Kotlin Libraries team, where he is focused on development and maintenance of multi-platform foundational libraries for Kotlin programming language. His main contribution in this role is design of Kotlin coroutines and development of the Kotlin coroutines library. In 2000, Roman graduated from St. Petersburg ITMO and started his career as a professional software developer. During his undergraduate study, he participated in International Collegiate Programming Contests (ICPC). Since 1997 and, until now, Roman has served as a Chief Judge of Northern Eurasia Region of ICPC. He also maintains his academic ties and now teaches a course on concurrent and distributed programming at ITMO. Roman worked for most of his career at Devexperts, where he designed and developed high-performance trading software for leading brokerage firms and market data delivery services that routinely handle millions of events per second. He is an expert in Java and JVM, particularly in concurrency, real-time data processing, algorithms, and performance optimizations for modern languages.

> " *If you're hiring a person to do some specific assignments using a specific framework for a library, then you might just test a person's knowledge of this specific practical task. But if you're hiring a person for advanced status to do something that wasn't done before, you'll want someone with the key fundamental knowledge.* "

You have a very strong algorithmic background. There has been a large controversy in terms of interviews for software engineering jobs—some people are in favor of having algorithm content in those interviews, whereas some other people prefer to focus on more practical issues. There will be some white-boarding. There is homework to implement at home. There is bare coding. What is your opinion about this? What is the method you have found that works best in your career?

This is torturous because there is no one simple answer, especially when you are hiring a person. What kind of skills, experience, and knowledge are you looking for in a person you are hiring? So consider algorithms as an example, especially in terms of global content. I worked all my life with all the high-performance, high-level, low-level stuff, and we were developing software in which these aspects were critical. But now I'm working on core foundational content libraries. Millions of people will be using them and, with all the different use cases, every small detail will matter in these libraries.

So, for hiring, we are looking for people who understand all those low-level details, and these aren't just about algorithms. It's actually quite an extensive body of knowledge that we're looking for a person to have—that includes some parts of algorithm design and implementation. But it's not the only skill we're looking at. The difference I think, and why many people are asking about algorithms, is that, unlike different technologies, they don't just come and go.

Once your library percolates, in five, 10 years, there are different levels of framework, and this changes every time. In our careers, you always learn new things, but there is certain fundamental knowledge that's algorithmic in design; it's one of those things that never changes. It does progress, but it progresses in a more specialized areas—it's not like the fundamentals, which do not change.

Algorithms have been there for 50 years. And it's the kind of knowledge you're supposed to acquire early in your career. It's supposed to stay with you for the rest of your career.

If you're hiring a person to do some specific assignments using a specific framework for a library, then you might just test a person's knowledge of this specific practical task. But if you're hiring a person for advanced status to do something that wasn't done before, you'll want someone with the key fundamental knowledge.

There's a current trend of placing a job candidate on the team for a few days and paying them as freelancers or contractors for their time. What do you think of this approach?

When I'm hiring a developer, I want them to write code. So, whatever the strategy, by the end of the interview, I should be familiar with or what kind of code they are writing. But you also want to know how they fit with your team and how comfortable you feel with them. But there's a lot of approaches. Eventually, there's some moment just to stop and make a decision. I don't think one strategy is superior than the other; it's just whatever companies feel they like doing.

You're also involved in functional programming, which isn't as well-known in our field, especially with enterprise software. How would you explain functional programming to people who have no experience with it?

Functional programming is one of the things a software engineer must know. It's something that they should have been learned when the person was learning how to program. It's really pitiful that it's not a universal knowledge still nowadays. And the reason for that? When you teach people programming, it's typical that you teach people imperative programming first and, in some sense, that's essentially whether it's fundamentally easier to accept.

I haven't seen any research into this, but it seems the educational courses today—like any computer science 101, or any introduction to programming course—are structured to start with imperative programming. We teach loops. So this is how we, as an industry, are teaching people to code: imperative comes first and then, somewhere later in education, people learn functional programming. And, so, some people just never get to learn functional programming, which is understandable.

But project programming is when it's repetitive; you end up writing the same things over and over again. You need to filter objects, and you go write this loop that does filtering—and you do it again and again and again. It's very predictive; it's time consuming. So functional programming helps avoid this repetition; instead of repeating the same thing over and over again, you extract it through a function. This was known before as a kind of procedural programming.

The key difference between procedural programming and functional programming is that, in procedural programming, we would usually extract some operation to a processor, and then we use it to repeat. In functional programming, we go a step further. We make higher-order functions. So we don't just extract a function to filter this particularly, under this particular criteria, because this particular operation is unlikely to be repeated in the future. But we are extracting a high-order function or filter that takes another function as a parameter that configures exactly you want to filter.

So it's not just introducing new function procedures. It is basic imperative programming 101. It's about a program with higher-order functions that we use to avoid this repeating boilerplate. We use algorithms that you read just once. Then it goes on from there, and you can then increase those levels of abstraction further. But from a practical standpoint, you're just reaching higher in terms of code reuse.

Your work with functional programming has made you one of the direct contributors to the success of Kotlin. What would you say to a person interested in adopting this language?

There are many reasons I'd advocate for adopting it. Something interesting is that every person is different, and every person has at least 10 reasons why they'd do what they do. I think that's the key to Kotlin's success. Kotlin has dozens of things that it does better than other languages. It's better on so many aspects overall that I see no reason not to adopt Kotlin.

66 *Kotlin is pragmatic. We solve. We're not into any kind of pure theoretical computer science. We're not here to do any religious wars. We're not here to promote our vision. We are here to solve problems developers face day to day.* 99

Tell us about the Kotlin team.

Right now, we have a team of more than 60 people working on the language—just a core team. We have a really great community of contributors who help us with things like feedback and code. And I think that's important to success. Nowadays, you can't succeed in a project like a programming language without a community, without being open and not just open source, but open and working with this community.

Regardless of how big a team you have, you can't know everything. You can't foresee everything. You can't take every use case. You can't know every use case by heart.

Kotlin is pragmatic. We solve. We're not into any kind of pure theoretical computer science. We're not here to do any religious wars. We're not here to promote our vision. We are here to solve problems developers face day to day, and to make their life in Kotlin simple. That's our mission. That's all it is about. There's no hidden thinking about that. There's no hidden agenda.

Do you think most languages are working toward a specific goal and long-term vision, or are they responding to what the community needs at that time?

If you look at modern languages designed 10, 15 years ago, you see lots of common trends, and this is kind of converged with the old. I see that the times change, how people write code changes. There's no surprise that this drives the change in programming languages, because programming as a field is evolving quickly. Twenty years ago, we were writing desktop applications and there were microservices. Nowadays, we are writing mobile applications. And there are way more people programming right now. Projects are becoming way bigger than they used to be—20 years ago, big projects were the exception. It's no surprise that programming languages need to change to meet these new challenges, and no surprise different languages come to similar conclusions, to how these challenges have to be met.

One of the problems we seem to have is that a student starts in the university, and then will begin their professional career in five, six years. What can you recommend to these students to focus on in order to have a successful career?

Balance your education. Remember that the fundamentals are important because they stay with you forever. While you're studying at university or in school for that matter, that's where you should really focus on fundamentals because, as you grow older, it's hard to pick up fundamentals you missed. So those fundamentals not only stay forever with you, they also form how you think about different problems and that's important for the rest of your life. But, since when you graduate to get an excellent job, it's important that you also get yourself familiar with whatever programming languages are out there.

While in university, you should not miss things like summer internships and practice time because they explore the actual technologies that are important right now. Software developers are so much in demand right now and there's software all around the world in every conceivable niche. So lots of people find development easy—especially bright people who have a knack for it.

They find it so easy to find a good job early in their career that they might think, "Okay, I'm fine. I don't need the rest of it. I'll just do this. I have a job now, I'll do it." But then the problem is that technologies will change over time. They will in five years, in 10 years. The old ones will wither, the new ones come, but the fundamentals are there forever. So, again, while in university, you should not forget that you should learn—that's your chance to get your fundamentals straight. And then if you get them straight, you'll be able to find a good job for the rest of your life.

Are there any books that you could recommend to a fellow software developer that had a lasting impact on your career?

One book I really loved as a kid was *Algorithms + Data Structures = Programs* by Niklaus Wirth. This is a classic book. It's quite out of date right now. I wouldn't recommend starting with it right now because algorithms that are explained there are out of date. But that was my go-to book that basically taught me the basics of algorithmic design and how to think about writing code and even structuring code.

Do you think there is a concept that most software developers don't pay enough attention to when they're trying to grow their careers?

Something I think people miss when they get into industrial programming is depth of knowledge. When they get a job, they just start doing new things and are under pressure to do them quickly. So they usually make a mistake of growing their knowledge upwards as they learn how to use these technologies. They learn tips and tricks, and this is great, but what lots of people miss is the fact that they have also to study in-depth. The question they should be always asking is how it works, what it does inside, and what's inside of that?

We develop in abstractions. There is a good post by Joel Spolsky titled, "The Law of Leaky Abstractions," which I would again recommend anyone to read because it explains the importance for a good software developer to always question everything they use and to always learn how it works inside, what it does, why it works this way. And that's universal advice for any kind of things.

The software development career moves very fast regardless of the fundamentals. There are new libraries, languages, and we need to understand the fundamentals. We need to master them. However, we need to use current tools because it's part of our day-to-day work.

Being in this fast-paced environment, how do you keep yourself updated in our industry? Do you have any particular system like mailing list, attending conferences, reading, etc.?

I don't have any single advice. There are many resources. You can use social networks. You can just talk with people. You can read books. There are so many resources out there that tell you what's new, what's in conferences, etc. I can't give universal ways that work for everybody, but I would urge every developer first to learn what's up, what's new and what's going on.

What's something you wish someone had told you when you were getting started that you had to learn the hard way?

Nobody taught me formally, for example, concurrency. At the time I was studying, this was not something people talked about a lot. So, at first, I'd stumble upon problems with concurrency in practice, and then I had to go back and relearn all the fundamentals, read papers, read books about it and then discover this whole world. So, concurrency, for me, even though I am now an expert in this field, it's not something I was formally taught. I practiced and then I went back and learned all the theory out there. It is important when you stumble into something in practice, don't always look for a rule because, when you know the basic principles, that saves you from having to know specifics.

What is the most undervalued skill among software engineers that you would like to see more?

People are so different. Some people lack knowledge, others lack compassion. Other people lack teamwork. I don't have any universal advice. People are so different.

ROMAN'S RECOMMENDATION

Algorithms + Data Structures = Programs | Niklaus Wirth

GETTING TO WORK

❝ *There's always going to be people saying, 'This is the one true way to do things,' and then other people saying, 'No it's not. This is the one true way to do things.' Being able to look at those claims dispassionately and figure out what actually works for you is the bigger thing to focus on in terms of learning.* **❞**

—Ellen Shapiro

JOHN SUNDELL

" Hold up your side
of the deal. "

🐦@johnsundell   🐦@swiftbysundell   swiftbysundell.com

John builds apps, games and developer tools. He also makes Swift by Sundell—a series of weekly articles and a podcast about Swift development, and co-hosts the Stacktrace podcast.

You have switched from a large company, Spotify, to work as a freelancer. What are some of the non-obvious ways that working as a freelancer differs from working at a company?

Freelancing offers a lot more freedom, but with this freedom comes a lot more responsibility. You not only manage your own time, but you also manage your clients and the quality of the work that you do.

When you work in a company, there is usually a supporting structure around you. For example, there might be a manager who helps the team manage its time and tasks, or there might be testers to test the team's newly built features. But when you work as a freelancer, many times you are responsible for those things. That means that you have to schedule when to work on your tasks in order to fulfill your agreement as to what you'll build and when it should be delivered. You also have to deliver high-quality work, because that's what clients will expect. Overall, being a freelancer is like running your own small business, and you need to make sure to deliver on your promises and to keep your customers happy.

What kind of qualities do you think it takes—professionally or personally—to work successfully as a freelancer?

I think it mostly comes down to being very organized. You need to manage your own time and to make sure that you spend your time on the right things—but you also need to maintain great relationships with the people and clients with whom you work. Managing expectations is a big part of that. People need to know when and what you are going to deliver, and they need to be able to trust that you'll stick to your deadlines. The classic phrase "under-promise and over-deliver" is key here.

Being a successful freelancer has as much to do with business practices as it has to do with the code that you write. When I was a freelancer, I would often spend hours dealing with contracts, emailing clients, and attending meetings. However, while some people can be frustrated by having many meetings and doing administrative work, I don't mind it at all. Whenever I'm sending invoices, doing administrative tasks, and responding to emails, it feels like I'm moving my business forward, and there's something incredibly satisfying about that.

How did you know it was time to become a full-time freelancer, and how did it feel to make that transition? What was your catalyst?

I became a freelancer to have the ability to work remotely. While a lot of companies offer remote work, I felt like taking on my own clients and working on multiple different projects would be an excellent fit for me, since it wouldn't tie me to any specific location or any strict working hours. I thought working on my own would enable me to travel a lot more, to work on things like open source and community initiatives, and give me the power to organize my time. That was all very appealing to me, so I decided to give it a try.

As a freelancer, one of the key aspects is to secure a steady flow of clients and projects. How did you achieve this? What would you recommend to a developer thinking of going freelancing?

Keeping a steady flow of clients can be incredibly difficult, and "client-hunting" is something that can take up a lot of your time if you're not careful. Before I made the transition to become a freelancer, I made sure that I had one long-term project lined up already. That project gave me 30 hours of work per week, which was great since it gave me the flexibility to do other things on the side—while still giving me a steady flow of income from day one.

Having that initial client was key for me, and it heavily reduced the stress-factor of going freelance. So my greatest advice for anyone who's looking to become a freelancer is to do something like that—to find a first project *before* making that jump. If you're lucky, you might even be able to convince your current employer to convert your employee contract into some form of freelancing arrangement.

You are also working remotely and advocating strongly for remote work. Remote work seems to be a trend that has come to stay: Not only do developers have more freedom and flexibility, but companies also benefit from a wider hiring pool. Any tips for companies thinking of going remote or trying to implement it?

To make remote work successful in a company, one of the most important things is to treat the whole company as if it were remote. Even if you're just hiring one or two people who are going to work remotely, pretend like everyone on the team is working remotely, too. If people are coming to the office every day, whenever there is a meeting, ask everyone to call into that meeting separately from their computers. Try not to put the whole team—except for one remote person—in a single room and ask that one person to dial in. That person will feel like an outsider who doesn't have the same level of influence as the people who are in the office every day.

Use small little tweaks like that: everyone dialing into meetings, all the conversations about code happening on GitHub or Slack (or whichever other tools that you use) instead of discussing those things ad hoc at someone's desk. All of that can make remote working not only possible, but also enjoyable. However, making such changes can be a bit awkward at first. Someone might wonder, "Why can't I just go talk to my coworker who is right there? Why do I need to get on a Hangout?" I think after you overcome that awkwardness—which is usually just something you have to get used to—these remote-friendly routines really help.

As you say, making a company remote-friendly opens up a wider pool from which you can recruit, and it gives everyone on the team a lot more flexibility, even if they go into the office every single day. If you set up the proper working environment, then everyone, even people in the office, can work remotely whenever they want. Guess what? If you're going on vacation, you could extend that vacation by a couple of weeks and work from there. It gives everyone a lot of freedom. Establishing remote-friendly routines can not only make a big difference for the individuals who are already working remotely, but it could also accelerate an office-based company's transition to a fully remote company very quickly.

> **“**I use a system to organize tasks that I call 'Quick Wins.' I try to split all of my tasks up into pieces that are as small as possible. **”**

In your independent work, how do you start your day and stay productive?

I use a system to organize tasks that I call "Quick Wins." I try to split all of my tasks up into pieces that are as small as possible—whether I'm building a new feature, sending an email, or scheduling something. These small tasks then go into my "Quick Wins" list and every morning I try to do at least one Quick Win just to get started with the day. That gives me a sense of success at the beginning of the day, which then makes it so much easier to move on to bigger and more complicated tasks.

I start almost all of my productivity work—like organizing my time, ideas, and schedule—by using Apple Notes. I use Notes for everything: for all of my different TODO lists, for ideas, for article drafts, and for preparing my next podcast episode. The reason I still stick with this app even though there are so many more purpose-built ones—like Apple's own Reminders app and other ones more geared towards TODO lists—is that I love the freedom of being able to make a note and then add TODO lists inline. I also like being able to take my iPad and my Apple pencil and draw and place images within a note or list. I basically "dump" a lot of thoughts into this application every single day, and then organize them afterwards.

I do most of my development in Xcode. Xcode has a feature called playgrounds, which lets you write Swift code in a way that continuously executes it to show you the the latest results, and I use this feature all the time. I do a lot of prototyping, I write a lot of sample code, and even when I'm doing something like building a new piece of UI, I like to do that using playgrounds. It gives me a very quick feedback loop, and I like the lightweight nature of this way of coding.

How do you manage your time and distribute it among your personal projects?

When I left Spotify at the end of 2016, I made a deal with myself: from now on, I'm going to dedicate 20% of my time to working for the Swift community—whether that's by writing articles, contributing to open source projects, or something else.

That might not sound like a lot of hours per week, but over time, it adds up. Like always, if you try to make the most use of your time, then even a small amount of hours can have a big impact eventually. Whenever I start a new project—whether that's for my business, for the community, or just for fun—I always make sure to set aside dedicated time for it. That way, I prevent myself from overworking, while also being able to juggle multiple projects at once.

So I did that 80/20 split between working as a freelancer and working on my website, articles, podcast and open source projects for about two years—and now, since the first of January 2019, I've been able to make Swift by Sundell and my work for the Swift community my full-time job, which honestly still feels a bit unreal and incredibly exciting.

For me, it has really taught me that even if something starts out as an experiment, or as a hobby project, if you dedicate enough time to it, and if you keep working on it through all the ups and downs—amazing things can happen, even things you didn't plan for or dream about.

What would you recommend to people who are new to engaging this community? Where should they start? Any tips?

My biggest recommendation would be to start small. Sometimes, when we think about these things—starting a blog, starting a podcast, making a YouTube video, or whatever it might be—we might think that the thing we're making must be big and revolutionary, something that'll have a big impact on the community. However, most projects don't have that kind of impact when they're started—and it's not really necessary. The important thing is just to get started, however small the first step might be.

For example, my first article was only 500 words. In my first podcast episode, I was the only one talking for half an hour. That was it: no guests, nothing, just me. And my first conference talk was just a 20-minute lightning talk.

The key is to remove that constraint that you need to make something big. An article can be short, a podcast episode can be simple, a YouTube video can just be you talking over a deck of slides, a talk can simply be about sharing something you've learned recently. The main thing is to focus on sharing something that you are passionate about.

I don't recommend starting to share things just because someone told you that you need to write an article in order to become a Senior Developer. I don't think that's true, and I don't think everyone needs to become a blogger or a podcaster. But if you do have something that you want to share, like a cool feature that you built, or some hard technical problem that you solved, try to do that in the simplest possible way. Don't try to build a huge audience or to become the next big blog, because that kind of thing takes so much time and effort.

Building up a big website with lots of content takes years, so I don't think anyone should have that as a goal or expectation when they're going into it. It should be more about building what are you passionate about, sharing what you'd like to share, and doing so in the simplest way possible.

As an independent contractor, what do you do to keep yourself updated with the latest development trends?

I'm a bit old-fashioned when it comes to things like that. I read a lot of documentation, but I feel that documentation is something that a lot of developers, especially people who are learning development now, are dismissing. They tend to go directly to a blog, to YouTube or Stack Overflow. That said—there's nothing wrong with that. I mean, I'm writing a blog, so I do like that people read blogs!

However, the documentation from platform vendors, such as Apple and Google, is usually of really high quality, especially when it comes to the high-level concepts of a tool or framework.

There is usually great documentation on everything from the UI layer and the various UI libraries that each platform offers, to things like audio and graphics frameworks, and I try to read almost all of it. If a new framework comes out during WWDC, I will take a look at the documentation, I will read through it, and then I will try it out by building a few experimental things. For example, I will open up a playground, import the framework, and try to write some code that uses it just to familiarize myself with the API, and to figure out how it works.

When it comes to understanding trends in particular, I mostly focus on talking to other developers, to hear what they are interested in right now, and what challenges they are solving on a day-to-day basis. For that, I use social media like Twitter, attend conferences, try to go to as many meetups here in my local city as I possibly can and, in general, try to stay in touch with the community as much as I can. These connections give me a lot of input in terms of what people are interested in and where the industry as a whole is going.

What is a current industry trend that you think is wrong?

I think big companies monetizing user data is one of the biggest threats that we're facing in the technology industry right now. Big companies that are harvesting user data without users knowing about it, and then using it to manipulate people or content for profit—or for creepy advertising that's following users around, tracking every move. I personally think that those kind of practices are morally wrong, and we, as an industry, are obligated to move in a direction that is more transparent, that is more responsible, and that is more user-friendly.

It also seems like the general public is becoming more aware of where their data is, how companies are using it, and how the data is being exploited. Those are definitely steps in the right direction. As individual developers, we have a lot of power and responsibility here, because all of those creepy analytics tools that are analyzing user behavior and tracking people in invasive ways, those are all algorithms implemented by developers—like you and me.

If you, as a developer, get assigned a task that you morally object to—then consider pushing back on it. Initially doing so might not be very productive because management might just find someone else to do it, but if you keep arguing your case about why user privacy matters—then that can have a big impact in the long run.

In terms of other sources, what podcasts or books have had a lasting impact on you or how you work?

Right now, I work a lot with website, article and podcast production. I run my own site, and so I am very inspired by other people who do the same thing. For instance, I like to listen to people like John Gruber, Myke Hurley and Stephen Hackett, and Chris Eidhof—people who have done much of the same thing that I'm doing—building a business around websites and podcasts.

I particularly like John Gruber's podcast *The Talk Show*. It's not only a great show, but I also enjoy it from a sort of meta angle—how he deals with sponsors, how he organizes the show and his website, etc. That's all very inspiring for me.

What is something you wish someone had told you when you started software development that you learned the hard way?

Not to have too many strong opinions. Keep an open mind. It's very common for people who are at the beginning of their career to have strong opinions about the techniques or methods that they like—and that they feel compelled to defend those opinions. I've completely moved away from that and wish I had learned to do so earlier. Very specific techniques or patterns rarely matter in the long run, and there are so many different ways to solve a given problem, and all of them have pros and cons.

You have to learn to pick your battles. Ask yourself: is this specific pattern, or tool, or code style, really that important? If you think about it, the answer is probably no. You probably want to spend your time having more productive discussions. Also, once you stop having those really strong opinions, you open up your mind to learning more about alternative solutions. Something that at first might not seem like a good solution may turn out really great, and might even become something that you'll learn a lot from.

What is an effective strategy to overcome this issue?

I think the best way to combat that kind of mindset is to try different things. If you're feeling that you could become a bit more open-minded, just challenge yourself to try something new. Even if it might not seem like something you'll like in the beginning, try it. I'd love for the industry in general to encourage that kind of thinking—especially when it comes to scenarios like deciding how to implement a given feature, or choosing which architectural approach that a team should take. Welcome as many different opinions as possible, build prototypes to try different things out, and encourage people to be open minded—don't just stick to one solution.

JOHN'S RECOMMENDATIONS

The Talk Show podcast | John Gruber

Accidental Tech podcast | Marco Arment, Casey Liss and John Siracusa

Connected podcast | Federico Viticci, Myke Hurley and Stephen Hackett

FELIX KRAUSE

*" Learn along
the way. "*

🐦 @KrauseFx   github.com/@KrauseFx   krausefx.com   whereisfelix.today

Felix is the founder of *fastlane*, an open-source tool for iOS and Android developers focused on making building and releasing apps easier. Just last year, fastlane has saved over 15,000,000 developer hours and is used by tens of thousands of companies around the world. He's also the founder of iOS-factor.com, an open-source best-practices guide on how to build high-quality iOS apps. He was named as one of Forbes 30 under 30. He has published various privacy-related essays on the iOS permission system. As a result, his posts reached #1 on HackerNews multiple times and got covered by major media outlets. Felix speaks at various conferences around the world, most recently Tel Aviv, Oslo, Tokyo, Melbourne, Bangalore, Vienna, Berlin and San Francisco.

Felix, you are very well-known for being the founder of fastlane, an amazing open-source tool for iOS and Android developers with a focus on building and mobilizing apps with ease. The tool boasts incredible numbers—it's estimated to have saved 15 million developer hours. It has since been acquired by Google. What was the inspiration to develop this tool?

Back home in Austria, I started a company that was providing an app builder for sport clubs. Back then, it was one of the first ones out there. It would automatically fetch all kinds of information from Facebook and RSS feeds, like the news items, images, videos and more. The great thing about this concept is that you only had to build it once, and then you could sell it to multiple types of sport clubs. I wanted to build it in a way that, when I changed the core, I could update *all* the modeled apps without a lot of extra work. I ended up automating 100% of the process—meaning when I changed a line of code and then pressed the Deploy button, it would push 20 updates to the store that hosted the app. That's kind of how I got started with the automation piece of my work.

Selling the resulting app was actually quite difficult. At some point, I decided, "Okay, let's focus on the automation part." So I built an actual product around the automation of the deployment process, and that's how *fastlane* got started. I started it as a college project while I was doing my Bachelor's degree in Software Engineering.

It's really interesting that you knew it was time to make your app / project be something else. How did you know you had to let go of the original idea of your app and focus on something else with it— the automation? Was that difficult?

It was a challenging decision to pivot. There were two components to it: First, selling the sports app was more difficult than expected, and I noticed I didn't enjoy doing it at all. Second, for my Bachelor's degree, I needed a project that had the right-sized scope.

Thanks to the university, I had the time to put into starting a new project, for which I chose the iOS build automation.

From there I naturally invested less and less time into the app builder, which then slowly faded out.

In all the work you do, you are also known for leading a nomadic lifestyle—moving to a new place every month and carrying what fits on your back. Is this difficult to do while also working professionally as a developer and entrepreneur?

My nomadic life is slightly different from other nomads in that I usually stay within the same city. I spend most of my time in New York City, where Google has an office. So while I move to a new apartment and a new neighborhood every month or so, I still go to the same office. I still get the job done. I still get to hang out with the same group of friends and so on. I agree that, if you to relocate to a different country every week, it's more challenging to be as productive, but that's why I made the conscious decision to move within the same city. While I travel for conferences from time to time, I usually stay in the same city—I'm in between New York and Austria, where I'm from, where my family is, so I spend some time there also.

How do you deal with lacking a physical office when you're traveling? Is there a place that you like to go, namely cafés or workspaces, etc.?

Actually, my favorite place to work is always in my own apartment or hotel room, because that's where it's quiet; that's the only real thing I care about when I want to get actual work done.

There's a big difference between writing emails and attending meetings— versus actually solving problems. Whenever I want to solve problems, I need a quiet surrounding, so I never work from coffee shops or the like. I prefer just my own apartment. When I travel, I always have a Bluetooth keyboard, Bluetooth trackpad, and a MacBook stand with me to lift up the MacBook—a traveling workstation. The one I have is the Roost stand; it's super small, and I always have it with me. It allows you to build up your workstation wherever you go, so you don't kill your neck when you work from your laptop.

Do you have any sort of ritual when you are starting the day?

My mornings are not the best. I generally don't like waking up, so there's nothing that I can recommend there! But the number one thing that has helped me a lot when it comes to daily productivity is going to the gym—usually at about 3 or 4 PM, which is a little after half the workday. The reason why I do this is because, at that time, it's usually already a little harder to focus; I might be a little tired or something, right? And so I always go to the gym during that time, and it clears my head. I shower again, and it kind of feels like having a second day. At least, that's how I see it, because, afterward, I go back to my Mac with a fresh mindset.

If you can do something like this when it comes to your job, I recommend doing that.

In working with other people remotely, how do you deal with the common problem of working with teams and people in different timezones?

Though, most of the time, I work in Eastern Standard Time, in New York City, it can still be complex. When it comes to scheduling, I use everytimezone.com; the site lets you visualize time zones more easily. But, also, to schedule meetings and video calls, I use Calendly, which allows you to send a link to someone else, and they can choose a time slot on your calendar. I don't use it too often. I also try to avoid meetings and calls as much as I can, and I always prefer asynchronous communication.

Why do you try to avoid meetings and calls? Why do you prefer asynchronous communication?

Many forms of communications, in particular, Slack messages, meetings and calls, encourage (or allow) a lazy communication and working style. Some people then make use of this, at the costs of your co-workers. If you use emails to communicate, it requires the author to provide all the needed context and detail to be able to reply to the problem, and it forces the author to properly structure their thoughts.

At the same time, once something is nicely written down in the form of a doc or email group, it allows other team members to read up on how a specific decision was made, etc.

You seem to have discovered what works for you in terms of productivity. Do you have any habits that are uncommon or very particular to you?

One habit is writing down ideas when I have them; I use an app called *MajorKey* to do that.

Another habit is listening to audiobooks. I live around 40 minutes from the Google office in New York City right now and I just walk and listen to audiobooks every day unless it's raining. If you walk for almost two hours a day and you listen to audiobooks, you can finish one book in a week, which is pretty impressive!

Which books have had the biggest impact on your life that you would recommend to other developers?

All the books I read are non-technical. A book I read recently that I enjoyed was *Homo Deus: A Brief History of Tomorrow* by Yuval Noah Harari. It's about the future of humankind, a little bit about the history of mankind over the last million years, and what the future problems will be in the next hundred, two hundred years. That was a really interesting book, and it was written in a way that it's applicable for us engineers, but also the non-engineers. It's a very good book.

In addition to audiobooks, what other habits have you developed?

I've developed some habits for when I have a project on which I have actual coding to do. Day-to-day, you contend with a lot of emails, meetings, documentation, etc. But sometimes you just want to solve technical problems. You just wanna write code. I usually clearly define that zone; it helps to have a ritual around that. For me, that was always Club-Mate—a German sparkling tea drink—that I usually have at home. It's just a caffeinated tea. But my rule is that I only drink it when I close my email apps and disable notifications to get coding done. I put on my headphones. I usually eat a piece of chocolate for some extra sugar, and I drink the Club-Mate, and that's the sign to myself that I'm going to get stuff done.

Aside from the ones you've mentioned, what other tools do you use daily that make your life as a developer easier?

I have several tools and processes that I use. The number one productivity tip that I can recommend to every professional developer is to set up shortcuts for literally every Mac app they use. The Mac operating system is built so that it's easy to use for new users and advanced users. But we sit in front of our Mac so many hours a day, doing so many things, that we can learn shortcuts. I have a shortcut to launch specific Mac apps.

When you think about it, you use, say, 15–20 Mac apps every day, right? You use Xcode, you use Simulator, you use Spotify and so on. You can set up a shortcut for each of these using various tools. You can do it in Alfred app, you can do it in BetterTouchTool, or there are probably other apps also, and then you can switch instantly between the apps. It's a ton faster than Spotlight, of course, but also it's a lot faster than using Command-Tab. I wrote a blog post about this, on how to set it up. It takes a few days to get used to it, but it really changes the way you work on your Mac, and I'm always surprised that not more people make use of it.

I recently started using a new tool for Google Chrome, but it's also for Safari, called Vimium that also make use of shortcuts. The app allows you to control any website using keyboard shortcuts, and it allows you to navigate without using a mouse. I just started using it. So far it's been working well. I believe that the longer you use it, the more important it becomes for your workflow.

Another tip is to practice inbox zero. I make heavy use of this concept in which I work through emails in my inbox. It means that every time I'm at my desk, no matter if it's at home or work, I open the inbox and see if there's anything new coming in that I need to look at. And, then, whenever there is some fallout work that I have to do, I move it to a TODO; I use Trello.

Keeping track of your TODOs and ideas is important. One thing that changed the way I work and live day to day is an open-source app I published called *MajorKey*. It's an iPhone app on my home screen. When I launch it, a big text field and a big text box appear. The keyboard is already there, and I just type down whatever thoughts I have. So let's say you are walking on the street and you're like, "Oh, wait! I can build this or I can solve it like this," or, "Oh, when I'm back at home I need to do this thing!" You just write it down, you tap the *MajorKey* button, and it sends an email to your inbox to remind you of the thought later.

It's so simple and so useful; so often when I'm walking around, talking with a friend or I'm at a meeting, I want to write something down that's really important but I don't want to keep it in my head. I want to write it down so that I can forget it for now and then do it at work later on. The app is available on GitHub also at GitHub.com/KrauseFx/MajorKey. It's not in the App Store yet. I might publish it at some point, but, for now, you have to compile it yourself. I also wrote the same for Mac as an Alfred extension—Alfred is the alternative to Spotlight.

What would you recommend to prospective developers who have no experience with open source to get started with it? How should they start contributing? What should be their first attempt?

That is exactly the title of a blog post I wrote: "How to Get Started Contributing to Open Source Projects." The most important thing is to just submit for requests; that can be as simple as recommendations for changes. I always appreciate it when people submit core requests to improve or fix a recommendation. Even if it's just fixing grammar or spelling mistakes, that's all great because we need that, right? That is, of course, the best way to get started.

You can also subscribe to a GitHub repo, and that will give you a sense of what kind of discussions are currently happening—what are the maintainers thinking about? When building something, make sure to check with the maintainers—the owners of the project—because if it doesn't align with their vision, they might not accept it. And, finally, always start small, don't think about the crazy new feature you can build; maybe fix a bug or improve a recommendation, or build a nice little feature.

As developers work on their projects, it seems security and privacy are an important thing to consider. You've done a lot of research on privacy issues in the world of iOS and Macintosh. Do you believe security is an important field for the average company to consider?

Of course, security and privacy are expected, and it's a big investment for companies, especially startups, to spend money and time on it. It's tricky for a small company to justify spending a lot of time and money on security, but it's necessary—it's very necessary. I do believe that GDPR is kind of tricky. GDPR is great in that it exists. I think that some engineers might not agree because they got hit by it pretty hard and they have to buckle up now to comply with it. But many of the rules themselves make sense, and it's good that there's some movement there. The problem is that it is easier for big companies like Facebook and Apple to follow the rules because they have the resources to do it. For startups, it's a little more difficult. But, on the other hand, if they cannot comply with the rules, do you, as a user, actually want to use those products if they don't have the right backups and security systems in place?

What security tips could you offer to developers? Particularly, mobile developers?

Third-party SDKs are important. Every dependency you add to your app adds risk because it runs in your app. The trickiest piece is that every SDK that you bundle in your app runs in the same permission scope as your app, which means that, if the app has access to the location data or photos, every SDK also has permission to those. This is something that can be abused very easily. Be very careful of all code that you include in your app, especially if it's binary post source, because there's no way for you, as a developer to verify the integrity of the SDK.

The second piece is your actual Mac. If your Mac becomes compromised in some way, and if it's a good hack, there is almost no way for you to find out. Then, you're in serious trouble because hackers can access your API keys and your build secrets. They can access your source codes and so on. Just don't trust any Mac apps on your Mac. The MacOS X is very new and not very stable yet. It's going in the right direction, but it'll take a few more years until that MacOS X is usable. Every Mac app, even if it's sandboxed, has access to your whole screen at any time on your Mac, even if the app runs in the background—without permission dialog.

66 *Let's say you have an idea for an app that you want to build. I would recommend you start building it and then learn along the way in the process of building the app.* 99

As a very senior developer that has gone through many stages, what other advice could you give to people who are starting in coding today?

I would tell them that there are *so* many good, free resources out there. Stanford University offers iTunes iOS development classes. MIT publishes a bunch of sessions. I recommend to everybody to make use of those. And, at the same time, I believe that learning is one thing, but, more importantly, you must use those skills for something. Some people constantly learn and learn, reading and reading books, but they never actually build, say, an app; they just learn. I think that it is really important that you build something.

Let's say you have an idea for an app that you want to build. I would recommend you start building it and then learn along the way in the process of building the app. I think that's cool, and then you also have something to show once it's ready! Having something to show, even if it's just this small sample app that you build and publish in app stores, is already very useful. It didn't take me long to build *MajorKey*, but that's already something that I could have shown if I were interviewing at a job.

Another thing I always talk about, of course, is the contribution to open-source projects. Let's say you apply for a job you want— it's a really cool job and you can imagine that a lot of people applied for that role. But let's say that you contributed to a project like CocoaPods, that forced you to learn about the spheres. You contributed to this improvement and that makes you stand out, right? Those things are always good, and it shows that you not only know about systems, like CocoaPods, but you know how to work on an existing code base, existing project, understand how it works, and work on a solution. Collaborating in open-source projects is great, and you get to work with some cool people who help you get that pull request merged.

FELIX'S RECOMMENDATIONS

How to Pick a Career (That Actually Fits You) | Tim Urban

Travel Is No Cure for the Mind | Lawrence Yeo

Your Life in Weeks | Tim Urban

JOE BIRCH

" *Trust is essential.* "

🐦 @hitherejoe   in/joe-birch-80392157   M @hitherejoe

Joe is an Android Engineer and Google Developer Expert for Android Assistant, Flutter and Google Pay based in Brighton, UK working on the Android team at Buffer. Passionate about engineering, he loves to create robust, polished and exciting projects for mobile and beyond—in fact, he'll probably be toying with whatever the new thing is at the time you're reading this! Joe is also a prolific public speaker and keen writer, he loves to share his learnings and experiences with others wherever he can.

You're tremendously prolific when it comes to writing articles. How do you manage to write articles with this frequency? Are there any tips that you would like to give to potential writers to achieve the sort of productivity you have?

I often start a draft on my blog based on something I'm doing at work. Even if it's just a little writing or a few notes, I start something. I go back later in the day or a few weeks later and finish the article. The list of articles I've started drafting on my blog contains ideas that are three or five months old that I haven't gotten around to working on, or things I started but wasn't in the mood to finish. I always come back to those things. My style is to make notes and start drafts and add things and then I come back to articles when I feel like I'm in the mood. This process keeps me going and provides a regular cycle of subjects to write about.

So I can imagine your drafts list is probably half-full with articles that have not been finished yet?

There are some that just have the title, and maybe I'll finish, but maybe I won't. Some are halfway written. I try to do at least one article a week, and sometimes I manage a couple. I feel that it's good to get into that habit of sharing ideas often and in the open.

How do you negotiate between wanting to put out polished work and wanting to share ideas frequently?

I prioritize getting things out there and focusing on what I think will be useful for people. Of course, I want to make sure what I contribute works properly, with regard to open-source code. When it comes to writing, I do a quick proofread, but I like just putting things out there once they're done. Sometimes I'll go back and change things around. Most of the time, I feel like they're good enough for people to learn something from.

Another topic where I feel you are an authority is in remote work. You work at Buffer, which is a remote company. You're the founder of the *Remote Dev* podcast about remote work. What were the main challenges you've faced in getting the podcast off the ground?

The first thing we found difficult was finding the first guest. As well, we weren't sure how it would be structured or what the approach should be. Another challenge was our lack of experience with recording and mixing. How do we make sure everyone's recording? How do you get it in sync? There's a lot to learn. We've gotten the hang of it now, but it was a lot more difficult than we thought it would be. We thought it would be just as simple as hitting record.

Buffer, where you work, is entirely based on remote work. What's a regular day like for you at Buffer?

Yes, we're one-hundred percent remote and we have nearly 90 people working for us worldwide. As you might imagine, we're all in a range of time zones. The Android and iOS teams are small, and we also have a mobile engineering, as well as a designer. My Android team member works on a six-hour time difference from me, so I work alone through the mornings. There are a few advocacy team members who I might communicate with during the morning, but generally, this is the time of day when I get deeply into the work.

I tend to start quite early. I start at about eight o'clock in the morning, and then take lunch at noon. I do that because it gives me a two-hour lunch break. In that time, I do my own things, like maybe a bit of writing or open source work. I started doing that over the last few months and it helped to switch off a bit from work.

In the afternoons, almost half the company comes online. At that point, things start to pick up a bit more, and I have my calls and team syncs. We don't really do pair programming. Once a week we have strategy syncs with the team leads to discuss any ongoing issues.

I switch off at five, so it's a normal work day. I think most people are surprised by this. Honestly, I work the same schedule remotely as I did on a non-remote basis, but with added flexibility.

What are three tools you use in your daily work to communicate with your peers remotely?

Slack is the Holy Grail. We use it for everything. We try and make sure everything is in Slack, so everything's recorded and someone who comes online when you're offline can see things that happened throughout the day.

We use Zoom for video calls. It's great for one-on-one chats, but we also have our all-hands meetings in Zoom. It has two view modes, so you can view either the person who's speaking, or you can view every camera for everyone who's online.

A third tool we use at Buffer for remote work is Threads. Threads is a forum on which you can post a subject. You give it a description, and then people can comment on it and post images and hold a discussion. It has Slack integration. It's helping to improve our asynchronous conversations.

What do you think of the recent trend of making salaries public? Are there advantages that this practice can provide to the company or the culture?

Knowing what people earn can increase trust. At Buffer, everyone knows what everyone earns. No one wonders whether someone working in the same role makes more money. As well, this policy is great for hiring because your salary is predetermined based on your location. If you apply for a job, you know what you're going to be paid from the get-go. This transparency definitely brings a huge sense of trust to the team.

> *I also like to give people the chance to be challenged, explore problems themselves and find their own solutions.* **"**

What's your leadership philosophy? What core principles and beliefs guide you when you are in a position of leadership?

I value honesty. Honest feedback allows for the chance to grow. And I do the same with people who I've mentored along the way. Trusting someone who's helping you or someone you're helping is essential. I also like to give people the chance to be challenged, explore problems themselves and find their own solutions.

Should all information be public in a company?

I think it should be. It's good to know that whatever is going on, you're going to know about it. At Buffer, we see all the emails and conversations between the CEO and the investors. That's giving you the full context. Even when Buffer had previously made layoffs, there was full transparency around this topic during the time. There's a peace of mind that comes when everyone is in the loop.

How do you manage your productivity when you're programming? Is there any system that you particularly like and follow in order to be productive while you're coding?

At the moment I don't have any specific thing in place. I used to follow the Pomodoro technique, based on 25 minutes of work and interspersed with short breaks. I used to do that, but I kind of just grew out of the habit. When I stopped using the Pomodoro technique, I didn't feel any less productive.

In the morning, I tend to do an hour of deep work, and then I'll pop downstairs for ten minutes and just have a little break. That seems to give me enough time to focus and also refresh my mind. I tend to follow this throughout the day. An hour of heads down concentration, followed by a short break or stretch to give me that moment to refresh.

What do you wish that someone had told you back when you started your career in software development that you had to learn the hard way instead?

So this is to do with knowledge scope. I like to know a lot of things from a lot of different areas like technology. When I first started, I wanted to know everything. If I was working on Android, I wanted to know all the Android libraries. If it was machine learning or whatever, I researched these things. That's how I approach things. It's just taking anything on board and learning it.

And I think about a year before I left my last job, I was incredibly stressed and I was doing so much. I used to get home from work and I'd be writing open source code and reading up on things. I'd wake up the next morning and do writing before I went to work, and then it would just be a constant cycle of unending work. I was trying to know everything.

The truth is, you don't need to know every part of your sector. You're not going to use every part of the hundred frameworks and libraries that are available. I definitely learned that the hard way when I realized how stressed I was becoming and how it was affecting my life. I had a three week holiday and did some traveling. When I came back, I changed things around a bit because I saw how my workflow was affecting me, and I realized that it just wasn't worth that stress.

What books would you recommend to someone getting started in the industry?

First, *The Pragmatic Programmer: From Journeyman to Master* by Andrew Hunt and David Thomas. I'm due to read it again. I read it every so often just because it's just a nice refresher and it's got some advice that could definitely help refresh your mind and shape the way you do things. A book called *Design Patterns: Elements of Reusable Object-Oriented Software* by Erich Gamma and Richard Helm helped me understand what I was learning at university. *Clean Code: A Handbook of Agile Software Craftsmanship* by Robert C. Martin is really refreshing and helps to define how to approach coding.

Are there any negative trends you've noticed in the industry, and how would you fix them?

Flexible work hours are important for remote workers and can significantly impact employee satisfaction. In one of my previous roles, we had a typical workplace with a ping pong table and games and stuff, but we had inflexible work hours. Really, I just want to be at home for an hour in the morning to get a package, or to leave work an hour early or so.

How do you see the future of remote working?

I think it's definitely getting more popular. I think in the U.S. it's going to continue to grow. But I'd love to see it more in the U.K. It's definitely not as popular over here as it is in the States. It's a step in the right direction.

What are the first steps a company should take in order to implement remote work?

Try and cultivate a culture in which everyone is included. For example, if you have a meeting, be sure to remember about the remote workers. It's definitely important to get that right from the start.

There's been a lot of controversy over hiring practices. From your point of view, what ensures a fair hiring process?

I don't feel algorithms are a good way of measuring someone. I used to be a fan of take-home exercises, but you've got to be respectful of people's time. It can't be too time-consuming because people will spend as long as they can to get the job. Time is expensive. If onboarding takes a few days, you then have to expect people to be able to take a few days off work. I think that's a great way of making sure that people are right for the company because then you can get a feel for what it's like working with them.

I think pair-programming sessions are the way to go. Having a coding task or even better, a ticket in Jira or a small feature that you need to build and having a pair-programming session with the interview candidate. That way, they're working in your code base, and they're fixing a real problem representative of what their job would be. The task should be something that gives you an impression of what it would be like to work with them. That's a good way of determining whether someone's a good fit.

JOE'S RECOMMENDATIONS

The Pragmatic Programmer: From Journeyman to Master |
Andrew Hunt and David Thomas

Design Patterns: Elements of Reusable Object-Oriented Software |
Erich Gamma and Richard Helm

*The Effective Manager: How to Leverage Your Efforts in Software
Engineering to Make a Disproportionate and Meaningful Impact* |
Edmond Lau

GABRIEL PEAL

❝ *It doesn't have to be perfect the first time.* ❞

🐦 @gpeal8   in /in/gpeal

G abriel is an Android engineer at Tonal where he works on bringing strength training into the 21st century. He also maintains Lottie for Android, an animation library used by tens of thousands of companies as well as MvRx, an Android architecture library built on top of Android Jetpack. Prior to Tonal, Gabriel was an Android engineer at Airbnb where he worked on a variety of Android product and infrastructure projects. Gabriel was also one of the first engineers on Android Auto. On Android Auto, he owned a variety of projects including assistant, system UI, music and phone calls.

You are a very senior developer, having worked for some of the big companies in the Bay Area in California. What kind of leadership have you had to show in your role?

Making decisive decisions can be challenging up front but pays dividends in the long run. One example was the decision to sunset React Native at Airbnb. Even though many teams were successfully using React Native and we had some groundbreaking projects in the pipeline, it was clear that React Native was never going to gain significant traction beyond what it had already captured. Fortunately, we made the hard but unambiguous decision to sunset it. This required working with many teams using React Native to reduce the impact on their roadmap while communicating broadly and without ambiguity that React Native is being fully deprecated at Airbnb. It would have been easier up front to reduce our investment and allow it to continue organically. However, the result could have been hugely detrimental to the developer experience internally and the quality of the product externally.

What is your leadership philosophy?

A high-functioning team is greater than the sum of its parts. However, a toxic culture can grind an entire organization to a halt. Also, many people in tech are truly passionate about their work and make it a part of their identity. In doing so, a positive or toxic team culture can bleed into every aspect of their life. As a leader, you have to recognize the unique personality of every single member of the team to maximize their potential and enable them to do their best work. As soon as personality clashes and conflict start to arise, it is important to be direct and approach the problem head-on before it grows and affects more people on the team.

What is something you had to learn on your own that you wish someone had told you back when you started in this industry?

The code you write doesn't have to be perfect the first time you write it. When writing something new, I often like to write it a few times, making a huge mess in the process. In doing that, I'll try several different approaches, freely throwing away code and refactoring things until something feels right. Only once I have a full picture of what I want to build will I clean everything up and make it presentable. From my experience, useful insights emerge during the building phase of any project that would have made a meaningful impact on the original design phase. Constraining the building phase to the limited set of information you had during the design phase inevitably leads to a local maximum solution and prevents explorations into new approaches that may become clear while building.

In drawing insight from other resources, which do you prefer: podcasts or books?

I am a huge fan of podcasts. I think they strike a great balance of polish, relevance, depth and variety. I also find them highly practical because I can listen to them sped up while at the gym or driving. I have always aspired to read more but struggle to read more than a few books per year. It is really easy to stall on reading in general when you lose interest in a single book. Recently, I have gotten better at giving up on books that I am stalled on and am both enjoying reading more and finishing more books than I used to.

What are the three books or podcasts that have had a lasting impact on how you do your work?

I started listening to podcasts in 2005. One of the first podcasts I listened to was *This Week in Tech*, hosted by Leo Laporte. *This Week in Tech* was my first foray into tech. It got me thinking about the world of consumer electronics and helped me paint a picture of the state of the world.

More recently, I have been listening to *Masters of Scale* with Reid Hoffman. His podcast has an stellar lineup of guests who share their experiences scaling businesses. Not only do you get insights into the incredible things many of them have done but you also get to see how humble many of their beginnings were or how they recovered from serious missteps along the way.

One book that has stuck with me and is on a very short list of books I would reread is *How to Win Friends & Influence People* by Dale Carnegie. I have even set up a recurring daily notification for each chapter title such that I get one each day to focus on.

One major shift the book helped me internalize was how to shake the egocentrism with which we all view the world. There is so much stress and anger in the world built up around the fact that somebody overestimates their importance in a situation. Learning how to contextualize and frame why other people behave the way that they do is something that can have compounding positive effects on relationships and stress levels.

In 2018, you published one of the most-quoted articles in the IT world, "React Native at Airbnb," where you relate your experiences using the framework with Airbnb. The dichotomy of developing a native app versus using a multiplatform framework has been ever-present in this industry. What are the key advantages and disadvantages of each aspect?

Picking the right mobile framework to use for a new project can be daunting. At this point, there has been enough native, React Native, and Flutter projects to find confirmation or disdain for pretty much any framework. At a high level, React Native and Flutter excel because they truly let you write most of your code one time and both support hot reload. However, the relative immaturity of each platform means inventing solutions that have been done many times on Android and iOS.

React Native and Flutter are also easier to learn than Android or iOS. I have seen teams with very little mobile experience ship Android and iOS apps that would have been completely impossible to deliver natively with the same engineers and time constraints. Also, all cross-platform frameworks still struggle when introduced into a large existing app.

In migrating from a native architecture into a multiplatform, one brings not only technological changes but also organizational ones. What are the most significant technological and/or organizational changes you have observed?

Organizational alignment is an extremely important quality of a high-functioning team. You may find that a cross-platform framework has some technical advantages but members of your team actively don't want it, so be prepared to deal with those issues indefinitely or consider whether the approach is right for your team. You don't have to turn existing Android and iOS engineers into enthusiastic supporters of cross-platform before starting. However, a level of respect and cooperation will be required from the get-go.

How would you recommend a company tackle those changes effectively?

Tackling the organizational challenges of introducing a cross-platform framework requires an open and honest communication channel. If the introduction is painted as a top-down silver bullet that will fix every problem, it is bound to fail. However, approaching it with balance and as a pragmatic experiment where the pros and cons will be considered within the specific context of your organization, things are much more likely to go over smoothly.

It seems that the industry demands of us to change our development paradigm every few years or even months. What advice would you give to a software engineer or developer on navigating through all these changes?

Being an engineer can be exhausting. There are new libraries, architectures, and frameworks all the time. When deciding whether to introduce something new into an existing codebase, it is important to think about its implications not just within the context of what it will be used for but also how it will interact with the rest of the codebase and will affect other engineers on the team.

Considering the holistic picture is particularly important when introducing a new framework or architecture. I have heard of product teams at large companies who want to introduce something like React Native into a codebase because it will help them move faster. However, they fail to consider the impact on other systems such as build tools, internationalization, experimentation, and sharing state with other features.

However, if you are excited about something new, it never hurts to spin up a side project or convert some existing code to something new. Simply using something will give you more perspective than reading a dozen blog posts and tweets. Also know that if you don't use the latest trend that everybody is raving about, it doesn't make what you are doing today any worse.

What recent industry or technological change or trend do you find the most exciting or promising?

I love the trend toward reactive programming. Nearly every platform is moving in that direction. React, which is aptly named, have proven that reactive programming is an effective way to scale a maintainable and testable codebase. You now see similar reactive patterns being used in Flutter with StatefulWidget, and on native Android with MVI and other libraries such as MvRx. In my experience as an engineer and mentor, reactive codebases tend to be easier to learn and become productive with. The simplicity of most reactive frameworks is a testament to that. The API surface area of components in React, StatefulWidgets in Flutter, and MvRx on Android are almost entirely consumed by setState, getState, and subscribe, and it is no coincidence that their life cycles are vastly less complex than they are for native Android and iOS development.

Are there any trends that you feel are just plain wrong?

I think there is too much emphasis on testing up-front versus building out a robust metrics platform to track metrics in production. While testing can be crucial in specific and considered use-cases, I have yet to see their value when applied broadly when you consider not just the safety they provide but also the opportunity cost of writing and maintaining them. Some of the best and most stable codebases I have worked in have had close to zero tests while some of the worst and most error-prone codebases have had nearly complete coverage. On the flip side, it is incredible how few metrics people collect and actively monitor their users in production. You can have broad test coverage while leaving major features broken for some or all of your users for release after release.

What would you suggest as an alternative to this trend?

I think engineers should consider how to measure the performance and reliability of features in the wild. One reason measuring analytics gets less consideration than tests is that tests can be done entirely within the scope of a codebase. You can write code and immediately write tests. However, monitoring analytics requires continual effort. However, building out a proper data and analytics pipeline requires stepping outside the comfort zone of many engineers. Doing this right usually requires learning new tools, integrating with new services, or even building out new pieces of infrastructure on AWS.

Multiplatform frameworks have been ever-evolving: Flutter, React, Kotlin/Native. It is difficult to take a bet on a single platform. But what are your views on this? Should we, as developers, bet strongly on any of them?

It is too early to bet the farm on any multi-platform framework. The mobile community is large enough to support multiple large frameworks. It is very possible that native, React Native, Flutter, Kotlin Multiplatform, and yet-to-be-built frameworks can all live in tandem. To date, each framework has brought new ideas to the table. The more smart people you have contributing new ideas, the better the outcome will be. When writing Airbnb's blog post series about sunsetting React Native, my biggest fear was that if it came across as too negative, it could have a detrimental impact on the size and morale of the cross-platform community. This would have been a disservice to everybody. Great ideas can come from anywhere. We used some of the best parts of stateful and immutable programming from React Native as the inspiration for MvRx which is now the de facto way of writing native Android code at Airbnb.

With all these changes, how do you keep yourself up-to-date with your skills or career?

Twitter and YouTube and Medium are excellent sources to stay up-to-date in the Android world. My Twitter account consists of nearly 100% Android engineers so I find an incredible amount of high-quality content and collaboration there. I have also found that the Android community on Twitter is Twitter at its best. Start by following a few Android developers, then follow their retweets and Twitter's suggested followers to gain a broader reach within the community. Twitter will then become your source to discover the rest of the high-quality content that exists whether it be a conference talk on YouTube, a Medium post, caster.io course or anything else. The beauty of Twitter is that it is also a two-way street. You can use it not just to consume but also to share and build connections with other people in the community.

In working on your projects, how do you start your day off with a bang? Do you have any secret morning routines that set you up for success?

I treasure my morning shower. There is a r/Showerthoughts subreddit for a reason. Somehow, because of a combination of the warm water and a clean separation from all technology, I do some of my best thinking in the shower. I then try and arrive to work at least an hour before most of my coworkers. Head-down coding time is precious and it is amazing how productive you can be if you sit down with a specific goal and can work without distractions. This becomes an order of magnitude harder once the normal work day starts and the routine of meetings, Slack messages, and conversations fragments your workflow. On many days, I get about as much coding done in that first hour as I do in the rest of the day combined.

How do you stay highly productive for long periods?

There is nothing more satisfying than sitting down with the explicit goal of creating something and then achieving it. This simple fact is hard-wired into our brains and incentivized by the dopamine boost you get after achieving something. Luckily, the tangible nature of programming is perfectly geared to give you these dopamine kicks after fixing a bug or finishing a new feature. When I work, I like to set a clear series of goals for myself. This process of creating incremental and achievable goals can be so rewarding that hours and hours will fly by before you realize it.

Overall, what would you recommend to an aspiring software developer to get started in their careers?

Pick something you want to build and build it. You will learn more and be more satisfied building something you care about with the wrong tools than building something you don't with the right ones. It can be overwhelming to try and pick the perfect language, framework, and architecture of a project before starting. As you gain experience, it will be easier to anticipate the pros and cons of different approaches ahead of time but even years into your career, these types of choices will still not be black and white.

While using something for the first time, don't stress out about getting everything perfect. Writing code is an iterative process. It is easy to refactor things later. Accepting the fact that you will write imperfect code that you can refactor later is critical to getting over the writer's block that kills many ideas too early.

GABRIEL'S RECOMMENDATIONS

The Consciousness Instinct: Unraveling the Mystery of How the Brain Makes the Mind | Michael S. Gazzaniga

How to Win Friends and Influence People | Dale Carnegie

Unbroken: A World War II Story of Survival, Resilience, and Redemption | Laura Hillenbrand

SUNSETTING REACT NATIVE

A Reflection on Change

GABRIEL PEAL

Due to a variety of technical and organizational issues, we will be sunsetting React Native and putting all of our efforts into making native amazing.

This is the fourth in a series of blog posts in which we outline our experience with React Native and what is next for mobile at Airbnb. Where are we today?

Although many teams relied on React Native and had planned on using it for the foreseeable future, we were ultimately unable to meet our original goals. In addition, there were a number of technical and organizational challenges that we were unable to overcome that would have made continuing to invest in React Native a challenge.

As a result, moving forward, we are sunsetting React Native at Airbnb and reinvesting all of our efforts back into native.

FAILING TO REACH OUR GOALS

Move Faster

When React Native worked as intended, engineers were able to move at an unparalleled speed. However, the numerous technical and organizational issues that we outlined in this series added frustrations and unexpected delays to many projects.

Maintain the Quality Bar

Recently, as React Native matured and we accumulated more expertise, we were able to accomplish a number of things that we weren't sure were possible. We built shared element transitions, parallax, and were able to dramatically improve the performance of some screens that used to frequently drop frames. However, some technical challenges such as initialization and the async first render made meeting certain goals challenging. The lack of resources internally and externally made this even more difficult.

Write Code Once Instead of Twice

Even though code in React Native features was almost entirely shared across platforms, only a small percentage of our app was React Native. In addition, large amounts of bridging infrastructure were required to enable product engineers to work effectively. As a result, we wound up supporting code on three platforms instead of two. We saw the potential for code sharing between mobile and web and were able to share a few npm packages but beyond that, it never materialized in a meaningful way.

Improve the Developer Experience

The developer experience with React Native was a mixed bag. In some ways, such as build times, things were dramatically better.

However, in others, such as debugging, things were much worse. The details are enumerated in part 2 in this series.

SUNSET PLAN

Because we weren't able to achieve our specific goals, we have decided that React Native isn't right for us anymore. We are currently in the process of working with teams to create a healthy transition plan. We have halted all new React Native features and have plans to transition the majority of the highest-trafficked screens to native by the end of the year. This was aided by some scheduled redesigns that were going to happen regardless. Our native infrastructure team will support React Native through 2018. In 2019, we will begin to ramp down support and reduce some of the React Native overhead such as initializing the runtime on launch.

At Airbnb, we are strong believers in open source. We actively use and contribute to many open source projects around the world and have open sourced some of our React Native work as well. As we have moved away from React Native, we haven't been able to maintain our React Native repos as well as the community deserves. To do what's best for the community, we will be migrating some of our React Native open source work to react-native-community which we have already begun to do with react-native-maps and will do with native-navigation and lottie-react-native.

IT IS NOT ALL BAD

Although we weren't able to achieve our goals with React Native, engineers who used React Native generally had a positive experience. Of these engineers:
- 60% would describe their experience as amazing.
- 20% were slightly positive.

- 15% were slightly negative.
- 5% were strongly negative.

63% of engineers would have chosen React Native again given the chance and 74% would consider React Native for a new project. It is worth noting that there is inherent selection bias in these results since it only surveys people who chose to use React Native.

These engineers wrote 80,000 lines of product code across 220 screens as well as 40,000 lines of javascript infrastructure. For reference, we have about 10x the amount of code and 4x the number of screens on each native platform.

REACT NATIVE IS MATURING

This series of posts reflects our experiences with React Native as of today. However, Facebook and the broader React Native community are dedicated to making React Native work for hybrid apps at scale. React Native is progressing faster than ever. There have been over 2500 commits in the last year and Facebook just announced that they are addressing some of the technical challenges we faced head-on. Even if we will no longer be investing in React Native, we're excited to continue following these developments because technical wins in React native translate to real-world wins for the people around the world who use our products.

TAKEAWAYS

We integrated React Native into large existing apps that continued to move at a very fast pace. Many of the difficulties we encountered were due to the hybrid model approach we took. However, our scale allowed us to take on and solve some difficult problems that smaller companies may not have had time to solve. Making React Native work seamlessly with native is possible but challenging. Every company that uses React Native will have an experience that is a unique function of their team composition, existing app, product requirements, and maturity of React Native.

When everything came together, which it did for many features, the iteration speed, quality, and developer experience matched or surpassed all of our goals and expectations. At times, it really felt like we were on the verge of changing the game for mobile development. Even though these experiences were highly encouraging, when we balanced the positives against the pain points plus the current needs and resources of our Engineering organization, we decided that it wasn't right for us anymore.

Deciding whether to use a new platform is a major decision and depends entirely on factors unique to your team. Our experiences and reasons for moving away may not apply to your team. In fact, many companies are continuing to successfully use it today and it may still be the best choice for many others.

Although we have never stopped investing in native, sunsetting React Native frees up even more resources to make native better than ever. Follow along in the next part of this series to learn what's new in native for us.

This is part four in a series of blog posts highlighting our experiences with React Native and what's next for mobile at Airbnb:

Part 1: React Native at Airbnb
Part 2: The Technology
Part 3: Building a Cross-Platform Mobile Team
Part 4: Making a Decision on React Native
Part 5: What's Next for Mobile

CREDIT

A version of this article was first published on *Medium* (June 19, 2018). The original article can be found here: medium.com/airbnb-engineering/sunsetting-react-native-1868ba28e30a

MARIN TODOROV

❝ *Focus on what you love doing.* **❞**

🐦@icanzilb in/in/marintodorov github.com/icanzilb

M arin is one of the founding members of the raywenderlich. com team and has worked on seven of the team's books. He's an independent contractor and has worked for clients like Roche, Realm, and Apple. Besides crafting code, Marin also enjoys blogging, teaching and speaking at conferences. He happily open sources code. You can find out more about Marin at www. underplot.com.

Many of our readers are interested in other works that have had an influence on you. What are the three that have had a lasting impact on how you do your work?

If I were to highlight only three books that have affected my work culture, I would go first and foremost with *The 4-Hour Workweek* by Tim Ferriss. This book—regardless of its clickbait title—has really been essential to how I have approached work for years. It has taught me how to declutter my schedule and focus on the things I really love doing. Reading—and embracing—this book got me started on my path to finding my work/life balance; never waking up to an alarm clock, and more advice in the book, are pure gold.

The second book that I'd say was a game changer for me I, unfortunately, read some 20+ years ago and I can't remember the title; it was about rapid application development with the earliest version of Delphi. I was impressed not so much with the content but the way the book was written. Part of the book was a first-person story about a developer who was tasked with developing a database-powered prototype overnight. You could really put yourself in the person's shoes as they discovered Delphi and made the most out of its features. This book had a lasting effect on me—even now, I still always try to cover real-life problems and guide the reader through a real-life developing process in my writing—including creating problems and bugs along the way, and fixing them later on.

As third, I'd add *Writing With Style: Conversations on the Art of Writing* by John R. Trimble. It's an essential collection of writing tips for anyone, both native and non-native speakers, who'd like to put down clear and readable prose. I bought it when we started planning the first ever raywenderlich.com book, and I made a habit of re-reading it before starting to work on a new book.

In addition to drawing inspiration from these books, what about personal insight? What is something you wish someone had told you back when you started software development that you had to learn the hard way instead?

When I was young, I naively believed working on software means working with reasonable, nice, and caring people. I had this romantic idea that being with your own kind automatically means you share the same beliefs and a universal understanding of being and working together. Unfortunately, I got to discover that software companies are made up of people just like life is—mostly the same rules apply, too. I had the chance to work at some amazing companies but had my share of bad experiences in the workplace as well.

> 66 *I think starting a career with the expectation that one is entitled to success if they check off some kind of a list is probably setting them up for a failure as few people are really entitled to anything.* 99

There are many people starting into software development today, who don't have a clear idea of the direction they should take to set themselves up for future success. What would recommend to people starting out as a software developer today, that would give them the best start to a successful career?

I never planned my career; my family didn't have the means for me to keep studying—I had to figure out on my own how to get by. I'm not in a position to give any advice on what's the best way to "set up oneself for future success in software development." But I will say I always did what I felt passionate about—I truly and deeply love programming. At first, I did it in my free time and it naturally turned into a career for me. I wish everyone had the same luck as I did and could turn their passion into a career.

In any case, I think starting a career with the expectation that one is entitled to success if they check off some kind of a list is probably setting them up for a failure as few people are really entitled to anything.

As part of your career, you've written a number of books for developers. Writing a single book can be a life mission for many, but you have an impressive record of authoring eight books and counting. And anyone can write a book, but it takes something special to write a "good" book. What is your secret to writing so many "good" books?

I disagree that anyone can write a book; in the same way that not everyone can develop software or design buildings, it requires certain skills. To name a few of these skills: It takes perseverance, thorough planning and humility. What I believe makes for a really good technical book is for the author to be able to explain things not from the position of a teacher lecturing an audience but rather as someone explaining to their peers in a friendly manner.

Additionally, it's essential to have an amazing publisher. "Traditional" publishers often times outsource editing, slap a random cover, release without a beep on social media, and then pay pennies on a sold copy. I'm really glad to have had the incredible opportunity to be published by Razeware and to build a lasting relationship, which has helped me improve my writing skills and my books year over year.

What has writing books taught you that you think can't be learned anywhere else?

One of the takeaways from the *The 4-Hour Workweek* is to focus on the things one feels they are best at and leave everything else to others. Collaborating with Ray Wenderlich and the team on all these books through the last eight years was an invaluable example of this great rule at work.

Elsewhere, I've seen excellent programmers decide to write a book on a topic they feel strongly about and fail not because they aren't masters of their domain but because writing a book requires much more than being able to write code. There are many layers of putting a book together—illustrations, diagrams, technical editing, editing, planning, updating, marketing, print layout, and much more.

Going a few times through the process of putting a book out with Ray and everyone on this team has really taught me to focus on the parts I'm good at and support my collaborators and trust them with doing their part. This formula Ray envisioned some time ago proves to be a successful one year over year—it's amazing what the broader team can pull off in terms of putting out a crazy amount of new and updated books each year.

Your comments on traditional publishers lead me to wonder what other current industry trend you think is just plain wrong.

This question reminds me of that old Simpsons meme, "Old man yells at cloud"! Let's see. I wouldn't say, for example, that I'm a big fan of "the blockchain"—it seems to me it's been around for a long while and the only purpose it serves so far is financial speculation and scams. It almost feels criminal that it's a virtual thing produced by burning coal in developing countries to enable few folks to get even richer. I really wish we were better than that as a species.

Another is the fail fast startup culture. I don't believe any company's future is burning through human resources even faster than through its remaining cash runway. I think working this way robs people from the satisfaction of nourishing successful, long-term products, building long-lasting relationships, and maintaining happy healthy lives. I hope that sooner than later founders will begin to reject pumping cash into prototypes in favor of building lasting businesses instead.

What would you suggest is a better alternative to this trend?

I'd suggest that we need to move away from the fail-fast culture as a community. The only party benefiting of fail fast are the investors as this culture is designed to run their numbers and not to help products gets released, companies grow sustainably, or people build knowledge and teams.

In thinking of building your own sense of productivity and nourishment, how do you start your day off with a bang? Do you have any secret morning routines that set you up for success?

I mentioned earlier that never waking up to an alarm clock has done wonders for me personally. I'm absolutely not a morning person and having a solid, uninterrupted sleep each night until I naturally feel that it's time to wake up has played an essential part in pulling off great amounts of work while keeping a healthy work/life balance. Another tip that helps non-morning folks like me is to use an app to actively block social media before noon—it really helps me get rolling in the early hours while I'm still somewhat able to be distracted.

Once you're up and working, how do you stay highly productive for long stretches of time?

Less is more! When I can plan my time myself I try to work as little as possible and focus on things I really like working on. This way I'm super productive in short amounts of time while spending the rest of my day walking, going to the museum, or generally nerding out.

MARIN'S RECOMMENDATIONS

The Spring: Charity Water project | charitywater.org

The Power of Habit: Why We Do What We Do in Life and Business | Charles Duhigg

Kid A | Radiohead

MIKE WOLFSON

❝ Learn from everyone around you. ❞

𝕏 @mikewolfson   in /in/mswolfson   mikewolfson.com

Mike Wolfson is a product-focused developer working out of Phoenix. He has been working in the software field for more than 20 years, and with Android since its introduction. He is a Google Developer Expert in Android and the author of the book *Android Developer Tools Essentials* published by O'Reilly.

He has spoken about Android and mobile development at a variety of conferences and user groups (including Google I/O, Oscon, GDGSiliconValley, Droidcon NYC and Turin, AnDevCon, and others). When he is not geeking out about phones, he enjoys the outdoors (snowboarding, hiking, scuba diving), collecting PEZ dispensers, and chasing his young (but quick) daughter.

How did you become involved in mobile development?

I was excited about mobile, and I thought it represented the future. I picked Android for a variety of reasons, but mostly because it wasn't iOS. The next trend is clearly going to be machine learning.

When choosing a direction, it's important to follow your passion. I've never been passionate about databases, and that's not the approach that I took. I'm interested in mobile. Making an app is really exciting for me. It's something I was instantly passionate about, and then it became not only my hobby but my job.

What inspires you?

I like solving problems, which take many forms. What inspires me to start is really solving the right problems and solving user problems.

I know you listen to a lot of podcasts. Are there any that have had a lasting impact on how you work?

The first one that I really enjoy is *The Tim Ferriss Show*. The Rick Rubin episode about how to find your Zen is great. The Derek Sivers episode is really good, too. It's a great resource for anyone interested in productivity and systems and how to be more effective.

Another podcast I really like is *The Joe Rogan Experience*. Again, it's about being a better person.

A podcast that really impacts me personally is *Design Matters*, by Debbie Millman. She's a famous designer in New York City. In her podcast, she discusses unique perspectives on design. As a show, it's about how to look at the world with a unique perspective towards solving problems and keeping the human part of the computer equation.

Speaking of both sides of the equation, have you noticed any negative trends in our industry?

There seems to be a bias toward using machine learning for every problem.

What would you do differently?

The first question to ask in any situation is what problem you're trying to solve and whether machine learning actually solves that problem. It's important to be mindful of how machine learning might impact the solution. It's important to think not only about how to solve a problem using machine learning but also what unforeseen problems might result from applying automated algorithms. In essence, machine learning can have complicated consequences, so applying it requires significant forethought, as well as oversight of the process. You may not know how machine learning is affecting your solution in the immediate term, but you need to be very mindful over the lifetime of the application to do auditing and understand what's happening and how your decisions are affecting your outcomes.

Years ago, the trend was that everything needed to be mobile, no matter what. I think we may be in the same sort of situation now, where every problem looks like it has a machine learning solution, though it may not.

Mike, you're an advocate for remote work. What are the less obvious advantages of remote work?

The flexibility of work-life balance. The most unexpected benefit is the ability for me as a developer to get into a flow state, in which I can avoid outside distractions. As a remote worker, I often find myself doing concentrated work, which software engineering requires.

The ability to get into that flow state is much easier when you're remote. I think people don't quite understand that. They think about all the practical abilities of being home and being able to fold laundry. But the ability to concentrate deeply is key.

Are there drawbacks to working remotely? If so, how do you manage them?

The biggest drawback of being remote is being out of sight, out of mind. This can be problematic when decisions are made without your attention or you're left out of discussions. As a remote worker, you have to make it visible when you're interacting with your co-colleagues. You have to be present in a standup meeting or video conference. Even if you're not physically there, you have to make your voice heard. Your time to make that impact is much shorter than other people, so make sure that you take advantage of it.

That's a great insight. How can a company develop a remote-friendly culture?

I've given this a lot of thought. The best way for a company to go remote is to give it a try. Set up some sample projects with desired metrics and measure the result of remote work on the small, confined sample project. For example, start with a single sprint for a software release. I think it's critically important to start small and create metrics that allow you to demonstrate that you're still being productive while you're trying these new things.

Secondly, roll out remote work gradually. There's no need to convert full-time office employees to full-time remote employees in an instant. Some companies are trying "no-meetings Wednesdays." Having a policy like no meetings on a regularly scheduled day means people can anticipate and best make use of that "head down" time.

The idea of one regular day without meetings is fantastic, even for companies that don't have remote workers.

I think that has a lot of secret sauce built into it. Freeing up just that one day for people has a big impact. It allows them to get a lot done that time spent in meetings would have prevented.

In addition to working as a developer, you also find time for writing. You wrote the *Android Developer Tools Essential* together with Donn Felker. What have you learned from writing this book that you couldn't have learned as a developer?

I learned perseverance with that project. It took a long time to write, and I encountered many obstacles, but I was able to work through the obstacles and commit the time to get it done. Now I have a book on my resumé, and it's something I'm very proud of. I think I learned dedication from that project.

How can an aspiring writer be successful?

First, practice, practice, practice. Writing is like exercise, and you need to do a lot of it. Writing blog posts or other content that is related to the book content is a great way to get started. Writing a page or two daily really helps.

As well, find inspiration in other content that matches the style that you're aiming for. Find an author or content that you want to imitate, and tailor your own version of that product to create something awesome. It's much harder to start with a blank slate than to start with a point of inspiration.

You might expect great developers to have a similar daily routine, but it turns out that everyone has distinct habits.

When I've been at the Googleplex for conferences and whatnot, as you have been, I'm always surprised by the emptiness of the parking lot before 9:00 A.M. At my workplace, our core hours are from 10:00

A.M. to 3:00 P.M., but I think there is a lot of variation. I think it's best to appreciate that variation in people. I do my best work in the morning. At night I'm not so good, but I think a lot of other people hit their full stride in the evenings.

> 66 *The mistake is being closed off to alternative approaches. The older I get, the more I realize how much I have to learn from everyone around me.* 99

What's a mistake you commonly see developers making, and how can they avoid it?

Beginning developers seem to be less open to listening to other people, especially people who are younger or have less experience. The mistake there is being closed off to alternative approaches. The older I get, the more I realize how much I have to learn from everyone around me.

What's the best path toward cultivating seniority and expertise as a developer?

Create a portfolio and a public persona. I spend so much time with the people at my company who are writing documentation or libraries or other components for my company. That kind of work has no mobility outside of the organization and no long-term value. I tell everyone I know to write content for public consumption. It's fine to link it back to your company, but make it about you. That way, you can build a portfolio of products, whether that's talks you've given at conferences, blog posts you've written, or code snippets you've created. You own it, and you can use it to promote yourself.

In some instances, I've used my portfolio to avoid doing software coding challenges. I can supply a code repo that has a recycler view that downloads from a restful interface and demonstrates all the same things that their code challenge wants and avoid doing additional work. Creating a public persona has been the single best thing that has allowed me to demonstrate my expertise.

Practically speaking, people tend to change jobs frequently in the software industry. Having an online portfolio helps to establish credibility despite frequent career moves. Instead of being new at every job, you arrive with a demonstrated knowledge base that people can review and use to get to know you without your having to reestablish your expertise.

MIKE'S RECOMMENDATIONS

The Tim Ferriss Show podcast | Tim Ferriss

Design Matters podcast | Debbie Millman

The Joe Rogan Experience podcast | Joe Rogan

TY SMITH

66 Your growth is your responsibility. 99

🐦 @tsmith   tysmith.me

Ty lives in San Francisco and has held team lead and engineering management roles at many unicorn startups including Uber, Twitter, and Evernote. He has specialized in building scalable mobile apps and developer tooling since 2009. He is passionate about software craftsmanship, engineering sustainability, and building teams focused on delightful user and developer experiences.

He's an active angel investor and advisor focused on helping startups scale their mobile and open-source strategies. He cares deeply about the open developer community, is a member of the Google Developer Expert program, regularly speaks at international conferences on Android, as well as organizes the SF Android Google Developer Group and Droidcon San Francisco conference. He's an avid enthusiast of biohacking, longevity, and transhumanism, and, with his spare time, he enjoys science fiction, cooking, traveling, wine tasting, snowboarding, and scuba diving.

You've been working as an Android engineer since 2009. Tell us a bit about how you got started and what the process was like developing applications for Android?

In 2009, I was graduating from college and had been working full time as an engineer, going to school during the evening. It was a very, very stressful time in my life. I was working for a small consulting company doing Ruby on Rails development; the company was targeting mobile customers, really for the first time. So we had a handful of iOS engineers, but iOS was very new at the time, especially its third-party app development. Android was just really coming out into the public, too—I think 1.5 or 1.6 had just dropped.

The tooling was awful, and I hadn't had any mobile experience. I was a little more interested in iOS development at the time because we had some iOS engineers around, but I was happy to do my server-side development on Rails. We had a pretty large customer, Zagat; it was a restaurant review service, later acquired by Google, subcontracting their mobile apps to this company. So we had a third-party contractor for the Android development side of it; we'd been doing the iOS side. Unfortunately, the contractor had to step away from the project early on. So this left a small consulting company with a very large client and no Android resources.

My boss at the time, Mekka Okereke, said to me, "Hey, Ty, we have this big client. We don't have any Android resources. We have this timeline of about three months. What do you think about learning and shipping the Android app at that time?" And I think my response was something along the lines of, "I don't think you're asking me to volunteer. I think I'm being volun-told, here." He shrugged and we got on with it and it was a hectic project.

I was learning and he was learning, and we were trying to ship it very quickly. But it was a very successful first launch of Zagat. The clients were happy.

Once I picked up Android there, with that first app, I did a couple more at that small company. The main contractor who hired us for Zagat reached out to me and offered me a job to work for them full time at their company Handmark. I was in Dallas then but had been taking to heart the idea of moving to San Francisco, California. I'd been doing Android for three years at that point—the tooling was still awful, it was still Eclipse and very slow, no dependency management, etc. They were not fun times. So I started reaching out to companies in the Bay Area.

I was hired by Evernote and relocated out to the Bay area. That was my first real Silicon Valley experience, seeing that startup grow from right under a hundred people to maybe 400 people before I left. I developed a lot of my technical chops in a way in which I had a lot of other peers that were pushing me that were much more driven than what I had experienced in other areas of the country working.

That also got me introduced to working on development tools. I worked on their single sign-on client and their external APIs. That was an opportunity for me to start doing developer advocacy for the first time and discovered I loved it. I joined Twitter for a few years. The tooling kept improving, and Android finally started to become something that our iOS peers didn't make fun of all the time. We started to see a lot of maturity in the tooling. After about three years, I moved on to Uber, continuing to do developer tooling and external advocacy. I started doing external API work—things like deep links and single sign-on and our API usage, speaking at conferences and doing open source. Eventually, I moved on to lead our mobile platform team and spent some time managing them as well.

So it's been an interesting journey. I've seen Android mature a lot over the last 10 years since I've been working on it. It started as a very painful toolchain. But a lot of people worked on it just because of the idealism of an open-source mobile experience, as well as a very limited market size at that point, and it has become a booming mature developer ecosystem at scale, and we see a much better developer experience for our Android engineers than for our iOS engineers.

What considerations would you offer to a developer who is thinking of making a move to Silicon Valley?

I think it's a personal decision for everybody. But Silicon Valley is still a unique place with this incredible amount of opportunity and energy. And some other great areas of the world have a big tech field, but it still doesn't compare to what you will see here. It is not for the faint of heart. When I was living outside of Silicon Valley, I was a tech enthusiast and I consumed the tech news and I always felt like an outsider reading about it or hearing about it or whom you know is impacted by it.

It wasn't until I was living here and my friends became the thought leaders that you regularly listen to talks by and read books by. Very quickly I started to feel like, oh, I am contributing to this community. I didn't feel like that was something that I could have bridged the gap between before I was here and I had the incredible support network that was pushing me in that direction as well.

It's not a cheap place to live, so there are sacrifices to be made, especially in your first year or two. A lot of people move out here and they say, well, I've done the math on what I can get as a salary out there, and it doesn't financially make sense. I would say that's often true for the first year or two that people live here, but the opportunity and the network that you build as well as the eventual equity that is often much more competitive out here often offsets that in the long run. That's something that a lot of people should consider when you're coming out here, not to compare your first year of work to the standard in Silicon Valley.

Some argue that one solution to this problem is remote work. What are your thoughts on this?

I am a huge proponent of remote work. While I am a big believer in living in San Francisco and the Bay Area, and I did mention there are many other great places for opportunities as well—Seattle, New York, Denver, all have very booming tech scenes. Something to consider, when you start looking at remote work, is if a company hasn't designed their culture around that from the beginning, it can be pretty frustrating for all the parties involved—things like if the meetings are remote-friendly or water cooler chat is done over Slack. At the first company I worked in, we were all remote, and it was a great experience. We felt a lot of camaraderie. We felt a lot of collaboration. A lot of alignment.

Since then, I've worked at companies that had various perspectives on remote workers. The more common Silicon Valley perspective is hesitant about remote work. The preference is for people to work together. Then if someone has a lot of leverage, they can negotiate to be in a remote role. I see the trend moving in that direction, but it's starting in the smaller companies first. I've seen several friends who have started startups and they have a much greater talent to pool from so they start with remote only. They don't have to worry about the cost of an office as well. So it's a great idea.

What would be your recommendation for a company that wants to go remote?

Starting early is much better for the culture, otherwise, you're going to end up with a lot of teams that try to shift; a company may say they are going to hire one remote person and that one remote person then feels very isolated because the team continues to have the chats in person, just casually. I just turn to my neighbor at my desk and we talk about something for a while. Maybe at the end of that conversation, I post a one-line status update in the group for that remote worker to follow along. But that's not the same experience.

So designing inclusive communication very early is necessary.

Second, it's much more difficult to have remote higher-level management folks. So often, I've seen that roles that allow for more independent work are sometimes more remote-friendly—engineers, designers, etc. Then, when you start looking at management, directors, and founders, having them be co-located, working with teams, is more common. Co-location allows that in-person collaboration that's needed to drive the strategy and the vision of the company, but it does potentially isolate those remote individual contributors. It also, in many ways, limits the career growth of those individuals because, to advance the career ladder as an engineer, you hit a point in which, even if you're not managing folks, you need to broaden your scope and use other people to broaden your impact. So one common complaint that I've heard from long-term remote individuals is feeling limited in career growth because it can be difficult once it's time to move past these areas of technical collaboration to strategic collaboration.

You've mentioned the career ladder. You've been a person that has been working as an engineer, later on, you've been a lead engineer and you've also been managing other engineers at Uber. How easy is the transition between those positions? What recommendations would you give to other engineers looking to manage others?

I spent a lot of years in different tech lead roles, leading teams, mentoring folks, and wanted to build out some experience managing and helping folks grow in their career directly, and being accountable for that. So I spent a little over a year in a role at Uber called a tech lead manager. The tech lead manager role is available at some of the bigger Silicon Valley companies. But it's not a full engineering manager. So we have three roles in the tech ladder. We have the individual contributor, we have the engineering manager and we have the tech lead manager.

The tech lead manager differs from an engineering manager in that they should have a much smaller team, ideally three to five people, and they are still responsible to be technical, to contribute code and design reviews and architecture reviews and have those technical conversations.

But they are also managing folks and responsible for the career growth of those people. So that's the role that I stepped into. As a former tech lead and as a mentor to many folks, that seems like a pretty natural career progression. There was a lot to learn as an engineer, the engineering manager would tell you. I read a lot of books. Fortunately, I had a great team of folks that I was taking over, where I had some previous interactions with them. There was already that trust that had been built. I spent the year honing the management side of it. Now I ended up stepping out of the tech lead manager role back to just pure engineering, more of a tech lead role. I did that with a lot of deliberation and some hesitation. But I felt like it was the best path forward for the team and the best path forward for my well being in the short term.

Usually, I don't think a tech lead is a the right role for managing teams. It's better to split the role to two different people. That allows someone to avoid context switching and focus on what's important to grow the team in two completely different directions. I needed to decide between committing fully to being an engineering manager, stepping away from the technical side or stepping back into a tech lead and engineering role and giving up the management. And based on what drives me, where my interests lie, I committed to stepping back into an engineering role and letting the team be managed by an experienced manager who could take on a lot more folks than I was able to as a tech lead manager, and really grow the team to what's needed for the amount of responsibility that we had.

For the long-term career of a developer, is it compulsory to move into the management ladder?

I think that is a stereotype. I think that, at many companies, it's true. I've been very fortunate to see a lot of the top tech companies that I've worked for have very defined career ladders for both and define it deliberately as two different skill sets. I'm very glad that I built the skill sets of being a manager, and I will very likely manage folks again at some point in the future, but I don't see that as a requirement to progress my career, nor do I see it as a requirement for most folks at these big companies.

I can continue to impact strategically on a large scale and have those conversations that I was empowered to have as an engineering manager, as a tech lead, as a high-level individual contributor. I think a lot of people don't do that, by default, but that's often there and just is kind of a thing that needs to be taken. And my experience as an engineering manager, the connections that were built there, the skills that were learned, will be very valuable in me being a regular engineer again, in stepping into those conversations and having a position of authority in understanding what I can be impacting.

So I see a great path to grow past the stereotypical aging-out range, 35 or 40, as an engineer, but I think the experience a person brings is most valuable in the scope they can impact. Higher-level engineers aren't just programming; they are spending a lot more time organizationally impacting. They are doing larger architecture. They are getting folks aligned on the technical strategy of what the company should be doing. They are establishing new processes. They are reviewing a lot of what is coming out from the lower level engineers. Those require a lot of experience in a position of wisdom and that's where you see a lot of older engineers, naturally, fall into this. Will every engineer want to stay on the engineering track? No; a lot of folks want to build that experience. They want to build their own little empire. They want to hire out a group. They want to become a director. They want to become a CTO or something like that. But I don't think that's necessary anymore.

We're talking about an experienced manager and leaders. How do you define a good leader?

I think that a good leader spends most of their time empowering their folks to grow and become self-managed. I've seen great leaders and I've seen bad leaders. Great leaders recognize the strengths of the folks and they try to give them opportunity to take advantage of those strengths and manage themselves. When they recognize the weaknesses, they try to give an opportunity that will grow that person past their weakness.

I've seen way too many bad leaders micromanage and not adjust their management technique to what each person needs, and they would talk a lot more than they listen. I would think, especially as a manager, you need to be listening about 80% of the time. Bad leaders are blind to the empathy that a leader should be demonstrating and not demonstrating that servant-leader mentality that needs to be had.

Those all create bad team dynamics to work on. I think as a crux of that, a lot of leaders, a lot of managers, are so focused on building their own career, that they just want to empire build. They want to take on new projects. They just want to set up new folks on their team to become managers, so they can have managers reporting to them, even if it doesn't necessarily make sense for that person. They are just doing what they can to aggressively move themselves up, and I think that that's an anti-pattern that's detrimental to teams. Your leader needs to understand what the team needs and what the person can do to impact that.

> 66 *It's critical to your growth to have a very good mentor to give you advice, push you in the right direction, set up accountability and give you the feedback that you need.* 99

Leadership is closely tied to mentorship. What are your thoughts on mentorship in our community?

The thing about a mentor relationship is it's volunteer time from both people, and the time of someone whom you would want mentoring you is extremely valuable. So, while some companies have mentorship programs and people can get involved with them, and they are very official, I've found that your career growth is your responsibility. Let's start with that. That you will have managers and you will have mentors and you will have senior engineers to try to push on you and to try to help you but at the end of the day, you are an adult with a career and your growth is your responsibility.

So recognizing this, it's critical to your growth to have a very good mentor to give you advice, push you in the right direction, set up accountability and give you the feedback that you need. But if we follow the idea that your career is your responsibility, it's also your responsibility to drive finding that mentor. I think it's especially important for a junior engineer. They need to step out of their comfort zone and they need to find someone and be active in advocating for that person to mentor them. They need to be extremely receptive to that person's feedback as well. What I found before is that as a mentor, your time is valuable. If this person isn't acting on your feedback and adjusting and making you feel like the advice that you're giving is being utilized, then you might not be interested in continuing that relationship.

We've touched on several trends, here—remote work, career growth, mentorship. Are there any other trends you think are problematic and what would be your solution?

One thing that I've noticed in the last few years in the mobile space is a lot of the big companies focusing on creating huge apps with many teams working and creating features for those apps. The apps get quite bloated; you see this in everything from Google to Facebook to Uber. Once we started pushing on further app adoption in the emerging markets, the biggest constraints that came up were lower powered-devices and lower throughput networks—just a lot of constraints where these large-featured apps were considered problematic. The apps were too big and people can't have them on their device, can't download them on cellular, or their devices are too slow to run these large bloated apps.

So you started to see this prominent trend of creating light apps that are specific to certain regions. And I think, in spirit, that's a good idea, recognizing that there are these other markets wherein you do have a large demographic of under-powered devices and trying to account for that. But what we've seen is that there's a demand for light apps in general; it's not just in those emerging markets. Because once those were available, once you had Facebook Messenger Lite emerged, for example, people in the United States, in Europe and other first-world countries with flagship devices began to prefer the Lite experience. They prefer simple, smaller apps with less bloat, less complex user experiences and fewer features—apps that focus on the core experience.

So, I think this Lite trend, in general, is a little bit problematic, but we should learn from that and try to move back to the core of products with the idea of simplification and creating lighter user experiences.

For companies that would like to move toward simplification, what would you recommend?

A prioritization of the company on the Lite perspective across their apps. Google, for example, released dynamic-feature loading for app bundles recently; I think that's a really good start. It takes quite a bit of internal work often to rearchitect and design your app in such a way that different chunks of it could be downloaded over-the-wire dynamically.

I've been a big fan of progressive web apps; for example, the Twitter mobile web experience is fantastic. Chrome's API and other general web APIs are getting better in areas like storage in the browser, rich notifications and more. There are several apps that I would be perfectly happy using a progressive web app, and I have been one of the biggest proponents of native performance best user experience, etc. I'm often the first one grilling React Native or some of the other cross-platform tools.

But I've seen some very lightweight and performant progressive web apps, and I think that would be a much more adaptable place for a lot of these companies to start with. One reason for this adoption is size constraints companies run into. iOS users are often throttled by the amount of bandwidth that they pay for per month, for example; they still have limited size on disk and they care about the performance in their app. Apple has certain size constraints that I've seen companies run into—their over-the-air-limit for an app, for example. The over-the-air update limit for an app was 50 megs, then bumped to a hundred, and now it's at 150. But several apps ran up against that size limitation and it became a huge problem.

At Uber, our rider app started getting very, very close to that, and it became a code red at the company with people trying to investigate how to trim off the size from the app so that we could continue downloading over-the-air and not require WiFi. Fortunately, Apple bumped the limit to 150 because some other companies were dealing with that at the same time. And things like bundling Swift just make iOS apps larger in general. But we've had a number of our very senior iOS engineers now take up the mantle of caring about the binary size, performance, etc.

And I think the progressive web app and mobile web, in general, can also solve part of that iOS problem as well. If you're doing something like dynamic feature loading or something that's very Android-specific, for example, in a company in which you're developing products across all the platforms, I've seen that it often becomes difficult to sell prioritization of network that is Android-specific. You go to a product manager and say, "Hey, we want to build up this dynamic feature loading for Android," and they say, "Great, how does that compare to these other features that we could be building that are in both iOS and Android?"

So doing something like the progressive web apps, when it makes sense, allows you to target both products.

And then once you've seen your market proof out, you've seen the metrics that you want, moving into the full Native experience when it's needed, is a great way to do that.

Is there something in your career that you have learned the hard way that you wish you would have known when you started in software development?

That a management role that requires a lot of technical contributions is often not the right role for a team. I think hiring a manager is hard, and often companies try to allow that role to exist as a way to fill a higher need because they have engineers who don't want to fully leave the technical track.

But, with some exceptions, I think that's the wrong role for most teams, and having a pure engineering manager and separate technical leaders that are solely responsible for those avenues of growth for the team is a much healthier position to be in and that's something that I learned by going through that for a year.

In terms of hiring, there is a lot of controversy about whether whiteboarding is an effective way to hire talent. How do we hire the right people for these roles?

That's a really hard question. I don't think there is a silver bullet, here. I think flexibility is required. Some folks thrive in an interview style, like a whiteboard style interview, who are extroverted. They are comfortable sharing their thoughts, speaking out loud, and they are very clear communicators. Those are skills that are important to understand when you're hiring a person.

But it also can exclude folks who are shyer, that take more time to warm up or are just very nervous in a high-pressure situation. So if you were to give homework or a project instead, it might empower that person who is shyer, who can work on their own and then submit it. That could be very valuable, but a lot of folks don't have time to do the homework; if they are working on homework, that's many hours out of their day, too. Not everyone has the luxury of that time. It's kind of a point of privilege that you can take out time in your evening or time off work to study. Imagine a single mother who works all day, comes home and takes care of her family is trying to change her engineering job; she has very little time to study data structures and algorithms, and to do homework, right?

So having flexibility and empathy in the interviewing process is going to take us a lot further where we can understand the constraints of a candidate and be adaptable to them. For someone who discusses their discomfort with the interview process, leaning more on the data points coming from a homework assignment is probably a great start. For someone who doesn't have the time to do the homework, figuring out how to get that data out of an on-site interview is valuable.

I think even when it comes to on-site interviews, there is quite a variety in how they are done. You have everything from purely whiteboarding to coding challenges or pair programming on-site. Candidates might use the whiteboard to diagram something but then hop onto a computer for implementation of the code. I think that having the flexibility and trying to reflect real-world working constraints is going to take us in a better direction in hiring.

At the end of the day, we're trying to get data about the interviewee, right? You want to have enough data that the candidate and your team are going to be good colleagues and collaborate well. You want to know that who you hire can be trusted to produce and be accountable for what they need to be. With that as the end goal, there are a lot of different ways we can take the interview process, and they need to account for the variability in the human condition.

You've been doing Android and other industry advocacy. How did you get involved in this?

When I was learning Android, I remember watching speaker videos of folks I looked up to.

But I also thought it was something I could never do—be at a Google I/O event, talking to a large crowd, explaining very detailed topics. I was at this tiny company in Dallas at the time.

Once I moved out to Silicon Valley and I started building my confidence, I voiced to a friend who was our developer advocate that it terrified me but it would be amazing if I could do public speaking one day. He pushed on me hard to commit to a talk. He said, "Okay, that terrifies you. The best way to get over that is to do it." And I took that advice, and I ran with it. There was one company event that we were hosting at our conference, and there was an upcoming joint conference in London, and I submitted talks to both. It was my first time speaking publicly and giving a tech talk.

I remember preparing a ton and being terrified. Public speaking is unique. A lot of people don't like public speaking. I was one of those people who felt like a deer in the headlights. But I prepped a lot, and I got up there for the first event, then the second event, and once I started getting into the content, it started flowing. By the end of it, I was feeling good and I had a huge confidence boost as well. So, with that, I started submitting more papers. Before I knew it, I was giving regular talks every year. Those folks whom I had originally looked up to in those videos when I was starting to learn Android in 2009 were now friends of mine whom I was spending time with casually and hanging out with at conferences. We were traveling together.

It was this moment of reflection, where I looked back at myself and I said, "Five years ago, you would never have thought that you were doing what you're doing now." So, really what got me involved was my fear of getting involved. It was a growth area for me, and by pushing on that growth area and fully committing to that I was able to create some velocity.

The second aspect of that, though, is that I care about working with other developers. So a lot of the tooling I am working on is developer tooling. I get to work with customers who are my peers, who give me great feedback, and who help me improve my craft. It's different than consumer products. So this idea of engaging with them in person, making personal relationships and meeting new folks has become an incredible draw, which reinforces the velocity that I wanted to have. I've never actually worked full time as a developer advocate, yet I've been in conversation with mentors of mine who are very, very established tech people who have introduced me as one of the best developer advocates they know—even knowing that I've never done that full time.

This has been a huge compliment to me, and it's helped me recognize that maybe, at some point, I do push fully into the developer side of things. A lot of this has been influenced by my wanting to push past this personal growth area, as well as finding love for working with other engineers.

What advice would you give to someone interested in public speaking?

When I started, I kind of followed a very stereotypical recommendation, which was to have a little bit of alcohol before you speak. Get a little bit of liquid confidence. So for the first few years that I spoke, I would often have a shot or a glass of beer right before I went up. Just enough to cool the nerves. What I found is that you will build this confidence on your own and that, at some point, being in front of people will be very comfortable, and you can be your natural self. But in the beginning, it's okay to help bootstrap yourself. So account for the fear and push through that, understanding that it will eventually be comfortable.

Do you think that public speaking is for everybody? Is it something every developer should try to do?

It's a skill to develop. I don't think that people are a natural fit one way or the other. I think some people are more natural fits, but I don't think it's mutually exclusive. It is a healthy skill to develop because it pushes on your ability to communicate ideas, to grow as an engineer, and to be able to engage and empathize with other people. I know most engineers won't click on those set of skills, and they will keep things very technical. But one of the biggest growth areas from moving from just a high-performing senior engineer to a much higher-level staff or principal is being able to step out of working purely in your technical domain, purely on your own, and start to empathize and have those soft skills to work with other folks. I think that external advocacy and external presentations are a great way to help build some of those skills.

Folks who went through a traditional computer science degree at a university did get some communication classes or humanities classes in other "softer" areas outside of computer science. We engineers have used bad communication as a crutch to not develop professionally because we put our value into other areas. I think that's toxic to our industry. If you were working in other non-technical roles, and if you were not able to work well with others, you'd be out. You'd either have to fix that or be out.

Yet, as engineers, we've had this stereotype of being a bad communicator because we are engineers. We just don't understand people. And I don't think that's true. I think that a lot of people embrace that stereotype as a reason not to grow those skills because they don't have to. But that's a problem for our industry. That's not a natural state.

What insight do you gather from other resources? Are you more into books or podcasts?

I'm a really big fan of audiobooks. I found that I have very limited time as it is and I prefer the substance matter of a full book with a longer narrative. I can dive in and explore a topic. I can fit audiobooks a lot more easily into my life; I can listen to those while commuting, at the gym, etc. I've been pushing on increasing the speed for listening to those slowly over time so, at this point, it's become a very efficient way to absorb that information. I only reference back to hardcopy books when necessary for diagrams or specific things that are not capturable in an audiobook.

What are some books that have had a lasting impact on you as a developer?

A book that's helped me frame how I communicate is Marshall Rosenberg's *Nonviolent Communication*. It's a book about the language of communication and how to empathetically debate, negotiate and understand another person's point. It creates a framework for considering how you're interpreted and how to interpret someone else in the professional workplace and personal relationships with resounding effects.

Another book that probably had the most pronounced personal change for me was Mark Manson's *The Subtle Art of Not Giving a F-ck*. It wasn't necessarily the book itself that had this paradigm shift for me. He originally wrote a blog post about this a few years ago. And I read it at a time in my life when I had been over-indexing on idealism and caring about things being done the right way. I was spreading myself too thin and fighting way too many battles. And it was taking a really strong toll on my being and my health and I was at a place where I needed to make a major shift.

Reading this post and understanding this model of prioritizing the number of f-cks that you give was helpful—treat them as a limited currency. I started thinking about my life in that way, where I had a limited amount of things that I can care about. That was a turning point for me to have a bigger focus on sustainability, wellness, and health. Not only did that affect me in my personal life but it carried over into professional growth as well. I gained the ability to deal with conflict at work and understand the amount of skin that I had in the game. I was willing to be a lot more reflective and pause to be less emotionally tied to those conversations. With that comes much more measured persona, much more emotional detachment for conflict and things like that. And that's just helped me grow a lot.

On the technical side, Uncle Bob's *Clean Code*. I read this years ago and it just helped me start thinking about larger systems and the impact of tech debt, as well as how properly defined architecture allows for scalability, showing the ramifications of bad architecture.

The other is *Effective Java* by Joshua Bloch. I think that's one that a lot of Java developers will refer back to as the Bible of Java development. It has some of the normal problems with technical books of having content not reflected in a newer version of Java. However, there's a lot of very solid fundamentals that are communicated across many object-oriented languages. Having worked in many big companies where we're trying to understand how to speak in a common language and get aligned, I found that the principles that are communicated in that really go a long way in helping people get on the same page and get aligned in the sort of technical excellence that would be expected in a larger company.

In addition to your other industry contributions, you're also an angel investor. What does that mean and how can one become a good investor?

There's quite a variety in how people do angel investing—everything from going in with a micro VC group to individual investments in companies. My background, so far, with angel investing started when I was at Twitter, and I was put in contact with a few folks who were putting together a micro VC fund. That grew pretty slowly with members; I think we're up to 20 or so members. The name of that group is Specialized Type; what we do is invest alongside the big venture capitalists, joining different funding rounds with these companies.

So we go in alongside them and invest a very small amount, and our value-add is that the entire group of investors comes from a deeply technical background with domain expertise in one area that the company would like to use as an advisor. We have folks who have security expertise, machine learning expertise, and scaling storage expertise. My value adds to that group has always been the mobile experience, Android, hiring, and open source. So, over the last three years, we've added several companies to our portfolio, and I work with them off and on; the time varies month by month.

I work with the founders and the senior leadership of those companies to help them in those specific areas and in what their needs are. Now it's been really interesting because it's helped grow my career in a way that I didn't originally expect. This has been a nice way for me to take a slow ramp into the logisticals of investment; they have an incredible network to utilize to learn additional things about the investment process.

From that experience, I've then been able to take my knowledge and start to work with individual companies in which I'll personally invest and then come onboard to help advise them to work through the problems that they're having at an early stage. It's been very interesting, stepping outside of the normal perspective of engineering to understand the bigger company problems that these companies are dealing with, and to use the technical expertise that I bring to help them solve those issues.

What are the main benefits that getting into angel investing can bring into your life?

Ideally, financial if the investment works out. The entire idea of getting in on these companies and helping them grow is a return. But if you get past that, then it does help, with an incredible amount of networking potential, growing a lot personally and helping to grow others in your network as well.

TY'S RECOMMENDATIONS

Nonviolent Communication: A Language of Life | Marshall B. Rosenberg, Ph.D.

The Subtle Art of Not Giving a F-ck: A Counterintuitive Approach to Living a Good Life | Mark Manson

Clean Code: A Handbook of Agile Software Craftsmanship
by Robert C. Martin

YOUR BODY AS A SYSTEM

Getting Creative with Self-Care

TY SMITH

Silicon Valley is an industry typically known for its hustle, long hours, passion, constant grind and learning—and always having a side project. My growth was fueled by a mentality that was within that.

When I was in college, I was working full-time as an engineer and doing a full-time set of classes at night and taking up contract projects for clients. I was doing the hustle. I was trying to grow. Now I see that same mentality in folks who are entering into this industry. But there's a significant problem of burnouts, health issues, and mental health strain. I have gone through several issues that have helped me reset my priorities and understand that that hustle can be very toxic.

Several years ago I didn't feel very healthy: I was overweight; I have a family history of heart disease; I had gone through some personal tragedy; and I was feeling super, super burned out from work.

So I started to prioritize and focus on personal sustainability and what it means for a work-life balance. I wanted to explore wellness and methods like meditation, exercise, weightloss, and different diets. That just became this slippery slope for understanding me; it's possible to have sustainability and to have balance in your life while still executing well and still producing a lot—and still being recognized as a leader in the space that you're in. They are not mutually exclusive.

And that was an epiphany to me that I wish would have come sooner; I'm glad it did come. That has led me down a path of quantified self-improvement, biohacking, and anti-aging research. I've started getting into medical papers trying to understand the benefits of a certain diet, lifestyles, medication or other things in this space.

It's been a really interesting journey. Now, it's something that I actively mentor and advocate with the folks who I'm working with. I've had a lot of people for whom I've specifically advocated to take a more moderate view to their work and to try to remove their sense of urgency around projects—to coach them in their ability to say no to deadlines and push things back. I want them to understand the prioritization of stakeholders when they're trying to demand something.

And it hasn't just been effective for me, but I've had many folks I mentor who came back to me later and said, "Wow this was life-changing. And this approach has allowed me to continue to be a very-high performing engineer while being much healthier and happier." So my passion is around shifting the industry in such a way that we can have a more moderate view of work, and we can have companies that understand, even from the beginning in a start-up, that work-life balance is important and folks spending time on their health is important.

And I'm glad to see that we are starting to see some of the shifts in the industry, but there's a long way to go.

Companies can start to do this by recognizing the difference in the maturity and seniority of their employees. I'd see a lot of new grads and younger folks who have a ton of energy, motivation, and ambition; they end up spending a ton of their hours working to try to get promoted, impact their environment, and even just build stuff. And if you let them just run with that, it can be detrimental to themselves. Some of them probably haven't learned quite yet that it's not a healthy approach to be taking.

It is problematic when you have someone newer to the industry and they're told that they have a timeline or a task to deliver—they don't feel comfortable pushing back on that. They want to prove themselves, so they'll go out of their way to work harder and make the thing happen and to make the deadline. They haven't learned the art of saying, "No" or, "I won't be able to make this." And if they do that, it becomes a big failure that they are dealing with guilt over and regret about it.

I say "no," or let things slip, all the time and that's fine; it's about setting the expectation with the stakeholders that it's going to happen, so it's about clear communication. Sure, a project manager doesn't want their thing to be prioritized over another, but at the end of the day, I'm not going to sacrifice my wellbeing to help a PM get to market three days earlier for an experiment that they want to run. That's not worth the toll to me and it demonstrates that the prioritization of the PM was off from that entire project as well.

But I've seen in folks who have been in the industry a while, who are more senior, that this realization starts to come naturally. They've experienced burn out. They have a prioritization framework. So one thing a company can do is empowering proper mentorship and push on the sustainability publicly from your leadership by getting the senior workers in your company to mentor the more junior team members.

So I think that the mentorship aspect is really important. I think companies need a public declaration from leadership and a focus on it through having normal hours that the leaders are working to set by example. Certain wellness programs, as well as understanding that some timelines are, for the most part, malleable. Communicating these values down to your team, as well as teaching them how to push back and prioritize, are all really important aspects that a company can help develop in their culture.

My focus on sustainability and wellness was the slippery slope into biohacking and transhumanism, which takes it from a focus on being healthy to a mentality around optimizing the human condition past what we currently do to what we do naturally. Biohacking and transhumanism are mostly around using technology or alternative lifestyles based on data, to significantly change certain properties.

For biohacking, I do a lot with anti-aging, trying to control my metabolism and then measuring the data on that pretty regularly. I've been doing a very low-carb diet with high fat, it's called a Ketogenic diet, for about five years, combined with intermittent fasting. Most days I eat once a day, and I limit that to an hour to two of an eating window; for the rest of the day, I'm in a fasted state.

I will periodically do longer fasts where I hydrate and have zero calories; I target once a quarter with a five-day fast. I've done some longer; I've done some shorter. Sometimes, it happens a little more frequently, but sometimes life gets in the way and it gets delayed a little bit.

I measure a ton of data. I take my blood multiple times a day, and I'm measuring my glucose levels and my ketone levels. There are weight and body fat percentage, heart rate, average heart rate throughout the day. There's the amount of sleep and REM that I'm getting. It's interesting to see how your body reacts and how you feel over this period. In the middle of the five-day fast, you might feel a little physically slower but your mind becomes extremely clear. It's like a deep state of meditation by default.

The science behind it demonstrates all the positive aspects of anti-aging efforts and decreasing cancer, diabetic, or cardiovascular risks.

So the biohacking scene is a diverse community—it's everything from folks putting chips in their hands to robot prostheses; it can be very extreme lifestyle approaches. My approach started with the question of how I can get healthy, lose some weight, and reduce my heart attack risk when I'm older. It evolved into a deep rabbit hole of information and optimization of humans.

As engineers, we are always questioning how we optimize our systems. I treat my body as a system and my mind reflects that. The healthier you are, the clearer your mind is. It's a lot easier to perform, debate and have the high-cognitive ability when your body is in a healthy state. A lot of people have standard lifestyles when it comes to diet and exercise, and they live a sedentary lifestyle. Until you've started to pursue something like this—understand the nuances of the resulting feelings and improvements—then assign data to that, it's very difficult to identify those benefits. But they start to become extremely pronounced the longer you do this sort of thing.

In addition to all of this, there are a lot of other lifestyle choices that I've made to try to increase my lifespan—again, through the research that's been done.

For example, I do cold shock therapy, which is getting into a cold-plunge pool; your body benefits from that. It increases your immune system and hormone production. I regularly try to start my morning with a cold shower, then I'll often use ice packs to try to reduce my body temperature for a while, trying to get into a deep shiver state. In addition to all those positive impacts like the hormone production, it also is an incredible way to boost your metabolism for the day.

Seeing my body as a system was a natural extension of the engineering mentality of dealing with systems and trying to optimize them. It took me a long time to get there but, once I was in that place, it became an almost natural way to think about it.

Too many people in our industry focus a lot on their craft and programming, but that sometimes comes at the expense of the balance that you might expect of a lifestyle. But learning to develop yourself in such a way to push those lifestyle changes to get yourself into a more balanced healthy place, reinforces your ability to be a good engineer. It brings a new experience that you can take to the problem; it brings new ways of thinking; it helps bring clarity to your mind; it brings new ideas from other people. It brings more impact and growth in your career as more people seek you and your advice, or they want you to work on their projects because they perceive a more developed sense of balance from you.

CREDIT

This content was developed from an interview with Enrique López Mañas, first published in *Living by the Code* (July 2019).

MARCIN
MOSKALA

❝ Keep trying and learning from your mistakes. ❞

🐦 @MarcinMoskala

Marcin Moskala is an experienced developer and Kotlin trainer. He is the founder of the Kt. Academy, an official JetBrains partner for teaching Kotlin, author of the books "Effective Kotlin" and "Android Development with Kotlin", a speaker at many international conferences, and a programming library creator and contributor.

How do you start your day off with a bang? Do you have any secret morning routines that set you up for success?

I generally have a morning routine, but it changes over time. I usually start my day with water and either a morning workout or a run. Then I eat my breakfast, and I take a shower.

I start my day with the most important task. Not the most urgent one, but the most important. It is generally a deep-work task—a task that requires a lot of concentration without any disruptions. This is why I don't let anyone disturb me, and I don't check email or any other communications.

If it is programming, I often work until evening. When it is a book writing or a presentation preparation, I am generally out of ideas after 3–5 hours, and then I switch to shallow tasks like emails or all the small things I need to do every day to maintain and develop Kt. Academy.

How do you stay highly productive for long periods?

I have quite an obsessive nature, and I need to force myself to remember about breaks and exercises. Otherwise, after a few weeks of obsessive work, I get totally out of energy, and I need a few days of absolute chillout. It is good to have some quiet time during the day. When you need a break, instead of some news or media, choose a walk or meditation. When you watch a short movie, you might think that it takes only a few minutes, but your brain still processes it for hours. It steals your concentration and tires your mind. If you have too little stimuli in your job, then it might be helpful though it is rarely an issue for programmers.

I recommend a few different books for when you are thinking about being more productive. *Deep Work: Rules for Focused Success in a Distracted World* by Cal Newport, for keeping yourself in a good state for work. *Flow: The Psychology of Optimal Experience* by Mihaly Csikszentmihalyi, which is about finding and enjoying the right state of mind when you work. And, finally, *Getting Things Done: The Art of Stress-Free Productivity* by David Allen for better task management.

You were working remotely for several years, and now you have settled in Poland. Do you think remote work and traveling has made you a better developer?

Working remotely for a long time is an important experience. When you work remotely, you need to show that you've done something every day, because otherwise, some people will suspect that you are slacking. They cannot see that you are working at something all day. So you end up doing more. On the other side, it generally takes less time because you don't waste so much time for driving, meetings, lunches, coffee talks, etc. Using all this time to work more is a sure way towards burnout—everyone needs social interactions and breaks. Spending it on TV or games is extremely dangerous. The art is to use it wisely.

So I discovered that the two most effective ways to recharge are having a walk and a nap. Both are nearly unimaginable in a company, but very efficient when you work from home. Though you still have some extra time you don't waste for driving, and you need socialization since you spend most days alone or with your loved ones. My solution was to get active in the programming community. I started writing articles and attending conferences. It was well-directed energy.

For people interested in being a nomad and working remotely, I'd tell them to try it! It is not as hard as it looks like. Plane tickets are cheap nowadays. For most countries, getting a visa is easy or not required at all. You can either find a remote job or just save some money. Both options are not a problem for programmers.

In drawing insight from outside sources, which do you prefer, podcasts or books?

I am an absolute bookworm, and there is no comparison. I like podcasts when I am running because I can deconcentrate at any point and, after that, quickly get back on track. This makes them perfect when you are doing something else like listening, like driving or household duties. Most podcasts forgive missing a few sentences, while books do not, because books generally build knowledge brick by brick. They require more concentration, but in return, they can dive much deeper into the subject. They can truly teach and change the reader's understanding. Books are generally more demanding than other sources of information, but it pays off. There are concepts that I can't imagine learning in any other way but by reading a book. This is why I recommend everyone spend at least 15 minutes every day reading a book.

What are the three (podcasts/books) that have had a lasting impact on how you do your work?

My work today is twofold. On one side, I am a programmer. On the other, I am teaching programming, speaking at conferences, and writing books. So I will give two answers.

About programming, I was strongly shaped by the absolute classic, *Clean Code: A Handbook of Agile Software Craftsmanship* by Robert C. Martin. I still believe that this book, together with the rest of the "Clean" trilogy, which includes *Clean Code, Clean Programmer*, and *Clean Architecture* is perfect for young developers. As a more advanced Java developer, I was strongly shaped by *Effective Java* by Joshua Bloch, one of the most important best-practices book for Java. And about the philosophy of being a good programmer, I was strongly influenced by *The Passionate Programmer: Creating a Remarkable Career in Software Development (Pragmatic Life)* by Chad Fowler.

About being a speaker and entrepreneur, there is a book that initially inspired me to start this journey: *The 4-Hour Workweek* by Tim Ferriss. It inspired me to travel and start my first business. Both turned out totally different than I expected, but they were both great journeys that changed me positively.

The main reasons for travel in the book were that you can learn a lot from other cultures and that in some countries your money is worth more because prices are lower. If you want to build a startup and you won't earn money for some time, this can be a great advantage. I felt fascinated by this idea, but in the end, both statements turned out to be only partially true to me. It's true that local food products like veggies and fruits are much cheaper in Asia, but to find high-quality food you need to pay similar prices to Warsaw, where I am from. We came across similar situations with a good standard flat.

During our travel, we discovered new things and learned how other cultures can be different—it takes you out of the box and makes you rethink your beliefs. I recommend this experience to everybody, but it also has some drawbacks. You cannot participate in a long-lasting stationary course so there are things you cannot develop during travel. Also, you cannot do your hobby if it involves some community or special equipment.

In the end, long travel turned out to be a great adventure for me, but not the way to live. I recommend everyone experience it, see both the bright side and the drawbacks, and then make your own decision on what suits you the most.

Another really important book to me is *The Lean Startup: How Today's Entrepreneurs Use Continuous Innovation to Create Radically Successful Businesses* by Eric Ries. It is often known as "the Bible for startups," and it changed my thinking about how to do business. I recommend it to anyone starting any project. And the last book that helped me in the chaotic world of business and self-employment was *Antifragile: Things That Gain from Disorder* by Nassim Nicholas Taleb. It helped me understand chaos; it's a different work and we aren't used to it. It is not that bad. It just has its own rules, problems, and strengths. But, this is a topic for another interview.

> *The hard way is an excellent way to learn essential lessons. There are many mistakes you have to experience or, otherwise, you will never fully understand what to do and how to avoid them.*

Beyond the insights from these books, what is something you wish someone had told you back when you started software development that you had to learn the hard way instead?

I believe that the hard way is an excellent way to learn essential lessons. There are many mistakes you have to experience or, otherwise, you will never fully understand what to do and how to avoid them. I made a lot of mistakes, and those experiences are my most valuable assets.

An example of a hard mistake was my first business. There is no better school of humility then truly believing in something and spending all your time and energy on it, and then seeing how it slowly fails. I started questioning all my beliefs, and it made me much more rational in the long term.

Your career is focused on teaching and providing training to folks around the world. You are a JetBrains certified trainer, founder of Kt. Academy and a frequent workshop instructor. What are the mistakes that people keep making when trying to acquire and apply new knowledge? How can this be fixed?

I believe that our community managed to create really good ways to gain knowledge. I suggest using these solutions, and remembering a few things. The social aspect is crucial in learning. Discussions between programmers are a useful way to share knowledge and news from the industry. I've also noticed that conferences are much more efficient than learning alone in the home.

If you want to migrate to a new technology with your whole team, workshops are much better than everyone learning separately.

Moreover, there are tons of useful materials for each technology—courses, books, meetups, webinars. Many of them are free. Choose those that fit you best and use them. Articles are perfect for staying up-to-date, but they never go deep enough. To go deeper, it is better to choose books, workshops, or courses. Practical courses or katas are important to practice real skills. Doing a bigger project by yourself in a newly learned technology is another important skill that should be practiced. If you want to learn something and stay truly up-to-date, do not rely on just a single kind of knowledge, but instead use them all.

And, of course, practice, practice, practice. Whenever I learn a new language or technology, I do a small project to practice my new skills. It can be anything. I enjoy making applications for workout management, but I sometimes also do games, news, or to-do lists.

As an expert in education, what are some lesser-known sources of information you rely on for learning?

In our industry, information flows very fast, and so good sources of information are generally well-known. To summarize the ones that I believe are the most influential: an RSS feed with the best blogs in your discipline is excellent as this is something we develop through time. Books, of course. Reddit, forums, Facebook groups, Twitter, feeds on Slack, or other social channels are a great community source. Stack Overflow and Quora, as well as other online resources like online courses from websites like Coursera, Udacity or edX. As I mentioned, conferences, meetups, and workshops—especially ones that get you out of your bubble. And, finally, documentation, katas, example projects on GitHub.

One way of learning I actively use, and that is not well-known is a spaced repetition applied for learning programming. I use a program called Anki. It has a significant base of free decks created by the community, of which many are about programming. They generally teach about nomenclature, functions, or technology characteristic behaviors. Though there are also some funny decks that show programming using small challenges, this technique is known as the Anki method. I have used Anki for over six years, and, according to my statistics, I used it on over 70% of days. After this time, I can recommend it as an excellent way to learn.

In terms of a knowledge base, you are an established expert in Kotlin. In what ways do you think Kotlin is shaking up the industry?

A characteristic of Kotlin is that it is not trying to be original. Just the opposite—it uses well-established solutions in the best way known to the industry. It is well-designed. The two features that are genuinely shaking the industry are Kotlin Coroutines and Multiplatform development capabilities.

The idea of coroutines is pretty old, but it took a long time to implement it properly. They did a fine job, but their solution has some limitations. Kotlin pushed it way forward. Kotlin Coroutines are an ultimate solution for concurrency, which gets more and more important with more and more cores in our processors. The Kotlin Coroutines library gives us a powerful concurrency model, but the real revolution is built-in support that can be used to reproduce any other concurrency model known in other popular languages. This gives huge freedom to library creators, and I hope that it will help us finally establish a concurrency model that is intuitive, safe, and readable.

Another huge advantage of Kotlin is that it allows multi-platform development, meaning that it can be compiled to JVM bytecode, JavaScript or native code. Therefore, we can have a full-stack project all in Kotlin, with, for instance, Spring on the backend and React on the frontend. We can also have a common module written in Kotlin that is used both on Android and by Swift on iOS. We can extract common logic or even network or database operations; there are common libraries for that. It also provides great power for library creators because they can implement a library in Kotlin once, and distribute it in a way so that it can be used not only in Kotlin, but also on all JVM languages (Java, Scala, Groovy), JavaScript languages (JavaScript, CoffeeScript, TypeScript) and even in native languages (Objective-C, Swift, C, C++, Python, Go etc.).

What do you think are the best ways to learn Kotlin, if you are coming from a different language background?

For an individual, I would recommend a combination of books and Kotlin Koans. Then migrate your project to Kotlin or just create a new project in Kotlin. There are also free online courses available on Coursera, made by the Kotlin team, and on Udacity, made by Google. When you need your team to move to Kotlin, workshops are very efficient. This is why I devoted myself to conducting them. I often stay in touch with companies, and I was always informed that after a three-day workshop the whole team moved to Kotlin, and they are happy with this transition.

How do you manage to be a prolific contributor to the community?

I believe that everyone needs to find their place. I did many different things including library development, community discussions and event organization. All those activities are very important, but in the end, I discovered that I feel best in teaching. This is something I truly enjoy. I believe the key is to find what you enjoy and are good at, and just do it as much as possible.

What do you consider as the biggest failure in your career? What did you learn from that failure?

I started a company selling a brain supplement. It was called Nootro, and the product was a bit similar to Nootrobox, now known as HVMN. The product was good, but we knew nothing about selling in the supplements industry. In the end the company failed. Now, I am happy about that. This failure was the best business lesson in my life. There is nothing so much eye opening as truly believing in something and seeing how your vision brutally crashes with reality.

MARCIN'S RECOMMENDATIONS

The Lean Startup: How Today's Entrepreneurs Use Continuous Innovation to Create Radically Successful Businesses | Eric Ries

Clean Code: A Handbook of Agile Software Craftsmanship |
Robert C. Martin

Antifragile: Things That Gain from Disorder |
Nassim Nicholas Taleb

IÑAKI VILLAR

66 *Communicate and
learn from others.* 99

🐦 @inyaki_mwc   github.com/cdsap/   medium.com/@inyaki_mwc

Born in the beautiful island of Majorca, Iñaki is an Android Developer since 2011. He has worked in different industries such as banking, airline companies and tourism. He is a Google Developer Expert in the areas of Kotlin and Android and an open-source contributor with projects like Kakao or Talaiot. He has participated as a speaker in more than 50 conferences in 20 countries. He currently lives in Los Angeles and is a Build Engineer for Tinder.

You have been focusing recently on testing, being a net contributor to the Kakao library. What is a common misunderstanding about testing?

I meet developers arguing that they don't have time to write tests or their managers don't give them time to write tests. This is wrong. Testing is an intrinsic part of software engineering and you must test your code.

Another misunderstanding is the abusing of mocks in your tests. The first rule is "don't mock classes you don't own" but I want to rise to the impact on a large suite of tests using mocks. Mocking is an expensive task, and you can face OOM easily in your build tests.

How is testing properly done? Are there any aspects we overlook?

It is vital to keep a good architecture in your project. The separation of responsibilities in different layers will allow you to write more specific tests. Having a pure Kotlin module will help you in writing host tests. When you want to use more advanced Testing like E2E tests, your architecture will play an important role because you want to hook easily into different scenarios.

Then it is essential to understand the difference between unit, integration and E2E tests. Testing is not only a technique to write tests under the JUnit runner. You have to follow different strategies to write the code when you want to apply more UI testing patterns like Page Objects.

Regarding overlooking, I would say code coverage. Coverage is a great tool that measures the degree to which the source code of a program is executed when a particular test suite runs. For instance, since the adoption of Kotlin, some of the fixed rules of having a specific percentage of coverage on your project don't make sense.

Kotlin compiler generates the bytecode and you don't have to spend time covering code that you haven't generated. As an example, you can create a simple class with a lateinit variable, write a simple test and apply for the coverage to check why it doesn't make sense having a fixed coverage.

You are well-known as a speaker in the community, giving insights such as this. Is there any procedure you follow to prepare your sessions? Is there any trick you have before presenting at a conference?

In the preparation of the session, I like to back the presentation with a story, such as a plot of a book or movie. My procedure is splitting the presentation into three to four essential sections. After that, and before working in the slides, I write a script with the content and the references for the presentation. With different iterations, I try to fix and update everything in the following weeks.

> 66 *It's important to review the state of tooling and testing of new technology. When you are working in medium-to-big teams, the adoption should be escalated and measured.* 99

Android is a key topic for you in some of your talks. You have been an early adopter of Kotlin, which came to revolutionize the Android world. How does one decide on adopting new technologies? How do you deal with the risks of jumping too early, too late, or jumping in a technology that ends up falling short?

Always, the adoption should be a trade-off of measuring the risk and impact in your product and team. It's important to review the state of tooling and testing of new technology.

When you are working in medium-to-big teams, the adoption should be escalated and measured. You can choose and experiment with a feature or a team in the organization. Once it is validated, you can escalate to other teams or features. In negative cases, you won't expose the other members of the team.

Tell us about the cheapest professional investment you have made in your life.

Regarding professional investment, the subscription of SafariBooks. It gives you access to thousands of books and videos of different technologies. Monthly, I choose one topic far from my current tasks and try to learn new things.

What would you recommend to a fellow software developer that is starting their career?

Software engineering is one of the most in-demand careers nowadays—you have positions like machine learning, mobile development, devops, backend or frontend, but the fundamentals are the same for all of them. I recommend having the Swiss Army knife of skills: data structures. I know it sounds boring, but they are present everywhere. Then you should know networking and containerization technologies. And, finally, invest time to learn one typed language and one dynamic language.

We have more resources than ever today to improve in our career, GitHub and StackOverflow, newsletters, even Slack groups are perfect sources to learn more. I would suggest to pick up a repository on GitHub and start learning the internals of the project. Also, you should join communities, events or meetups. The social part of your job will help you meet other exciting engineers and projects. And who knows? Maybe you will give a talk at these events.

You also have a unique track of working with different cultures in the same company. How do you bridge these cultural differences? Is there any tip you could give to people working or aiming to work in a multicultural environment?

I remember counting 24 different nationalities in the Mobile Team in the last company. I enjoy these kinds of environments. Of course, you have to be open-minded, but sometimes it is inevitable to fall victim to some cultural shock. The important thing is always communication and aiming to learn from others.

As a fun fact, a very good friend, Leonid Olevksy, organized a monthly event to know more about the cultures of the team. We learned about Nigeria, Indonesia, Israel, Russia and other countries, and I enjoyed helping us to understand each other better.

Tell us three technical tools not widely known that you use frequently.

First, SdkMan, which is a tool for managing parallel versions of multiple Software Development Kits. It provides a convenient CLI and API for installing. Next, Gephi, which I've used lately when I'm working on projects with data structures like graphs, and I need to analyze data. It helps you with visualization, and you can also provide different graph algorithms to better understand the composition of the graphs. And, finally, Koshry, which is associated with Kotlin projects. It gives your team the ability to monitor pull requests and take automatic actions, depending on your rules result. It helped me to define a better process in the team and is easy to extend. It's similar to Dagger but Kotlin oriented. You can extend the fu switching, remove and list candidates.

What are the three additional resources—such as books—that have had a lasting impact on how you do your work?

First, *Domain-Driven Design: Tackling Complexity in the Heart of Software* by Eric Evans. This is an essential book for designing software applications. The book talks about using model-driven design to create a domain model and ubiquitous language that everyone in the company can leverage.

Another is *Your Code as a Crime Scene: Use Forensic Techniques to Arrest Defects, Bottlenecks, and Bad Design in Your Programs* by Adam Tornhill. With a funny story behind the main topic, it provides powerful tools and techniques to successfully maintain your software.

And, finally, *Designing Data-Intensive Applications: The Big Ideas Behind Reliable, Scalable, and Maintainable Systems* by Martin Kleppmann. The book gives a comprehensive overview of design aspects for systems working with data, systems, databases, tools and techniques.

In working with these tools or others, how do you keep yourself productive through the day?

I like the Pomodoro Technique applied in 60 minutes. I also plan personal sprints of two weeks of things I want to learn and continue improving in the skills. Exercise is also essential. It doesn't matter if you can run 10 km or 2 km, the important thing is to clear your body and mind to be more productive every day. And to make things more fun. I try to explore new sports in which I have to learn and listen from the professionals.

IÑAKI'S RECOMMENDATIONS

GDG communities | developers.google.com/community/gdg/

O'Reilly books | oreilly.com/online-learning/individuals.html

Uber Engineering blog | eng.uber.com

OLUWASEGUN FAMISA

❝Structure your own self-learning.❞

🐦 @segunfamisa

Segun is a Google Developer Expert for Android, based in Berlin, Germany. Although originally trained as an electronic engineer, he has taken on the challenge of developing for Android for around seven years. He has previously worked at Andela as an Android Consultant in Lagos, Nigeria where he worked with various partners on their Android projects. He also worked at Konga as a Software Engineer in the Android team of KongaPay. He is passionate about Software Engineering and loves to share his passion and findings through technical articles on his blog as well as speaking about the platform. When he is not writing code, he is playing the bass guitar in local bars around where he lives or trying his hand at painting.

AN INTERVIEW WITH SEGUN FAMISA

Like many in this industry, you've been a global traveler. You moved from Nigeria to Germany. Tell us, what would you recommend to a fellow developer that is thinking of switching countries? What are the hardest problems you encountered, and how did you solve them?

I would recommend living abroad for anyone who is thinking about it. The biggest benefit for me is the fresh perspective it gives about life in other cultures. I am constantly learning about people's ways of living in my host country. This is also the first time in my life that I am part of a minority population, and the entire experience has been humbling and has provided new insights, especially on the topics of inclusivity.

Moving to another country also opened doors of travel opportunities to neighboring countries and environments, since they're closer to me now than they used to be. All of this adds up to the wholesome experience of living abroad, and I would 100% recommend it to anyone willing and able to do it.

For me, however, the hardest challenges are, first, the process of actually settling into the country—paperwork, finding my own apartment, etc. I think there is no way to solve these problems aside from getting them done and out of the way. For some, it takes a long time; for others, it takes a short time. But once it's done, it's done. A second challenge is that I was an active person in the developer community back home, and it takes me a while to get into the developer community in my host country. The way to solve this was to find someone also interested in this, and they introduced me to other people in the community. I was also able to meet people myself and I attended more meetups like Google Developer Groups, Kotlin User Groups, etc. I also followed some of the developers in my immediate community on Twitter. And, finally, socializing. At some point, the only people I knew in the entire city I lived were my colleagues, so I decided to join some meetups and after-work events and that helped improve my social life.

In terms of getting insight or help from resources, which do you prefer: podcasts or books?

I prefer books to podcasts. Podcasts are great, and I do listen to a couple of podcasts. This is probably a personal issue, but I'm usually tempted to multitask—do things while listening to podcasts, and I often zone out and lose track of what is being said. I'm able to get right into the content when reading books.

What are the three podcasts or books that have had a lasting impact on how you do your work?

Two books that come to mind are *Effective Java* by Joshua Bloch and *Working Effectively with Legacy Code* by Michael Feathers. There's also an Android developer podcast I like called *Fragmented*, hosted by Donn Felker and Kaushik Gopal.

Which other resources do you rely on heavily to keep yourself up-to-date in your industry?

I use Twitter, my most active social media account. I follow a lot of experts and new developers in my field and get to learn about what they're sharing. I also use newsletters and am subscribed to a couple of weekly newsletters, like *Android Weekly*, *Kotlin Weekly*, *Android Developer Digest*, etc. And YouTube; I watch talks from different conferences, I am also subscribed to a couple of developer channels like those from Google, Android Dialogs and other channels.

> 66 *There is an unwritten rule or law that, as a developer, one has to be constantly coding... This is not very sustainable and at some point in time, one may suffer from burnout.* 99

In keeping up with industry trends, are there any that you think are just plain wrong?

There is an unwritten rule or law that, as a developer, one has to be constantly coding. Some people even have it as a slogan and on t-shirts: ABC—"always be coding."

This makes people subconsciously spend their weekends and all of their free time writing code—I'm not saying this is bad—when they could be going to the park, reading a book or just resting. This is not very sustainable and at some point in time, one may suffer from burnout. Developers and indeed, all workers in the industry should encourage and adopt the concept of leaving work at work, and taking personal time off during the weekends and holiday periods.

What is something else you wish someone had told you back when you started software development, that you had to learn the hard way instead?

I wish someone had told me that it was beneficial to have a structure to my self-learning process. As a newbie, I kept gathering resources and studying materials, and I would jump from one resource to the other. There was no structure to my learning, and I missed a lot of important things I had to catch up on much later. I also sometimes suffered from information overload and I would get discouraged. I wish I had a learning curriculum that I had stuck to.

What do you think is one core concept that most software developers don't pay enough attention to when they are trying to grow their careers?

Product thinking. I think the ability to contribute beyond code to the product being worked on is really valuable and important as a software developer. Unfortunately, many fine software developers do not contribute beyond the acceptance criteria on the tasks they work on. I believe that as one is growing their software development career they should also pay sufficient attention to their product thinking skills. This makes them wholesome value contributors to the teams they work on. It also opens up the possibility to transition into technical product management roles later in their careers.

Which advice would you give to someone who is starting his or her career?

For anyone starting, I would say that consistency is key. For anyone starting their development career, especially if they are self-learning, there's a chance that they will want to jump from framework to framework, or from stack to stack. I think it is best for them to be consistent in which development stack they start with, until they get comfortable, before switching to something else.

Which is the cheapest investment you have made that has provided you the highest ROI in your career?

My first Android device. Well, it was not originally an Android device, it was a Windows mobile OS device, but I was able to sideload Android OSes on the device. I was able to use this as my testing device when I was learning how to build Android apps, especially as my development computer was slow and emulators were heavy and slow back then.

Currently, multiplatform development is the Holy Grail of our industry. What are your views on frameworks such as Kotlin/Native and Flutter?

First of all, I think Kotlin should be the de-facto language of every native Android development—the features of the language contribute immensely to productivity and app stability. But on the topic of multiplatform development, Kotlin/Native is an amazing feature that allows you to write code once and deploy to many platforms including the iOS platform. I like this feature because teams can easily share common business logic between their Android and iOS teams. Flutter is another great platform for multiplatform development—unlike many other similar solutions, it is native on both platforms, which is great for performance. On the other hand, it does not completely remove the requirement to understand native development. My biggest reservation with Flutter is that the libraries and support packages are only just growing. Overall, I think they're both great approaches to multiplatform, but for now, my bet is on Kotlin/Native.

In your daily work, do you have any secret morning routines that set you up for success and how do you stay productive for long periods?

I do not have any strict morning routines, per se, aside from trying to wake up at the same time every morning and sleeping at the same time at night. But staying productive for long periods is a bit of an oxymoron! Taking breaks is what helps me stay productive. Every time I walk away for a short break and come back to my work, I come back with renewed energy and focus much longer than I would have if I didn't take the break. This has been theorized into many productivity concepts, one of which includes the Pomodoro technique, but mine is not as short as the traditional 25 minute-long deep work sessions.

SEGUN'S RECOMMENDATIONS

Effective Java | Joshua Bloch

Working Effectively with Legacy Code | Michael Feathers

Android Backstage Podcast | Tor Norbye, Romain Guy and Chet Hasse

FERNANDO CEJAS

" Be open and try new things. "

fernandocejas.com   github.com/android10   f/Penano

Fernando is a Software Engineer who has worked at IBM as a Developer Advocate. He has also spent time working at SoundCloud as a Mobile Core Engineer and, prior to that, at Flomio and Tuenti as a Mobile Software Engineer. Fernando is a huge fan of agile methodologies, programming, and tech in general. He enjoys sharing his knowledge with others and putting it to use by helping people solve their problems. His urge to share what he knows has turned him into a prolific public speaker.

AN INTERVIEW WITH FERNANDO CEJAS

You are one of the most senior and well-traveled people in the industry—tell us a little more about yourself.

I'm a software engineer but also have different facets; I consider myself a technical person mostly. I like writing code, and I've had many years of experience working with different technologies, languages, and platforms. Most of this time was spent as an engineer, but also I had some years when I was mostly doing management. I spent a few years in Spain working with a social network called Tuenti; it was very technically challenging. Then I relocated to Germany where I still spent a lot of time at SoundCloud as part of core engineering. Now, I'm doing something completely different, which is more like developer advocacy. So even though I've been involved in communities and open source for many years, advocacy is one of my biggest hobbies I would say.

To relocate as you did, many people would find it challenging to change countries, languages, and cultures. Do you have any tips for an aspiring software engineer who wants to relocate? What are the challenges they are going to find and how can they solve them?

The biggest challenge is at the start when you first relocate. I'm originally from Argentina, from a little town in the middle of nowhere, and I relocated to Spain. Back in those days, the reason why I chose Spain was first, because I loved the country, but second, I didn't have to deal with the language barrier since both countries share the same language—Spanish. Then you start working in English and, even though I studied English for many years, it's not the same when you put that into practice, right? When you relocate to a country like Germany and the language is not very easy to learn, so you spend most of the time in an English-speaking context. Once there, I would advise not to be shy.

In order to learn you have to make mistakes all the time. You ought not to be afraid of making those mistakes. Just talk, talk, talk. In my case, of course, I definitely had to learn some basics. But go for it. And, sometimes we feel like we can survive with just English because English is kind of easy to learn. But you will definitely go a step further if you learn the host language, and you will integrate into the country, which is super important when you're living abroad. It's important in order to open up your mind, to evolve your mindset, and to really understand what's going on around you. Sometimes it feels like I don't know what's going on here, but sometimes it's the language barrier that is holding you back. So don't be shy. Go for it and keep in mind that there are other people who have gone through this process. Just speak words out—it doesn't matter.

My doctor, when I first tried in German, said, "Oh, you speak like a three-year-old kid,"—but in a sweet way. Now, she has seen my evolution, even though it's not perfect.

Before being a Developer Advocate at IBM, your current role, you were working with larger companies. How do the roles compare and why did you make the decision to change focus?

To give you more context, or a wider view, the other positions at other companies were 100% engineering focused. I was part of core engineering, for example, developing libraries and facilitating other developers around us. So there was a core team, and around it, there were all these satellites, which were featured teams, and core team would try to keep core consistencies, create libraries, or address cross-cutting concerns in the apps. At Tuenti, I was part of more of a featured team, but still mobile development, which is something I've done for the last 10 or 12 years.

I always liked being involved with communities. I've done organization for Google developers in Barcelona, for example, for something like G-Talk. I've also done open-source writing. It's something I've been doing in addition to my day job, while also working on engineering.

Here's the thing: At some point, I wanted to turn that—or to try to turn that—into my day-to-day life. I said, okay, so, I've been doing engineering 100% for a while. Maybe it's time to change a little bit of my career path to see how it feels. Going to a conference and creating a relationship with others and being active in the community is something I really enjoy. There are pros and cons, and I'm still working out what parts I like the most.

I consider myself a team player. I like to work with people, I like to communicate, I like to create stuff. I like to, for example, chat with someone or go to the whiteboard and come up with a solution, write down the stuff do some collaborative programming. That's something that is more likely to happen if you're an engineer in an office—or even a remote engineer. You have a team working on a specific bunch of nationalities within the codebase, for example. But this developer advocate position is kind of more isolated.

You probably have more flexibility in your work, and the work is more research related. You're understanding a product—you're understanding the need and you're trying to create relationships. But, in the end, you do this mostly by yourself. When you have to showcase something, you create a presentation. Of course, you have a team and you collect some feedback, but the creational part, working together with someone else, like doing some pair programming, doesn't really exist. Maybe this is the way how the company is handling this position, but that's what I'm seeing in the community overall while exchanging feedback with other developer advocates. It involves a lot of travel as well. Sometimes, it feels like you're not at home. But sometimes you want quiet times and a routine—that is less likely to happen in this position.

If you want to write code 100% of your time, a developer-advocate position is not one you would go for. It involves all these aspects that are very time-consuming. Of course, I always said the more senior you become, the less code you write like an engineer. You do have initiatives and are still in touch with the code itself. But this position is more about organizing, preparing presentations, emails, creating relationships, talking to many people, organizing events, and more.

You're mostly a remote worker in this position. Is remote work something you'd recommend companies implement for their employees? If they are interested, how should they get started?

This is the 2.0 way of working nowadays. I would say if you're not going remote, you're missing a lot of talented people out there because not everyone is likely to or has the chance to relocate somewhere else. But moving in this direction is challenging, and I've been doing some advising on this. One of the challenges is if you have part of your team on site and the rest is remote. When you have a very low number of remote workers who are part of a team, they can feel outside of the team. If you think of your team behavior, for example, when you talk to someone from the team, if you're in an office, you might not start a video call. You'll probably just gather whoever is in the office together then and go to a room and to have a discussion.

That's what I've been seeing so far. It's very important for remote workers not to feel isolated and that they feel part of the team. There are tons of tools out there, especially for communication. A company itself must be prepared for remote work and to have the tooling and organization to handle different time zones, for example. Overall, I'd say it's easier when 100% of the company is remote to avoid these issues.

Instead of "remote," I'd call this kind of organization "distributed." I would definitely encourage any company to have employees distributed as you're missing a lot of opportunities if you are not doing that. Something surprising to me is the big players who don't allow remote work; my company does. It's surprising because they're supposed to have the young mentality and so forth, but they're not in the present or the near future. It's not like the old days when we suffered from a lack of tooling. It's easier now.

What are some tools you use daily that you would recommend to others?

Slack, of course; it's such a simple tool capable of PTOs, conferencing, chat or even just phone calls. That's my main communication tool.

For development, as I'm a big fan of mobile, in this case of Android, Android Studio is my tool; there pretty much isn't a time when I do not open it. I like the tool Visual Studio Code. I think it's very lightweight—kind of in the middle between a powerful text editor and IDE—so it's kind of a hybrid. It's super fast and there's a big community around it.

I would also have to say my terminal. I mostly picked Linux as my operating system for the last couple of years. I had been a Linux user in the past, but then, you know, you take the chance to change your machine. I've been using macOS, which is super good, too, and the core itself is Linux. But I like communities. I use ArchLinux, and my command line tool. I'm not the most expert Linux user, but I like doing things on the command line. I'm basically using Bash, so not a big deal. Not these fancy terminals that exist nowadays, but my own customized Bash terminal.

With whatever tool you use, how do you start your day to set yourself up for success?

I have two techniques for staying productive that I use that are lessons learned. I try to avoid things like procrastination that we all suffer from sometimes; it's impossible not to procrastinate at all, but at least you can minimize it. The first one is a personal routine. When we are talking about actual methodologies, I use a Trello board. This is a personal board. Every day, by the end of my day, I just take five to 10 minutes to plan out my next day. Sometimes, of course, there are things that come up out of nowhere, but most of the time you have this structure and, after your coffee, you know what you will be working on. For productivity itself, I use the Pomodoro Technique— these windows of time of 15 minutes, then you stop five minutes.

Then you have another 15 minutes, and so forth until the fourth time when you have a bigger rest. That's something that helps to really focus me and minimize the amount of procrastination. Those are my two main tools.

In addition to tools, are there any resources, like books or podcasts, that you'd recommend that have had an impact on your life?

I do listen to podcasts, but I'm more a fan of books. I have a visual memory, so I memorize more when I read rather than what I hear. That's why I struggle more with language learning. I prefer going over books first—understand and create a relationship and then keep it in my mind. So for books, more technically, I'd first say *Refactoring: Improving the Design of Existing Code* by Martin Fowler. That book was a game changer for me; it's when I understood how important testing is. It was about changing all this internal structure and extraction with all these patterns for refactoring and making your code better. *The Pragmatic Programmer: From Journeyman to Master* by Andrew Hunt is another classic.

When I was a teenager, a game changer for me was El Principito—The Little Prince. It's one of those books that doesn't have one read—"Oh, this is about love and this is about that." You could relate that metaphorically. In this case, it focused on the human relationship with someone you liked or loved so much, and someone who is an important part of your life.

You've been influential in the community with the blog posts you have written, especially in the Android ecosystem and your post on

clean architecture. What's the origin of the clean architecture post, specifically?

I remember the days of facing some challenges with other colleagues working on a social network we were starting to scale. We found that the architectures out there were good practice but would not really fit within our needs. We needed a new way of architecting mobile applications, in this case, Android, that would definitely fulfill what we were needing back then.

We had a lot of discussions on the board and basically grabbed other good practices and experiences from other areas, in this case, backing. At some point, I was interested in what Robert Martin, Uncle Bob, was saying about clean architecture, and I saw it as a very simple way of separating concerns. That would give us a code base that would make our lives easier in terms of firsts—problem-solving, scalability, modernization and testability—and that would mean that this architecture would be independent of frameworks. At the time, we were attached to frameworks. We didn't have enough tooling to test and refactoring was a nightmare. At some point, we said okay, we need to rethink this. To be honest, that took time. I tried to evolve what we did in the company, and I spent some time at home thinking and trying to come up with something simple, as well.

I learned a lot in the process. It evolved super fast and people were coming up with new ideas and things. In the first version, failing in many different ways, I learned a lot. I think that's the most important part, here: seeing the learning process and how people have been modifying that code and adapting it to different areas. It turned out it worked. It was about bringing already-proven things from other technologies to mobile legacies.

You're a very seasoned speaker, traveling the world, sharing insights like this. How can a new developer unfamiliar with public speaking get started?

I think this is a recurring topic nowadays because of the content consumption and content generation. There is so much information out there, and many people are jumping on board saying that you should talk at conferences or write articles. In my opinion, you should only talk if you really like it, and if you have something to say. Some people just ask me, "How can I start?" And my answer is always: "Do you really like it? Or is the environment is pushing you towards this direction?" One of the things I have in mind is I get it out whenever I have something to say. I think, for me, it's mostly about giving back to the community.

But if you really want to try it, I'd say start simple and work towards complexity. So if you haven't tried it, but you want to know whether you would like it or not, you can start by starting with your company in front of a tiny meetup. For example, in my company, I implemented something that is called a five-minute talk. Once a week, we prepare a concept or something new to learn that would take five minutes to explain. So we spend half an hour and there are four speakers, let's say. It's a cool starting point for speaking and sharing ideas, and then you will realize whether you like it or not. Maybe then you could go after showcasing something to your colleagues—then going bigger and bigger if you really like it. If you don't like speaking, you can apply your ideas to some papers, blogs or articles.

There is so much out there when we talk about content generation. Again, with public speaking, start from the little stuff five-minute talks maybe, or just maybe one day take the lead in a big meeting—a meeting with five to eight people maximum. As developers and engineers, we have a reputation for being introverted, and many people struggle with speaking in public, with communication, and so forth.

I used to be shyer, myself. But you can also go to conferences and start socializing, trying to make yourself a little bit more extroverted by sharing what you know.

What is something that you didn't know when you started as a software developer that you wish someone had told you that you had to learn the hard way instead?

I wish someone would have pushed me and convinced me, when I began my career, that testing your code is important. I'm pretty sure we all started writing code without tests, and I would say, "Yeah, this is not worth it. Why should I spend time on this?" But there are so many benefits, and, of course, asserting that your code behaves as expected is something that we should always keep in mind. Writing tests for me should be something that is part of our engineering process. It should be implicit when we are writing code. We shouldn't talk about testing and talk about writing code. They should be together. You want to make sure that the code you're writing is behaving as expected and that would help out with refactoring. Nowadays, you know that refactoring is about changing the internal structure of your code and not the behavior. That means you still want the same behavior, which is internally asserted by the test battery that you have.

I wish I would have known that before because I would have avoided many issues. I would have avoided wasting my time on so many occasions.

❝ *For any tool, we, as professionals, need to be open, to collect feedback, and to try out new things.* ❞

What are your thoughts on test-driven development?

TDD is one of the more useful things I've found in the last few years. I'm not an expert, and, most of the time I don't do it. But it's nice for super complex development. Sometimes it could be a little bit more challenging, but it's one more tool in your toolbox. But if you're strict with the way you write code, it's also possible without TDD. Sometimes people don't feel comfortable by just following this red/green/refactor, like writing your code, make it fail, refactor it, and make the test to pass. So use it if you feel comfortable with it. It can depend on my mood! It can also depend on the programming language or platform.

For any tool, we, as professionals, need to be open, to collect feedback, and to try out new things.

FERNANDO'S RECOMMENDATIONS

SoundCloud Developers site | developers.soundcloud.com/blog

The Netflix Tech blog | medium.com/netflix-techblog

IT IS ABOUT PHILOSOPHY... AN ORGANIZATION'S CULTURE AND THE POWER OF HUMANITY

Making the Best of Your Organization's Culture

FERNANDO CEJAS

Philosophy is the study of general and fundamental problems, such as those connected with reality, existence, knowledge, values, reason, mind, and language. In my mind, when looking at this definition, this question arises:

How can all this be linked to an organization's culture?

True fact: There is a proportional relationship in being happy and getting things done, which again brings up another topic to the table: How can we achieve such happiness and motivation in order to create a working environment full of good vibes?

66 *There is a proportional relationship in being happy and getting things done.* 99

In order to answer these questions, let's walk together through a bunch of aspects, that in my opinion, are key in order to construct a culture and environment based on human values which will facilitate working in harmony, thus, contributing to achieving that mentioned happiness.

Human Values

We can learn pretty much every technology out there and predict its behavior, but unfortunately people are unpredictable and that is why I encourage building up a working culture based on a set of very important human values:

- Respect
- Honesty
- Communication
- Humility

From my perspective, these are the pillars of any relationship or interaction: family, friends and human beings in general.

Applying them all is not straightforward, but understanding them is a big win, and trust me, it is the way to go, otherwise much of our energy will be consumed trying to fix friction and conflicts bubbling up from people interacting with each other.

❝ Computers are predictable, people are totally unpredictable. ❞

Here are a few tips that can help us to promote those mentioned values:

- Respect other opinions: In the end these are opinions and we could agree or not, but listening is always a must.
- Accept feedback without being a smartass: We are not all-knowing and we must be always open to receive feedback in a constructive way.
- Understand we make mistakes: There are always good intentions but we are human beings and we are not perfect.
- No finger-pointing: Learn out of failure and create retrospectives in order to not repeat those failures again, but please do not blame people, we are always together

either in both the good moments and when going through difficulties.

- Be a team player: Communicate properly and be honest and transparent.
- We all have our bad days, right? Learn to separate what is personal and what it is not.
- Be open-minded and understand other cultures: Most of the time we work in a multicultural context and that is why we must keep it in mind. For example, what could be super nice in one culture, could be rude in another.
- Listen and be patient: We all deserve our time to express ourselves.
- Be positive: There is always light at the end of the tunnel.
- Be friendly and help: when we ask for help, we want to see that big smile which makes us feel way better.
- Treat everyone the same way: No one is better than anyone, no rockstars. (Personal experience: people in upper layers of the company/organization, I'm looking at you.)
- Do not be shy: Voice your opinion and ask anything, dumb questions do not exist.

❝ *No one is better than anyone; no rockstars please.* **❞**

This sounds good on paper and also normal right?

Unfortunately, at least in my experience, I have not found many places where this is respected. That is why taking this attitude is a good starting point and a game-changer for our working culture, and the first step is to apply them ourselves and be an example for the rest.

Favor Leaders Over Bosses

The very first and important point here is to differentiate a leader from a boss. Both roles take responsibilities but the main difference sits on their attitude and way of working.

In my opinion, a leader is someone I see as a reference, someone I trust and rely on, a person I can also learn a lot from, with high human qualities and values. She/he should point us in the right direction, and also defend and protect us if we are under difficult situations.

> 66 *A leader is someone I see as a reference, someone I trust and rely on, a person I can also learn a lot from, with high human qualities and values.* 99

Another feature a good leader should offer is the ability to make us feel that we are part of the project, by letting us participate in the decision making without doing micromanagement, thus, trusting and letting us do our job.

> 66 *The concept of a boss is prehistoric and should be eradicated.* 99

On the other hand, we have the concept of the boss, which from my point of view, it is prehistoric and should be eradicated. Tons of red flags in people with this mentality 200 years old, pushing and giving commands as if we were machines causing burnout and demotivation.

I think the choice is clear: favor a leader over a boss.

Communication and Transparency

It is evident that the smaller your organization is, the better the information flows, that is why we should favor flat hierarchies as much as we can.

This is not easy, especially if you start growing up exponentially, but minimize the number of communication layers to facilitate transparency and a good flow in the information transportation across the organization.

We should also try to avoid secrets and hidden information in general, especially since this might lead to mistrust.

Anyway, it is totally valid if some information is critical and should be not exposed or kept safe: one clear example is regarding NDAs or partnerships with third parties that are out of scope and control in our organization.

66 *We should try to avoid secrets and hidden information in general, especially since this might lead to untrust.* 99

Here are some tools that facilitate transparency:
- All-Hands
- Internal Wiki/Blog
- A People's Team (HR could also take this role)

In the end, a rule of thumb is that we should feel free and comfortable to ask any questions to anyone. If we want to feel part of a project, we need to feel it in all senses at all levels: that is why it is important to communicate properly and efficiently in a transparent way.

Career Path and Continuous Improvement

With this world changing so fast, we all love to learn and make progress in our careers, that is the main reason why one of the fundamental building blocks of any organization's culture is guidance and career path.

> **"** *One of the fundamental building blocks of any organization's culture is guidance and career path.* **"**

Both People's Team and (Engineering) Managers should help with the task:

- Establish policies for mentorship: Continuous learning and knowledge sharing.
- Define policies for career guidance: Follow up closely employees' motivations with tools like 1:1 meetings for example.
- Conduct regular employee surveys: Nothing can be improved without constructive feedback.
- Nothing better than celebration. Anything would be the same without celebrating our achievements: Recognition of the effort. In my opinion, this one is one of the most important ones: Celebrate your achievements.

> **"** *Anything would be the same without celebrating our achievements: Recognition to the effort.* **"**

We should always reward employees who do a good job: recognition to both the individuals and teams who work hard will encourage them to keep it up, plus it will also spread out the notion that hard work is acknowledged and appreciated.

Engineering Culture

Now it is time to switch gears and go deeper into what we can do in terms of engineering. (Although I guess these principles, or part of them, could also apply to any other area.)

❝ *Foment continuous learning and sharing.* **❞**

Here are a bunch of key points:
- Defend code quality and good practices.
- Accept challenges: Do not be afraid of making mistakes.
- Be prepared for the change: Everything evolves.
- Foment continuous learning and sharing.
- Share experiences: Blog entries, promote conference attendance, etc.
- Continuous Learning: One day per week or sprint of "hacking time."
- Use Post-mortems: Learn out of mistakes.
- Retrospectives: Another tool for continuous feedback and improvement.
- Have fun.

❝ *Defend code quality and good practices.* **❞**

Hiring

Hiring is important and a lot of time and effort must be invested in order to develop all these ideas mentioned so far. We should be involved in the hiring process, especially if the person who is going to be hired will work with us: We want to avoid people who do not fit with the culture we are encouraging. We should be involved in the process in order to hire the right people who are going to work with us.

So here is my advice: If you have the chance to participate and combine efforts with the Human Resources team, do not doubt and go for it: It is very likely that it will require a bit of effort and time investment but you will appreciate it, and in the end, it will contribute to building up such organization's culture we are looking for.

The Power of Happiness and Motivation

Building an organization's culture with all the ideas above is not easy (and there is a long path towards it) but we can always contribute from our tiny position. These points should be taken into consideration when it comes to happiness:

- Start from the trenches: Build your own team's culture and infect others.
- Neither impose nor give commands: Spread and pollute the environment with good vibes.
- Become a reference and a game-changer.
- Create a context where the word pressure is forbidden: in the end, we put our own pressure on ourselves. We are not under the gun and knowing when to say no is an important part of happiness and being a good professional.
- Follow your heart: Many times the heart sees what it is invisible to the eye, especially in difficult situations.
- Equality in all senses for the win: Do not feel intimidated by anyone because no one is better than anyone.

Keep in mind that we spend so many hours in our lives working, so we should always try to find something which really fulfills us, and if you feel you have tried pretty much everything to achieve these goals, maybe you should reconsider whether your current place is the right one.

> **Equality in all senses for the win: Do not feel intimidated by anyone because no one is better than anyone.**

Be a Good Person Over a Good Professional

Prioritize humanity over technical skills. This is, in the end, my conclusion. Both are important, no doubt, but in my opinion, nothing is more fulfilling when you open your heart and help people, and you are appreciated because of that too.

> **We work with people, not with computers, they are the only means to reach out to people.**

And REMEMBER: We work with people, not with computers, they are only the means to reach out to PEOPLE.

CREDIT

A version of this article was first published on Fernando Cejas's personal website (November 10, 2018). The original article can be found here: fernandocejas.com/2018/11/11/organization-culture-and-humanity/

TANNER WAYNE NELSON

66 Gain the courage to try. 99

🐦 @tanner0101

Tanner is an American software engineer based in New York City. He started programming in elementary school and went on to study Computer Science at New York University. Tanner created Vapor in 2016 and now works full time maintaining the core framework and the dozens of packages around it.

You are the creator of Vapor, a very popular web framework. Tell us, how does Swift, a language originally conceived for a mobile platform, perform at scale for web development?

Swift is a wonderful language for web development. It strikes a unique balance between simplicity, safety, and performance that set it apart from other popular languages in the field. If you compare Swift to interpreted languages like PHP, Python, and Ruby, its performance will be unmatched. This is one of the huge benefits of being a compiled language. When you compare Swift to other compiled languages, like Java, Go, and C#, performance is more evenly matched, but Swift's expressive syntax and advanced type system shine. The ecosystem is still very young though and has its rough edges. We're definitely in this one for the long haul.

JetBrains is also experimenting as well with Kotlin/Native. What are your thoughts on cross-platform development? Will there ever be a Holy Grail that lets you develop once, and deploy anywhere?

I think there is room for code sharing—libraries and frameworks written in Swift or Kotlin that can be shared between mobile and backend projects, for example. However, I don't think there will ever be a good one-size-fits-all solution to developing for different platforms. In my opinion, a much better approach is to use the best tool for a given job. I think this is a big reason why the micro-service pattern has become so popular lately. Backend teams that utilize multiple frameworks and languages to solve problems can pick and choose the best tool for each situation.

How do you keep an open-source project successful at scale?

I think the main key to success in open source is embracing the community. This is something Vapor has prioritized since day one, and we are constantly trying to improve. A few examples come to mind. First, giving the project a simple, open license, like the MIT license. Creating a space where people interested in the project can communicate freely is key, as well as discussing the project's roadmap openly and always asking for input. You also want to make it as easy as possible to report bugs, request features, or submit code. And when someone does contribute, it's important to reward them with appreciation and status.

For those folks interested in free/libre and open-source software (FLOSS) but who haven't yet taken a step into this world, what would you recommend as a first step for them? In what ways do you find participating in collaborative FLOSS projects benefits people, career-wise?

If you haven't yet delved into the world of open source, the first and hardest step is probably getting over the fear of posting your code publicly. There could be some embarrassing mistake you made in your logic or maybe people will think your idea is dumb, right? This was true for me at least. And, as it turns out, I did make a bunch of embarrassing mistakes and some people did think my ideas were dumb. But the vast majority of people were extremely kind and helpful. They helped me improve my code and taught me so much along the way. I feel that I've learned more in these past three years working on Vapor than I have at any other point in my career. It's the people that make OSS awesome. Anyone willing to devote their free time to contribute to open source must be quite passionate about programming, and that passion is inspiring.

So my advice would be: don't worry too much about it, just post something—anything. The sooner the better.

A lot of the work you do happens remotely. What do you find are the best approaches for collaborating successfully with remote teams or people working remotely in very different time zones? Are there any tools that make your life easier in this respect?

For the core team, at least, having clear ownership over specific features or projects have been incredibly helpful. This reduces the amount of communication needed between us to complete tasks and minimizes blocking due to time zone differences.

However, Vapor is much larger than just the core team. We have taken code contributions from well over a hundred developers already, and the number grows every day. Luckily, GitHub provides a lot of great tools for collaborating on this scale. Our main strategy here has been to just keep things as simple as possible. We use many of GitHub's advanced features like Milestones and Projects instead of bringing in new tools like Trello or Jira. We also make sure that all of our developer resources, like our command-line interface, website, and documentation, are open source and just as easy to contribute to as the core framework.

What is something you wish someone had told you back when you started software development that you had to learn the hard way instead?

I was really into web development when I was in middle school, using languages like HTML, CSS, JS and later PHP. When I was starting high school around 2008, I remember watching WWDC keynotes, wishing that I could create iPhone apps. But Objective-C looked terrifying to me and I knew for sure I would not be able to learn it. Years later, and thanks to Stanford's amazing, free iOS lectures, I finally came around to giving Objective-C a shot. I immediately fell in love with iOS programming and it became one of my biggest passions for years to come.

I regret that it took me so long to gain enough courage to try, and I wish I could go back in time to tell myself: "Hey, it's not so hard actually, you can do it." Even after this lesson, and numerous more throughout my life, I still find myself doubting in my ability to learn new things. Luckily, it gets easier to overpower the self-doubt over time.

> 66 *As programmers, we stand on the shoulders of giants— the levels of abstraction between a web programmer and the logic gates on a circuit board are incredibly deep and complex.* 99

Are there any resources that have also impacted your work?

A few come to mind. *C Programming Language* by Brian W. Kernighan and Dennis M. Ritchie; *Structure and Interpretation of Computer Programs* by Harold Abelson, Gerald Jay Sussman and Julie Sussman; and *Beej's Guide to Network Programming* by Brian Hall.

As programmers, we stand on the shoulders of giants—the levels of abstraction between a web programmer and the logic gates on a circuit board are incredibly deep and complex. I think it's safe to say that no single person in the world understands everything from top to bottom. We learn a single abstraction layer well and spend most of our time being productive there. However, sometimes it's fun to take a peek behind the curtain and learn more about how these abstractions we use everyday work. Sometimes this knowledge can even come in handy.

Are there any current industry trends that you think are just plain wrong?

I find Google Chrome's ever-growing market share to be quite concerning. As it continues to rise, Google gains even more power to dictate how the web should work. This does not bode well, especially after seeing Google use its search engine's market share to push their terrible Accelerated Mobile Pages (AMP) tech. Recent developments, such as Microsoft replacing their EdgeHTML engine with Chrome, show no sign of improvement. People should give browsers besides Chrome a chance before it's too late.

In terms of preparing to do your work, how do you start your day off with a bang? Do you have any secret morning routines that set you up for success?

I wake up early and exercise every day. Programming is an incredibly sedentary job and you need to counteract that if you want to stay happy and have energy.

How do you stay highly productive in your work for long periods?

I think taking breaks from long projects is critical to keeping quality and creativity high. If you're finding it hard to "get into the zone" for a certain task, put it on hold and do something else that excites you for a bit. Maybe there's a side project you've been neglecting or a new framework you've been wanting to learn about. After the break, you'll come back to the problem with a fresh mind, and potentially a better solution.

TANNER'S RECOMMENDATIONS

C Programming Language | Brian W. Kernighan and Dennis M. Ritchie

Structure and Interpretation of Computer Programs |
Harold Abelson, Gerald Jay Sussman and Julie Sussman

Beej's Guide to Network Programming | Brian Hall

ANNYCE DAVIS

66 *Start each day with a clean slate.* 99

🐦 @brwngrldev   💼 /in/annycedavis

nnyce spends her day-to-day working as a Software Developer and Leader. She's specifically been focused on mobile application development for the past decade. Annyce is also an Android Google Developer Expert, developing videos, blog posts, and conference talks for the Developer Community. She's currently Director of Engineering at Meetup. There she uses technology as a tool to help others foster real-world connections.

You are a resource in the Android community, having been quoted across media as one of the key individuals to follow. In one of your blog posts, "So You Want to Be an Android Developer..." you give your readers a guide to get started or grow their current skills. What are the key takeaways from this article?

The key thing I want people to understand is that you need a good foundation in the basics: XML, Java, Object-Oriented Design and then you can add on to your skillset bit by bit. The other thing I've noticed with working on Android for so long is that eventually, Google will come out with their own version of the most popular libraries or patterns that the community is adopting. So sticking to the Jetpack toolchain is a good decision for the long run.

Overall, you are a very prolific contributor to the Android community through video tutorials, blog posts, and conferences. Where do you find your inspiration for new projects and content?

I get inspiration from my everyday activities. As I explore new technologies, frameworks, and design principles I always think to myself, "This might make a great talk/blog post/course." I love creating content as much for others as for myself. I find the creative process very rewarding and it helps me to solidify the materials in my own mind.

What advice would you give to developers interested in starting to produce and share their own tutorials, articles, or presentations?

One thing I do is keep a running list of things that I'm working on, or I've learned recently in a markdown file. This makes it easier for me to draw on when I'm ready to create a blog post or presentation. I've also written about my process for conference talks and course creation. I would recommend they check it out as it's still relatively close to how I execute currently.

In terms of your own development, what role models have helped shape your career?

Chiu-Ki Chan has had a huge impact on how I view myself as a developer and leader. When I first started speaking at conferences, she was the voice in my ear that told me I belonged and I had something worthwhile to say. I also appreciate how we can share ideas with each other and be open about our ambitions and goals. Hands down, meeting her turned my career in a whole new direction! Further, I appreciate my current manager a lot. His approach to dealing with diverse perspectives and personalities has really encouraged me to explore my own strengths and weaknesses when it comes to managing others.

Donn Felker, Florina Muntenescu, Ian Lake and Rebecca Franks are others who come to mind who have been positive influences.

Many developers rarely get any formal training during their education, relying heavily on soft skills in addition to their knowledge as developers. It seems soft skills are often underrated. What are the soft skills you consider more important when working on a team?

Being able to communicate effectively is key. This covers how you express yourself in meetings, technical documentation that you write, even how you come across on Slack. Being an effective communicator will help you to stand out from your peers.

In terms of using resources for your own development, which do you prefer: podcasts or books?

I prefer books. Although I listen to several podcasts, I appreciate being able to explore various topics in more detail and generally, books do that better. I also find it easier to grab a book off of my shelf and refer to something valuable that I remembered reading.

What are the three books that have had a lasting impact on how you do your work?

First, *Head First Design Patterns: A Brain-Friendly Guide* by Eric Freeman, Bert Bates, Kathy Sierra and Elisabeth Robson. Design patterns help you to apply software designs to your code to improve its flexibility and maintainability. I've read several books on the subject, but this one helps to bring it all together with a fun, quirky style. Instead of just tons of text explaining a pattern, it uses examples and silly scenarios to help you understand the reason for a particular pattern. In fact, I've found several examples in my current application where the Command Pattern has helped to clean up the code tremendously. I'd recommend getting the paperback version as this is one that you should keep in your library.

Next, *The Manager's Path: A Guide for Tech Leaders Navigating Growth and Change Paperback* by Camille Fournier. "Actionable advice" is the best way to describe this book. It starts out by explaining what you should expect from a manager and then goes into how to be managed. This section was great for me because it helped codify some thoughts I had around where I want to go next with my career. Especially the section on taking ownership of your relationship with your manager and not just letting it be a top-down exchange. I have recommended this book to so many people at this point. If you're still on the fence, just do it; you won't be disappointed.

Finally, *The Clean Coder: A Code of Conduct for Professional Programmers* by Robert C. Martin. This book really spoke to me. It aligned with feelings and thoughts I already had around professionalism in the tech industry and commitment to tasks. I appreciate the very conversational style and the fact that the author shares the times when he failed to do the right thing and the bad effects. I feel like this is great for people new to the industry to read and internalize so that we can have more professional behavior on software teams.

What do you wish someone had told you when you started software development that you had to learn the hard way?

I wish that someone had told me there's no such thing as just a minimum viable product, or MVP. Earlier on in my career, I would be asked to just put something together, simple, fast and does the job. We just need an MVP. But invariably it never stays as just an MVP and ends up making it into production and you have to live with that code for a long time. Although it's important to move quickly in many cases, you still need to use a good design and have tests. So now, if I'm asked to do an MVP, I always design it in such a way that I could live with that code for the next year or two.

What is a current industry trend that you think is just plain wrong?

One thing I wish would die is the tendency to "poo-poo" on anything that you don't personally agree with. For example, there is a resurgence of libraries that are based on the Service Locator pattern. There are die-hard dependency injection guys that make sure every chance they get they point out that something is not "real DI", etc. This just seems to miss the point for me, obviously, these types of technology trends surface for a reason. They point out that there's something lacking with the current, more popular choice.

What would you suggest is a better alternative to this trend?

I would love to see people engage in more useful dialogue. For example, if you see a trend that you don't personally agree with, why not try to find out why things are shifting. Why are people getting fed up with the current solution? What can we do to make things better for everyone? Just more of a community spirit, instead of "us versus them."

Currently, you are working at Off Grid Electric, which is a fully remote team. What are the most significant challenges of working on a fully remote, or distributed, team?

The biggest challenge is having visibility into what everyone is doing. When you're colocated with your team you can just walk over to someone's desk and check in with them. Or you can look over and see them deep in thought as they try to figure out a nagging bug. But when you're distributed you can't just do that, so it takes more effort to keep everyone in the loop.

> 66 *The best thing you can do as a remote employee is to be visible on your company's chat platform, contribute to virtual meetings as much as possible and keep confirming that the work you do is valuable to the business.* 99

What are the best tools you've found for working successfully in a remote position?

The best thing you can do as a remote employee is to be visible on your company's chat platform, contribute to virtual meetings as much as possible and keep confirming that the work you do is valuable to the business. I've seen many people leave remote positions because they started to feel that they weren't working on high-value items to the business. This can happen easily, so you have to put forth the effort to stay in sync with the direction of the company and advocate for yourself so that you are always working on things that push the business forward.

In setting yourself up for work, how do you start your day off with a bang? Do you have any secret morning routines that set you up for success?

I start each day with a clean slate. Whatever happened the day before is in the past. I don't like to let negativity linger in my life or in my mind. It prevents me from thinking creatively and from experimenting. I wouldn't really consider that a secret, but it's just something that I try to do and it helps when things get a bit crazy at work.

How do you stay highly productive for long stretches of time?

My favorite thing is to listen to brain.fm with noisli.com—the combination helps me to stay in the zone and I can easily focus uninterrupted for two hours at a time.

ANNYCE'S RECOMMENDATIONS

Head First Design Patterns: A Brain-Friendly Guide | Eric Freeman, Bert Bates, Kathy Sierra and Elisabeth Robson

The Manager's Path: A Guide for Tech Leaders Navigating Growth and Change Paperback | Camille Fournier

The Clean Coder: A Code of Conduct for Professional Programmers | Robert C. Martin.

SO YOU WANT TO BE AN ANDROID DEVELOPER...

Your Android Developer Starter Kit

ANNYCE DAVIS

I f I had a nickel for every time someone asked me: How do I become an Android Developer? Let's just say I'd have a whole lot of nickels! So as a gift to the world I've consolidated the various versions of my advice.

As an Android and Kotlin Google Developer Expert, I've created lots of content in this space, so where it makes sense I've included links to my relevant videos and courses.

First, let me just list out everything you would need to know to make a basic Android app:

- XML: It's what we use to configure resources and user interface elements.
- JSON: The preferred data exchange format for communicating via APIs.
- Java: The primary language that most frameworks, libraries and code samples are written in.
- Git: A version control system.

Second, what you need to know to be hired as an Android Developer:

- JUnit: A unit testing framework.
- Mockito: A mocking framework for unit tests.

- Retrofit: A networking library designed for working with REST APIs.
- Android Architecture Components: A collection of libraries that help you design robust, testable, and maintainable apps.
- Constraint Layout: Android View that allows you to create large and complex layouts with a flat view hierarchy.
- Recycler View: Android View for displaying a scrolling list of elements.
- Object-Oriented Programming: Simplifies development and maintenance.

Finally, here's everything you may need to know to make more complex Android apps:

- SQLite: The database that ships with Android to persist your data.
- Kotlin: A language that targets the JVM and eases the burden of programming on Android.
- RxJava: Library for composing asynchronous programs using observable sequences.
- Espresso: A UI testing framework for developers.
- Gradle: The build system used to package and deploy Android applications.
- Material Design: The visual language used on Android to express user interface components.
- Dependency Injection: A way to handle dependencies which makes it easier to structure your code.
- Design Patterns: General, reusable solutions to commonly occurring problems.
- Firebase: Firebase gives you functionality like analytics, messaging and crash reporting under one umbrella.
- WorkManager: Library to assist you in specifying deferrable, asynchronous tasks and when they should run.

How can you learn more about these things:
- *Kotlin Weekly*
- *Android Weekly*
- Android Dev Digest
- Android Podcasts
- Lynda.com
- Udacity
- Caster.IO
- Android Conferences

The most important thing is it to practice! You have to actually write some code and design a few applications to become a good Android developer. Here's a few app ideas:
- TODO: Allow the user to create a TODO and view their list of TODOs.
- Trivia Game: Present the user with a series of questions that have multiple choice answers.
- Remote Data: Download data from a remote API and display it.
- App Clone: Pick one of your favorite apps and make a clone of it.

Or think of something that you're passionate about and make an app for it. The key thing is that you want to gradually improve your expertise by creating more and more complex applications.

CREDIT

A version of this article was first published on Annyce Davis' website (May 15, 2018). The original article can be found here: adavis. info/2018/05/so-you-want-to-be-an-android-developer.html

RAÚL RAJA
MARTÍNEZ

❝ *Do what is important to you.* ❞

🐦 @raulraja   in /in/raulraja   47deg.com/team/raul   github.com/raulraja

Raúl is a co-founder and CTO of 47 Degrees and a member of the Scala Center's Advisory board. As a functional programming enthusiast and experienced engineer, he is a creator, maintainer, and frequent contributor to many well-known open-source libraries. He frequently speaks at technology conferences around the world and has developed free training assets to help ease the learning curve of a variety of programming languages and their related toolsets.

You're an influential voice in the industry. You co-founded 47 Degrees, and you're a contributor to the open-source community as well as several different projects. What are you reading or listening to these days?

I do a fair amount of both. I listen to most of the Functional Programming podcasts. I listen to three or four podcasts a week, and I do a lot of reading online. As I am developing and looking for documentation, I get interested in a topic. Then I go down the rabbit hole. When I see a new book that interests me, I pick it up, especially if it's about Idris, Haskell, Scala, or coding. I also read a lot of short stories and comics.

What podcasts or books have had a lasting impact on your work?

When I was a kid in Spain, I read a book in Catalan called, *L'esquelet de La Balena* by David Cirici. It's about a near-future when teenagers are stranded in the forest and technology helps them survive. As a teen reading this book, I realized there was a lot more out there than my kid's world. That got me interested in technology and learning more about computers.

As far as podcasts, I love the Scala podcast. The host is from the same company that I used to work for, and she does awesome work interviewing people from the Scala community, talking mostly about Functional Programming. There is another great podcast if you're interested in Functional Programming called *Scala Love* with Oli Makhasoeva. This one touches on different topics and more different languages as well, so it's not just tied to Scala or a language in particular. Sometimes they touch on Category Theory. There are a lot of great podcasts for people interested in our field.

How would you explain Functional Programming to a newcomer?

Functional Programming is coding with functions and creating pure functions. Pure functions are those that, given an input, always produce the same output. They are deterministic in their behavior, and they produce no observable effects on the external world. For example, if you insert a record in a database, every time you load the function and insert the record, it's going to produce an effect in the world. That would be an impure function. If you wrap that same computation into a data type, that function would no longer produce the effect. Instead, it produces a pure value to get a reasonable path around composing these other pure values. Finally, it executes safely when you're ready. That's what Functional Programming is about. It's about programming with pure values that are composable, and they are created out of pure functions that produce no side effects.

That's abstract, but if you're familiar with functions at all, thinking of a function producing an effect or not is going to help you. You're organizing yourself in a way where all your functions produce no effect; that is, they return a lazy computation you can defer invocation for instead of performing its effect eagerly.

Someone said, "I like Functional Programming because it takes people more talented than I am and makes them unemployable." It seems that Functional Programming has been relegated to academia despite being a smart programming choice. What's the relevance of Functional Programming for the commercial development environment?

If you're one of those supposedly unemployable people, you should come work for 47 Degrees. We are hiring those kinds of people. At one time, Functional Programming was a small niche, but something great has happened. Languages like Scala, Kotlin and many other mixed languages in the space have taken over teams and companies all over the world. Now, people are doing Functional Programming more than ever before. There are entire industries in which hundreds of people are coding banking and web services, older systems, orchestration processes, and so on. They're using Functional Programming. In the last five years, the rise of systems like Spark for distributed computation has brought broader adoption of languages like Scala. That has inspired people to learn Functional Programming.

In the same way, some industries are critical in terms of computation or numerical precision. They use libraries like Spire, libraries which employ Functional Programming, or are oriented towards the immediate use of the data. Streaming libraries like Rx lead to the development of Android. They have brought the functional combinators such as flatMap, map, filter, etc., which have been widely adopted and they are now in almost every language.

What was true five years ago isn't true anymore. It's time for everyone to move on. Functional Programming is increasingly adopted in backend development, and it's increasingly relevant to frontend (React) and even Android development (Rx).

Functional Programming is taking the Trojan Horse approach of assimilating everything that is around it and infecting those languages that are not functional with functional features. Anyone mapping an Observable today is doing Functional Programming. If you know how to do that, I don't think you're unemployable. There are a ton of companies that need you today.

How do Kotlin and Scala compare?

Kotlin and Scala are syntactically similar. Kotlin came after Scala. It copied a lot of the features that Scala provides. For example, in Scala or Kotlin, data classes and case classes are essentially the same. Sealed classes in Kotlin are the same as Sealed in Scala, for the most part. The features and syntactic sugar are very similar.

The differences are mostly on the Type System side of things. Scala has a more powerful Type System and can do a lot more in terms of path-dependent types, for instance. You can't do that with Kotlin today. Kotlin provides a different approach to some of those problems. For example, there are receiver functions or extension functions, which eliminate the scope of referring objects with dot notation. You can scope any block to an object, and then "this" pointer becomes the object reference, and therefore, you can access all its functions and properties with direct syntax. Scala does not have that ready, at least not yet. It will once they have extension functions, too.

In that sense, they both try to solve similar problems in different ways, when it comes to dependency injection or scoping. Scala uses implicits. Kotlin uses extension and receiver functions. Aside from that, Scala is less powerful in one thing. Kotlin has a suspension system. The suspension system allows you to encode IO continuations. That currently makes IO potentially faster in Kotlin than in Scala. We are trying to prove that in Arrow. I can talk about that later. In summary, there are things that Kotlin programming language has that work better than Scala, and there are things that Scala has that are more functional than Kotlin.

Kotlin is more oriented towards effects, and Scala is more about a Type System and being able to support polymorphism, higher kinds of types that in Kotlin are less of a problem. Once you have a suspended system, you eliminate IO. IO obeying Scala is the same as a suspended function in Kotlin. This eliminates the wrapping and the need to map, flatmap, and so on because you can just operate over imperative syntax suspended. That is huge for Functional Programming because you eliminate F. All of that is possible with Kotlin, but it's not so much in Scala because you are more guided towards the syntax of the type systems and suspension is effect suspension is not baked in the language.

Those things make Kotlin things easier in terms of F being oriented to effects. When it comes to being oriented to polymorphic derivation, generic programming or type-level programming, Scala is apter. I make money with both as a consultant, and both are great for different communities and purposes.

As developers, it's very important to keep an open mind because every few years things change. Kotlin is relatively new, and maybe in four years, we'll have something different. It's bad to marry any technology.

This is not politics. You don't have to take sides.

You are the maintainer of Arrow, a library for Typed Functional Programming in Kotlin. What are the spaces where a potential developer can find Arrow helpful?

Arrow provides a toolbelt for functional programmers. It includes type classes and data types alongside many utilities to make your code pure and composable. You have the guarantee that unless explicitly denoted, all Arrow APIs are pure and principled in terms of the algebraic laws that govern Functional Programming as a technique.

Arrow's goal is to provide a lingua franca—"One ring to rule them all." It'll be a single API composed of about fifteen different functions. Once you learn those functions, you can compose any program that can be written with those data types and those abstractions. You no longer have to depend on learning third-party framework APIs like Rx or whatever comes next.

Arrow tries to give you that math-fundamental language in which program composition is based upon. You can go full wild and do everything polymorphic, or you can use the Data Types that you care about. Arrow has small articles. It teaches you how to apply them to your daily programming and provides you the instructions to do so.

It's not an elitist framework like you would find in some languages. You can use it however you want. The foundations for each data type and the laws that it abides by are there. You don't have to use all of them.

You served as the CTO for 47 Degrees while you remained active in the developer community. How do you find the balance between being in a position of leadership and being a developer?

Once you're in management, you have the power to influence where money and time go. Any company that invests in open-source is going to attract the developers it needs as resources, and those developers are going to make money. That money is going to generate more means for resource acquisition, and so on. If your company doesn't have a balance, your capacity is limited.

A CTO in the tech industry has to be involved. You're going to sell consultant services for things that you are building—things that the community cares about—and that community that cares is going to help you build. The CTO can't stay in the corner punching a keyboard. A CTO has to manage resources for the company to keep it stable, healthy, and honest. It's all a matter of strategy, and at the same time, it's a matter of doing what you like and making that impact. Doing what you like and making money at the same time is awesome.

How would you advise a developer that wants a career path to a CTO role?

I don't know how you can climb to CTO from being an employee because I haven't done that. Being a CTO means being in a primary management role while staying current with technology. You have to be adaptive to everything in the communities you are working with, and you have to be looking for ways to do things that get people interested. If you want to be a CTO, you're going to have to do pretty much whatever it takes, and that depends too on the company.

You've worked for Boeing, one of the biggest companies in the world, and now you're CTO at 47 Degrees, which might be one of the smallest. How do the environments compare?

I worked on the 787 at Boeing. I worked with great people whom I'm still friends with. There are many reasons why I left, including bureaucracy. Bureaucracy is a part of every big company, and it makes it hard to get things done. That was my biggest problem there. That's not something you have in a smaller company. That's the main difference. At really big companies, you can never follow your own destiny. You might be there because they pay you well or you're working on something that interests you. Climbing the corporate ladder is something that I'm not really interested in. I'm interested in technology, and a small company is a better place for me. At a small company, I can create a bigger impact and work on what I like. In a bigger company, I couldn't.

66 *I dislike all the startups and companies that emphasize entertainment… When companies try to create a culture, it limits the types of people who want to work there. I think it's better to attract people by other means.* 99

Some people say life at a corporate institution is easier.

It's about the individual. For example, I dislike all the startups and companies that emphasize entertainment. Everything is about game rooms, and trying to keep everyone inside all the time. I value individuality. A lot of the problems that you might find in socializing as an engineer may be because your work requires you to be in front of a computer for so much time. I like the kind of company where people are just on their way. There's not this startup, millennial-style culture. When companies try to create a culture, it limits the types of people who want to work there. It's better to attract people by other means. Open stores, or build compensation packets, or whatever it is, rather than entertainment rooms.

Being able to contribute to open-source or being able to work remotely is also one of the big things today.

Remote is the future. People that are offered the option to work remotely tend to know the best way for them and tend to be very productive. I like to work remotely when I need concentration time without distractions.

What are the views of remote work at 47 Degrees?

We started remote work when we grew about 6–10 people. Then we went to fifteen, and at some point, we had one or two remotes. More people joined, and many of them were remote. Mostly, we went that direction because we got into Kotlin. Several of the coding guys we had in the company were trained in Scala from scratch. Many of the coding guys came in knowing Kotlin. For that reason, we hired different remote positions. We find that most people who live close to an office location work at the office a few days of the week so that they can get together with co-workers and share in-person, and they work remotely other days. Of course, there are some other people that are remote the whole time, and then they come to visit the office throughout the year. So far, it's been working great.

What was the hardest thing about starting your company?

We started in September of 2010. 47 Degrees was founded by the engineering team at our previous startup that closed. At that point, we decided to do it on our own and try to save the team. We took 50 bucks, got our business license in the city of Seattle, and decided that we were going to start doing work for free. We worked for free building websites and small projects until we developed a portfolio, at which point we started charging. That's how we got our financing. We worked for four or five months without getting paid. Once we had built a name for ourselves, we started getting contracts. We're unusual because we never took a loan or investment.

That is an unusual case. Did you have a plan B?

I have never been afraid because thankfully, until now, being an engineer has paid well, and it's been easy to find a job. I left for the U.S. with no money and tried to make a living there with my wife. Her parents helped us. What I'm saying is if you have some back-up plan, whether it's family or your job situation, you can always find another job. You can take those risks. Don't be afraid. If it doesn't work out, there are still many places looking for engineers.

How do you plan your workday?

I try to plan my weeks ahead of time in terms of meetings. I usually work during the evenings and in the mornings in random chunks of three or four hours. When I have meetings or things planned, then I follow more of a straight routine. At the end of the day, being a part of my family's routine is where my happiness lies. In terms of work, I think about what I'm trying to accomplish and by when. What resources do I need? I can plan all of that ahead, which gives me the freedom to move my routine for the convenience of my family. This gives me a good work-life balance.

How do you define success?

Success is being able to do whatever is important to you. If you're taking care of your family, that can be a success. You don't have to have a dream job. Your internal sense of satisfaction in life is what makes you happy. In terms of work, do what you like, or do what allows you to do what you like.

I would say those two things together equal success. As well, try and help others. Your success shouldn't depend upon others' failures.

RAÚL'S RECOMMENDATION

Essentialism: The Disciplined Pursuit of Less | Greg McKeown

PAUL BLUNDELL

" Be a thought leader,
not a user. "

🐦 @blundell_apps 🔗/in/blundell blog.blundellapps.co.uk

Paul is Head of Engineering and a Google developer expert for Android & IoT, based in Liverpool in the United Kingdom. He is a remote Android expert who enjoys innovating within his company and growing his engineering skills. In working with teams, he values communication, continued learning and mentorship.

You have over 57,000 reputation points on Stack Overflow, which makes you one of the top contributors. How do you find the time to contribute so much?

My Stack Overflow score has come over ten years of industry work. I started contributing answers about six years ago. That's 10,000 rep points per year—roughly 1,000 per month or 250 per week. You could provide two or three answers per week and with compounding interest get the same score. The point here is those big successes may look amazing, but they are made up of little steps. If you want to achieve something, take the first step. If you have never answered a question on Stack Overflow, start by making your goal to answer one question.

Contributing regularly and making it a habit is the secret. To form a habit, you have to do something repeatedly, and that means you have to enjoy it. I enjoy helping people, and I enjoy learning by getting to the bottom of problems. Combining these two things is what keeps me checking Stack Overflow every other day and contributing to helping others. Find something you enjoy, and then find an outlet for it.

You're the author of *Learning Android Application Testing*. What did you learn from writing a book that you might pass along to an aspiring writer?

Writing a book is hard work! The book I wrote was a revised edition, so I had a rough guiding structure in place already. I learned that writing a book is just like any other problem: You break it down into its smallest components and build it back up. The publishing team really helped with this. In general, when you write a book, there are a lot more people involved than just the author. My writing process went like this: I wrote a sentence or two about what I wanted the reader to have learned at the end. Then, I wrote a sentence or two about what type of reader would read this book, and then a list of bullet-point steps to get from the start to the end. Then, I took each of these bullet points and repeated the process: What is the end goal of the bullet point? I found the starting point for each point and generated a list to get the reader from A to B. That's the magic of writing a book! It's the same process I use when writing blog posts, just scaled up to many, many pages.

For an aspiring writer, I would recommend they drop all other hobbies while writing the book. You want to give the book all of your attention because you want to get it completed. A half-finished book would be a very heavy burden hanging over you, and once you put a project like that down, it's quite hard to pick it back up again. I'd also tell them that writing a book is entirely possible. Start by breaking down the problem into small chunks, and remember: No one writes for the money.

You've offered some concrete steps to tackling a complex project. Does that advice apply to leadership, as well? What does great leadership look like to you?

Leadership can come in many forms. It's not just about being in a management position or having control over people or budgets. Leadership is about helping people. It's about showing them the light at the end of the tunnel and showing them that getting there is possible. You can be a role model without realizing it and without being in a standard leadership position. I believe in servant leadership, which means enabling others and sharing power and responsibility. A good leader listens to those around them and makes sure team members have what they need to succeed. When the opportunity arises, a good leader finds the team best suited to succeed in the project and enables them to take ownership.

Are there specific resources that have helped shape your beliefs about leadership or that have had a lasting impact on how you do your work?

Turn The Ship Around! by L. David Marquet is a wonderful example of leadership, showing how to create a culture of leaders, not followers.

Clean Code: A Handbook of Agile Software Craftsmanship and *The Clean Coder: A Code of Conduct for Professional Programmers* by Robert C. Martin and have to be mentioned as resources. They set out what a professional programmer should be and how they should act. These books guided me and my early career a lot.

Introducing Neuro-Linguistic Programming: Psychological Skills for Understanding and Influencing People by Joseph O'Connor and John Seymour is an amazing book to open your mind to the other skills you need in the workplace. If you want to stick to programming books, *97 Things Every Programmer Should Know: Collective Wisdom from the Experts* by Kevlin Henney is also a great reference for improving your pull request conversations—it's like if you'd sat in the pub for the previous 25 years and heard great anecdotes from fellow developers.

What do you wish someone had told you when you started software development that you had to learn the hard way instead?

There are definitely lessons I've learned the long way around, but because of that, I'm a more rounded developer. Having a shortcut at the beginning isn't always the best idea. That said, I wish I'd known that programming is more about the conversation and expressiveness of the code than it is about a correct answer. If you can explain to those around you what the code is doing, then that code or project will be more successful in the long run than a project that works for reasons no one can understand.

What negative trends do you see taking shape in the industry right now?

Everyone is trying to solve problems. Some people may take a complex route to the answer, but they'll learn, so I rarely call people out as wrong. Also, history has a habit of correcting people. I'd rather talk about what I believe will be the most successful industry trends in the future.

There's a reason everyone is taking a functional approach to programming right now. The benefit I see in it is the immutability and the guarantee of a known state. Allowing people to debug and avoid crashes is much easier. This is possible in OO programming, but it's not enforced in the same way. On the other hand, OO programming is much better at showing what is going on in terms of the domain and the lexicon of the product and what the rest of the business is talking about. I believe most apps are going too far in the functional direction and too easily dismissing what object-oriented programming brings to the table. The future is some combination of them both.

Outside of programming, edge computing and IoT is so on-trend. There's a real push for cross-platform development to succeed, and the latest attempt at this is Google's Fuchsia OS. My understanding is that this OS is trying to be the answer to all hardware, from low-end embedded devices through mobile and all the way up to desktops. This new OS, combined with edge computing and computer-inference and machine learning required to be locally on the device rather than in the cloud—this is the place to be and the wave to ride for engineers in the next 10 years.

What would you recommend to a fellow software developer who wants to transition to a management role?

Remember that as a manager, you're there to make other people succeed. Managers succeed through others succeeding, and sometimes that means they leave their managers behind. Before becoming a manager, ask yourself whether being in a management role will motivate you.

Novoda, where I work, has an open-source learning program called the Novoda Crafter University. I've given talks on it including at Software Craftsmanship London. Novoda NCU is a guide to learning for our engineers, and just recently we added a module on Management. Two books from this I really recommend are *The New One-Minute Manager* by Ken Blanchard and Johnson M.D., Spencer, and *The Truth About Employee Engagement: A Fable About Addressing the Three Root Causes of Job Misery* by Patrick M. Lencioni. I would say, if you read these two books and embrace their teaching, you'll have a stable core of what it takes to be an amazing manager of people.

> ❝ *I often see developers favoring "new tech" over paying attention to the details... Attention to the details allows you to understand core concepts and the reasons behind shiny new libraries to become a thought leader rather than a user.* ❞

What is one core concept that most software developers don't pay enough attention to when trying to grow their careers?

I often see developers favoring "new tech" over paying attention to the details. It's great to stay current, but there's no point in embracing the latest reactive library or dependency injection framework if you don't try to understand the reactive paradigm at its roots or know how to do manual dependency injection. Attention to the details allows you to understand core concepts and the reasons behind shiny new libraries. This way, you can become a critic and thought leader rather than a consumer or user.

Another example of the importance of attention to detail is reading your own code over and over. Once your code works, don't just ship it, read it again for clarity. Ask yourself whether someone else will understand it. Walk away from the code for twenty minutes and see if it's still clear. This attention to detail is what separates good developers from great developers.

What resources do you rely on to stay current in your industry?

A strong peer network is always important, whether virtual or physical. There is always more information than you can consume; however, if you share the top ten percent of what you learn, and your peers around you do the same, then you're all learning from each other and helping each other.

I also rely heavily on learning through side projects. It's fun to create things that solve a problem. For example, once I created a script that parsed all pull requests in a GitHub repo and pulled out all GIFs to show a history of the product evolves. I solved that problem and also learned a lot about the GitHub API and recursion. Sometimes side projects can be directed learning. For example, I want to learn about technology X, so I think of a scenario that might be interesting to make an application about. Another time, I research what technology would be the best solution. If you're stuck on a side project, explore Stack Overflow, where other people share their problems or projects. Often, I have to learn about a new subject before I can solve a new problem.

What are three development tools you can't live without?

Google! Seriously, I google everything! Sometimes it's to use tools like formatting JSON, converting millis to dates or a regex helper. Other times, it's programming answers or tech insights. I come across my own blog posts or Stack Overflow answers sometimes, which reassures me that there is a known answer, though then I worry about having forgotten it.

Everyone googles, and googling efficiently is a skill to embrace!

The second go-to tool I use is Slack, formerly ScreenHero, which is used for remote pairing sessions. It makes coding in a pair so smooth. It's such an invaluable tool. The integration with Slack allows for more distraction when pairing, but the tool is still great for feeling that you and someone potentially across the world are working on the same problem.

The third is my IDE, IntelliJ or Android Studio. It automates so much about my daily tasks and is always improving, especially the refactoring menus. While refactoring is also possible manually, the power to inline classes or rename across a whole project allows me to concentrate more of my time on solving problems and therefore doesn't give an excuse or barrier not to refactor. Understanding the power of the IDE is understanding what it is doing for you. *Refactoring: Improving the Design of Existing Code* by Martin Fowler explains the mindset of breaking down problems, everything is step by step, showing how to tackle complex refactoring issues.

Speaking of daily routines, how do you set yourself up for success every day?

I don't! I'm a night owl. I stay up late tinkering and don't stop until I complete a task! Then I make sure I get my eight hours of sleep to be ready for the next day. The effort to make sure I get a full night's sleep is what I think is important.

How do you stay highly productive for long stretches of time?

For me, high productivity doesn't occur over a long stretch, but I know what high productivity feels like. When I'm feeling productive, I make sure I'm working towards a task I want to complete, versus when I am feeling unproductive I play around. I'm not highly productive for long periods, but I am highly productive for long sessions interspersed with downtime. Giving myself that downtime,to browse cat GIFs or play the Switch is what spurs me on to do the next iteration of productive work.

PAUL'S RECOMMENDATIONS

Your Money or Your Life: 9 Steps to Transforming Your Relationship with Money and Achieving Financial Independence | Vicki Robin

Blundell Android Developer tutorials and blog | blundellapps.co.uk/

CÉSAR VALIENTE

❝ *A career is a marathon not a sprint.* **❞**

🐦 @CesarValiente   💼 in/cesarvaliente/   cesarvaliente.com/

César is a passionate software engineer. He has worked in several companies and on many different projects, in startups, mid-size companies, and big corporations. He currently works at Microsoft where he also leads the Android community there. He has always been involved in communities and open-source, he enjoys sharing his knowledge with others and learning from others. He has spoken in some of the most relevant tech conferences in Europe. He loves to spend his time with his family and friends, and on his hobbies.

You've transitioned from the startup world into a big company, like Microsoft. What are the biggest differences between the two worlds?

The main difference in my transition from a startup to a big corporation was how different both worlds are in terms of size and resources. In our startup, the whole team was about 60 people, including engineering, management, and design. In Microsoft, we have more than 100,000 people. The difference is huge practically speaking. The biggest difference to me is that in a startup, everything is fast. It has to be fast because if you don't show numbers to the investors in a short period of time, you're probably going to run out of cash. For a big company like Microsoft, the need to move fast is lower than for a startup, although, of course, there are goals to achieve and numbers to show. Everything moves slower than in a startup because of the number of people involved, processes that happen, different levels decisions, etc. On the other hand, in big corporations, you have more resources. You have people and money.

Can you say more about the advantages the corporate world has over the startup world?

As we have said before, more resources are a significant advantage for big corporations. Also, these corporations offer many opportunities for career development. People can take different roles; you can work as a software engineer, but if you have the opportunity and want to take it, you can jump into management or even into design, all while working on different projects and technologies. For instance, at Microsoft, a developer might work on different projects and teams, from Xbox to OneNote, from Windows to mobile apps, etc. The list of projects to be involved in is nearly endless.

The financial benefits of working for a big corporation are significant, too.

What has your experience been with mentorship?

Prior to joining Microsoft, I never had a mentor. If I would have had mentorship, I could have made fewer mistakes early on. In fact, for me, the entire community has been a stand-in for a single mentor in my career. Mentors are important. A good mentor is knowledgeable and is a good listener. A mentor doesn't necessarily provide technical answers but helps you solve problems including career and even personal problems.

Can you describe how Microsoft's senior mentorship program works?

Traditionally, mentorship programs target junior developers, but in a corporation as big as Microsoft, even senior engineers have the opportunity for mentorship by talking to the correct people. This works because senior engineers aren't the top-level contributors. Above us are the principals, engineering directors, distinguished engineers, etc. These people have the most experience of all of us. Even if their experience is somewhat dissimilar to my own, their depth of knowledge makes them incredibly valuable.

How does a high-performing engineer like you balance the demands of having a family with the demands of a career in software engineering?

Before having a baby, I could spend the whole day working in the office and continue working into the evening. Now that I have a baby, I'm trying to keep to a more regular schedule so that I can spend time with my family. I wake up early and start, then stop working earlier.

Could you mention three must-have tools that you use on a daily basis?

As an Android Engineer, Android Studio is the main tool that I use every day. I use SourceTree as a source code repository management tool, and PowerShell and Mac terminals. My web browser of choice is Chrome because of the integration with my Google account and many different extensions. Finally, I think Visual Studio Code is an amazing product. It's open-source, and it's really powerful.

What three books have had a lasting impact on you?

There are several! *Clean Code: A Handbook of Agile Software Craftsmanship* by Robert C. Martin is essential for engineers. *Professional Android* by Reto Meier and Ian Lake, and Mark L. Murphy's *The Busy Coder's Guide to Android Development* have been a great reference for me in terms of Android development.

I'd recommend *Head First JavaScript Programming: A Brain-Friendly Guide* by Eric Freeman and Elisabeth Robson; I used this book when I was learning Java at the university. *Grokking Algorithms: An Illustrated Guide for Programmers and Other Curious People* by Aditya Bhargava and *Head First Design Patterns: A Brain-Friendly Guide* by Eric Freeman and Bert Bates have been influential for me. I'd also recommend *97 Things Every Programmer Should Know: Collective Wisdom from the Experts* by Kevlin Henney. The latter is comprised of 97 people responding to topics related to software development.

What do you wish you'd known at the outset of your career?

First, I've learned the hard way to implement good practices in software engineering. My understanding of architectural concepts has evolved over time, thanks to the community, and what I've learned from reading books and working with colleagues. Finally, nobody taught me about testing, and I really didn't understand what it was until I started taking care of that and learning about it.

There is a lot of controversy over how companies hire engineers. Traditionally, especially at a big corporation, there's the whiteboard and interview when we have to write algorithms. Other people advocate for what might be called take-home tests. Still, others prefer to pair job candidates with existing team members for a trial run. Which hiring practice is the best?

I've interviewed candidates for roles at both startups and big corporations. Each hiring committee took different approaches, but I'm not sure either has the best approach. Like everything, it's an iterative process. We learn each time we conduct an interview. Handing an interviewee a project to complete is compelling from the perspective of the interviewer, but it's important to be mindful of the candidate's time.

One exercise I like is to set up a playground for the candidate to work. The candidate takes different responsibilities, and as the person in charge of evaluating the candidate, you can step in and offer support and feedback. This system offers a hiring committee the opportunity to see how the candidate thinks and works. I have a lot of respect for companies that prefer to use whiteboard algorithms if it works for them, and I think that candidates applying for those roles know to expect that from the hiring process. However, if you're looking for experienced people, talking about their experience is likely more important than giving them a problem to solve. In general, a company should adapt its hiring strategies based on the roles they need to fill.

What would you recommend to a software developer starting his or her career in today's industry?

The first step is to join the community behind the project you want to be a part of. You're going to learn a lot from the people involved in this community, and also you're going to grow and meet people who may affect your career. The tech world is global but small, and a career is a marathon, not a sprint.

Any parting wisdom?

I would encourage anyone getting started in technology to find a mentor and get involved in the community. I think this is the best way to grow.

CÉSAR'S RECOMMENDATIONS

The One Minute Manager | Kenneth Blanchard, Ph.D. and Spencer Johnson, M.D.

Who Moved My Cheese?: An A-Mazing Way to Deal with Change in Your Work and in Your Life | Spencer Johnson, M.D.

"Stop Comparing" by Kristijan Šimic | http://krisso.net/articles/stop-comparing

MOYINOLUWA ADEYEMI

66 *Compromise goes a long way.* 99

🐦 @moyheen   🔗 /in/moyinoluwa/

M oyinoluwa is a Google Developer Expert for Android and a Software Engineer at Twitter. Before Twitter, she was a Senior Android Developer at Zola Electric where she worked in a team to enable people in Sub-Saharan Africa have access to clean energy. She has a bachelor's degree in Computer Science with Mathematics from Obafemi Awolowo University, Nigeria.

Moyinoluwa loves learning and sharing her knowledge about Android Development at local and international events. She is also very involved with the developer community. She started the first Women Techmakers group in Nigeria at her university in 2013, managed the Google Developers Group there for 3 years and she was a co-organizer for the Google Developers Group in Lagos for almost four years.

While she's not doing any of these things you'll most likely find her with her nose in a good book, speaking at a developer event, learning German or trying to beat her personal best for a marathon.

AN INTERVIEW WITH MOYINOLUWA ADEYEMI

You have experience having worked at a Udacity Nanodegree. It seems that the old paradigm of attending university, acquiring a degree and finding a job is no longer the most valid one for software engineers. How does your own experience relate?

I studied Computer Science at University, so I followed the traditional path of acquiring a CS degree. A degree helped me build the foundations of everything I do today. I also met the set of people who would eventually influence my decision to become a programmer and to program for Android.

While most of what I know today that's relevant for my current career as an Android Developer was self-taught, my university curriculum gave me a foundational knowledge and a generalist overview of computing.

I took Computer Architecture, Human-Computer Interaction (HCI), and project management classes. At the time, I wasn't sure how all these were going to be relevant, but looking back now, I see how it all fits together.

I found the Nanodegree to be more specific and tailored to my learning. When I started learning how to program for Android, I didn't have access to a curriculum. Instead, I consumed whatever resources I could find that were Android-related.

At the time, I didn't think learning through video tutorials was for me. That changed when I took the Android Fundamentals course on Udacity. What stood out the most to me was the fact that my learning was now directed. I knew what to focus on and in what order. The course also had short videos, unlike the other video resources I had tried, so it was easy to not lose concentration or get bored. I completed that and really enjoyed it. After that, it was a no-brainer for me to make the decision to sign up for the Android Nanodegree.

What would you say to a developer thinking of starting one of those degrees?

I think it depends. They should know whether that method of learning works for them. One of the major reasons I find this kind of certification path very interesting is that there's a curriculum. That's not always the case in a field in which a student is trying to plot a course for themselves.

Here's me acknowledging that what worked for me may not work for someone else.

To give the benefit of the doubt, all of these programs have a track record of success. Maybe they are on to something.

That's really interesting. I think most of us in the industry would say at least some of our knowledge is self-taught. A lot of what we learn comes from podcasts and books. Which do you prefer?

Books. I find that reading helps a lot with my writing. It also helps me stay focused on one thing at a time, which is becoming increasingly difficult for me. I also think that books contain more nuance than a podcast can have. One can argue that podcasts are faster to get through, though.

Speaking of efficiency, one of the trends that seems to be here to stay is remote work. What do companies often do wrong when they have a remote team?

One problem I see is companies not having a remote culture. Making remote developers feel included in the team is very important, especially when the team is partially remote and other co-workers are physically in an office. This includes keeping all conversation in a general place like Slack so that team members who are not physically present can have the context for all the conversations, ensuring that all activities are done online so that team members are not excluded.

I also think being able to reach a compromise on periods of overlap based on time zones during work hours goes a long way.

How does a developer start working remotely?

First, by getting the necessary setup in place—a dedicated room for work with a steady internet connection. They can choose to set that up at home or work from a co-working space. Because my team is really distributed, I use Clocker, an app that manages time zones to determine when to schedule meetings and when to send team members messages or expect a reply to an urgent issue. I enter the locations of my team members, and at a glance I can tell what time it is where everyone is.

How can we do remote work effectively?

Again, It's important to have a dedicated workspace. As well, it's important to build trust with the rest of the team since no one is going to be looking over our shoulders. Additional communication may be called for because remote workers are less visible to team members. It's also important to work towards maintaining physical and mental health. This might be easier to achieve with remote work because it enables us to become more flexible. We can fix healthy meals ourselves, and we have more space to schedule exercise hours.

You're a marathon runner, right? Does being a distance athlete have an impact on your professional life?

Yes, it does. Running has helped improve my physical and mental health and my sleep. The runner's high is a real thing, and that becomes very important to me when working solo for a long stretch at a time takes a toll.

I often experience a runner's high after I've pushed myself more than I thought I could go by increasing my speed or covering a longer distance.

While running, if I have a problem I can't figure out, I turn it over and over in my head and sometimes I find an idea for how to proceed. Also, with running, there's always a new goal to aim for. Similarly, I always aim to be better at work. Generally, running has helped me to be more patient and better at solving problems.

The funny part is the imposter syndrome. Sometimes I feel I shouldn't call myself a runner because I'm not very fast. That happens to me sometimes in my professional life, too. For example, sometimes I feel like I don't deserve the opportunities I get even after putting in the work to get them. The same way I've learned to dismiss those feelings with regard to running, I've learned to recognize and dismiss imposter syndrome when it comes up professionally.

> 66 *Programming is just one of the skills that makes one a well-rounded developer. The so-called soft skills are actually very important when you have to work in a team because development isn't done in a silo.* 99

Speaking of important lessons, what's something you learned the hard way? Is there anything you wish someone had told you when you started working in software development?

Software Development is not just about programming. Programming is just one of the skills that makes one a well-rounded developer. The so-called soft skills are actually very important when you have to work in a team because development isn't done in a silo.

How do we solve the problem of lack of minority visibility in software engineering?

I think being very conscious of it and explicitly reaching out to members of underrepresented groups helps. This can be applied when looking for speakers and attendees for tech events and during hiring. It's also important to make workspaces inclusive so that after putting in all the hard work to bring people in, they don't take the first door out. Being very particular about growing the skills of underrepresented folks when possible will also help.

What is one core concept most software developers don't pay enough attention to when they are trying to grow their careers?

For me, it's connecting with someone who's interested in my growth and helps me set goals to achieve them. This can be managers or mentors outside the company who are ahead of you in the field.

What other resources do you rely on heavily to stay current on industry knowledge?

I read the Android and Kotlin weekly newsletters and listen to podcasts including Fragmented, Android Developers Backstage, and Android Dialogs. I find published videos from conferences to be a great resource, and I follow a lot of Android developers on Twitter too.

What's the cheapest investment you've made that has provided you the highest ROI in your career?

My Macbook Pro 2015. I bought it for $694 four years ago. Before then, I was programming on a machine with poor battery life and not enough processing power to run the applications I installed on it. Setting up developer environments used to be a pain. The new laptop meant I could churn out work faster.

What advice would you give to someone starting his or her career?

Learn how to learn, and never stop learning because things change so fast. They might be overwhelmed with all there is to know, but they should take it one day at a time.

How does your daily routine reflect what you've learned over time about how to work effectively?

I try to start my day early. I usually complete a chapter of a book or think through any pending challenges I have to resolve, technical or otherwise. My concentration is at its peak early in the day, so I try to make the best use of that time. I also try not to check social media until later in the day.

How do you stay highly productive for long stretches of time?

I block out time and focus on completing one task at a time while listening to ambient music. Sometimes I'm interrupted during one of the time blocks but I've learned to schedule interruptions. I don't know if this is peculiar to me, but sometimes I have moments when I don't feel like doing any work. During those times, I've trained myself to just start and take it one line at a time, no matter how long it takes me instead of waiting to get in the flow or waiting for when I feel like it. I reward myself for any progress made during this period no matter how small it is and usually, before I realize it, I have churned out good quality work.

MOYINOLUWA'S RECOMMENDATIONS

Deep Work: Rules for Focused Success in a Distracted World | Cal Newport

It Doesn't Have to Be Crazy at Work | Jason Fried and David Heinemeier Hansson

I DON'T HAVE IT IN MY BLOOD

On Giving Yourself the Credit You Deserve

MOYINOLUWA ADEYEMI

'*ve never met a girl breaking Android like you. You have it in your blood,* said my friend Seti to me. I was on an African GDG Organizer WhatsApp group chat. GDGs are for developers who are interested in Google's developer technology; everything from the Android, Chrome, Drive, and Google Cloud platforms, to product APIs like the Cast API, Maps API, and YouTube API. The volunteer organizers were responsible for managing these groups. My Togolese friend, Seti was commending my recent feat of completing the Udacity Android Developer Nanodegree, which is a compact online curriculum designed to get you the skills that employers believe are key to get a job in technology. It focuses on learning by doing. It is typically comprised of five to eight projects with relevant courses to support the skills needed to complete those projects. This was remarkable to him and to everyone who knows what a Nanodegree entails. Immediately he typed that, I went down memory lane.

Three years ago, I was a 400-level student of Computer Science and GDG OAU—a Google-developer group based in Obafemi Awolowo University, Nigeria—organizer who hadn't fully discovered what she wanted to do with her life. This may be surprising to people who thought I already had my life together. But it was a lie; I was confused. The problem was that I started out with graphic design in Corel Draw, and I experimented with Front-End development using HTML and CSS. This was the natural path for a UI Developer, just that I wasn't sure that I wanted to be one.

I could use the tools fairly well and I was even ready to learn more to enhance the little I knew, but I hated that after spending so much time on one design, it could just get dismissed in a second. Statements like, "Make me options to choose from," got on my nerves so much then. I would rather focus on development where you worked based on existing principles to optimize whatever you were working on and everything you did had a logical explanation. But I didn't have major development skills then. I already knew I wouldn't get any job if I was to graduate from school at that moment.

GDG Organizers are supposed to organize some universal programs in their groups at specific parts of the year based on the recommendations from the Developer Relations team. Information about Android Study Jams, a beginner program for new Android Developers was one of such programs that were passed on the mailing list. There was a criterion for organizing this, though. One member of each GDG team was supposed to take the Developing Android Apps course on Udacity and get certified. That person was to be the facilitator for the remaining members of the group who signed up for the Study Jams series.

My own responsibility was to determine who took this course and it absolutely didn't have to be me. I decided to use this opportunity to hone my own skills so I thought seriously about facilitating it. One part of me thought "Moyin don't even try taking it. You are still struggling with design. You know that there are other guys you can call to do this." The other part was like "What do you have to lose? The worst that will happen is that GDG OAU won't qualify to host Android Study Jams because you did not complete the course." Thankfully, I listened to the part that supported me enrolling in the course.

I enrolled and started the lessons. I understood the first three lessons because they were on layouts and .xml. Then came lessons 4a and 4b with Content providers, loaders and sync adapter. It was mini-hell but I kept at it. I watched and re-watched those videos, and they slowly started making sense. I also had really experienced guys in GDG OAU who were always available to assist me.

I eventually finished with the lessons and it was time to build a final project. That's where the wahala—Nigerian slang for trouble—started. Me, a newbie, build a complete Android project alone? The fear set in. The crippling kind. It was December and I had a deadline of one month. I called my parents and told them I had a project to work on. That I was not going home for Christmas and New Year. Sounds crazy right? That was fear talking. Maybe it was also the challenge. I do not know again.

I decided to build a game because it did not really involve communication with a server, which was a requirement for submission. I won't start explaining what trying to work on a project that I had to learn alone felt like. The harmattan, the loneliness—it was December and every other sane person was at home on break from school, the frustration when I could not get some things right or Gradle was buggy and I did not know what was up, the annoyance when I realized I didn't have a test device and all my sane friends, both guys and ladies were at home for the holidays. Only Akapo was around and I borrowed his device to test. I was using a 3+-year-old Windows machine that ran Gradle builds in four minutes approximately. The emulators did not even start up.

January came around and everyone resumed. The deadline to submit the project was January 8, 2015, else the sponsorship would be lost.

I managed to wrap things up by January 6. That was exactly when OAU's power supply (that's usually very stable) decided to go faulty on me. I eventually submitted at one minute past midnight on January 9, California time thanks to Caleb and Ayodele Marcus who was flexible with the submission time. It was late, but I had achieved something no one could take away from me. I had built an app and we were able to host the Study Jams. A lot of what is happening in my life right now is dependent on the sacrifices I made then.

Fast-forward some months after that, I was browsing one Sunday evening when I saw this Udacity advert about the Android Developer Nanodegree starting in August 2015. As usual, the inner battles began. Should I, or should I not enroll?

The difference was that this was going to cost $200 monthly while I was sponsored for the Study Jams. I didn't know where I was going to get money to pay for it. But the daring part of me, the one that likes adventure made me apply. I remember thinking to myself that at worst, I'll cancel the subscription when I can't afford to pay for the remaining months. So I started. I remember dreading the beginning of a new month because of the $200 monthly bank alerts. I even had one that was exchanged by GTBank at 270 Nigerian Naira (NGN)to the dollar. But I persisted. All this meant no eating out, no random trips to the cinema to watch movies, no Coldstone icecream. Thankfully, I could hide under the fitfam tag.

At first, the projects were a bit tough, but with time I began to breeze through them. I had to re-submit more than one project because I didn't meet expectations, but I kept at it. In the last lap, I almost lost my motivation. I had to have one of my friends hold me accountable. I opted to send him daily .apk files with the latest updates, all to ensure that I finished the course in time.

It's over now, I finally have the Android Developer Nanodegree certificate. It's really not about the digital print but the journey to mastery throughout the whole process. I still can't say I know everything there is to know in this field, but at least now, I can commit to learning everything I can about it, as often as possible.

So Seti, I don't have it in my blood. I worked hard for it.

CREDIT

A version of this article was first published on *Medium* (January 9, 2017). The original article can be found here: /blog.devcenter. co/i-dont-have-it-in-my-blood-37fbdfbddfcc

LEADERSHIP

*❝I definitely think good leaders are made...
The biggest things I look for in a leader are
self-awareness and humility. These two
characteristics open people up to admitting and
learning from their own mistakes, which makes
them very coachable—the effort you expend on
coachable people is always multiplied.❞*

—Cate Huston

DR. JOSEPH HOWARD

66 *Lead by example.* 99

🐦 @orionthewake.

J oe is a former physicist that studied computational particle physics using parallel Fortran simulations. He gradually shifted into systems engineering and then ultimately software engineering around the time of the release of the iOS and Android SDKs. He's been a mobile, web, and systems software developer since 2009. He's currently a Senior Architect at CVS Health, helping people on their path to a better health.

In your current role, you have a diverse set of responsibilities. You lead a team of Android developers, write tutorials and books for raywenderlich.com, and you're currently the Android Pillar Lead for raywenderlich.com. How do you balance all of them?

In any role in which you're managing a team, it's important to have long-term goals and short-term goals. This is also true as an individual contributor when making applications or content. So I try to break things down to form long-term goals—the ones that I'm thinking about in terms of, say, a calendar year. We do that internally at our company, Razeware, starting in January and wrapping it up in December. But, to give more structure to the goals, I approach them on a week-by-week basis—how to go through each week to try to achieve those long-term goals. Then, each week I think of daily priorities. So I break down all the goals and try to prioritize them. What do I need to do week to week, then what do I need to do each day of the week to finish what I need to do for that week.

In terms of my specific responsibilities, there's a lot of context switching. I'm doing more now than just Android, leading other teams as well. So I'm building things on Android and building things using other technologies, some of which I'm brand new to.

I try to organize my week so that each day I'm within one context, whether it's making videos, writing content, performing editing tasks or whatever the case may be, I try to find tasks that will take a full day, to try to minimize the context switching. Rather than spending an hour on one thing and an hour on something else, I do what I can to try to spend a day on a given thing. It rarely happens that way. But, at the beginning of the week, I lay out what I'm going to do each day and then try to spend as many hours on any given day doing that thing. There are meetings and other things that get in the way, but I just try to take it day-by-day and build-up from those daily tasks I'm working on.

A few good weeks in a row lets me know I'm on the way to achieving the long-term goals that I set out for the year.

You've mentioned meetings and I think there is a connection between meetings and context switching and these might be a particularly important problem to solve in a remote company since communication is the key. So what are your views on the meetings between development teams? How often should they happen? How long should everybody be at the meeting? How do you operate?

I'm a stereotypical engineer that's not the biggest fan of meetings. Fewer meetings always sounds good to me. Meetings are necessary and, in certain situations, you need to have long meetings. But, for me, a working meeting should always be half an hour or less. People tend to schedule most meetings at an hour by default just to make sure they have time to talk about whatever they need to talk about. And then often that hour gets filled with stuff that wasn't necessary for that particular meeting.

I try to keep things short, be direct, talk about the thing we need to talk about and then let everyone go—go on and do what they need to do. Being remote, it's very nice in that you kind of strip down and just have the meetings that you need. For someone like me, it's great because we're using technology to have the meetings, whether it's Google Hangouts or Skype or something else, and that motivates everyone to have a good meeting. We discuss what we need and then go about our day after that.

In my role, I tend to have some weeks that have just one meeting—a weekly all-hands meeting. Other weeks, I'll have 10 or more. It varies week by week. The days when I have no meetings are the days I'm the most productive for sure.

Working remotely is going to be one of the future trends. Many companies are not yet prepared to work remotely. From your experience, how can a company start working remotely? What are the areas that they should start working on?

To start, finding the right tools that will help you work remotely is key. My previous position was full-time, working in the nearest city. The management team started letting people work from home one day a week. Remote workers would use Google Hangouts or the like to go to whatever meetings they needed to go to. If your company is trying to go in this direction, it's important to figure out what the tools are that you can use in terms of meetings and communication. Slack is another great tool to maintain communication between people. It's also important to set guidelines for communication—what's best communicated over email versus Slack? What's the right tool to use for a meeting?

For example, when I write someone a Slack message, I don't expect them to respond to me right away. Even if it says they're online, I assume, okay, they're going to get this and they're going to respond to me when they can. Making it clear to everyone what the expectations are is important so that people know what to expect. If you use email, for example, consider an informal rule that you're not expecting someone to get back to you for a couple of days, but then expect everyone to respond to emails within a couple of days so that you're not leaving people hanging when they send you an email. This kind of communication expectations can happen when onboarding people onto your team.

I also try to be very flexible because our company is remote and you have to be very flexible with scheduling, adapt to changing requirements and plans, and have different expectations over time. With each different group of people that I work with, I just try to be as flexible and understanding as possible and work with people in ways that are good for them.

You're leading different kinds of teams: writers, editors, instructors, and developers. What are the key differences in leading different kinds of teams?

Learn the terminology of each group of people that you're working with. For example, the technical language of a developer, or the terminology that a writer uses to communicate. And then also understand each person individually, what their background is, and what their role is. If I'm talking to an Android developer that I've worked with before, and I know roughly their level of experience with Android, then I can use certain terms and assume things about what they will know.

On the other hand, when I'm working with an editor from our site who isn't an Android developer and who doesn't have that background, I won't just throw out an Android term and expect them to know what it means, because they don't have that context. I try as best I can to treat people as individuals.

As you work for a global company, there is a lot of diversity in your team. How does diversity improve a team and how do you think we can increase the diversity in the tech industry?

Diversity improves a team because everyone has different experiences. Everyone has different backgrounds, education, and many other things that shape who they are. No one knows everything. Having a diverse team makes the overall team stronger because people can share their knowledge and experiences with one another. It's extremely important to be able to learn from other people and understand how each of us contributes. It's important to learn from each other and be open to the possibility that other people know more than you do on a given topic or area or life experience. You also need to be willing to share and be open with them about what your background is.

In terms of improving diversity, we try to make sure people have equal opportunity to excel. We need to try to engage communities that haven't been represented in tech and engineering, and then do everything we can to bring that opportunity to every community in ways that could help build that diversity over time.

> 66 *My job is to give the people that I'm working with what they need to succeed in whatever it is we're working on, but also beyond that in their careers, and, longer-term, as people. I work for them; not the other way around.* 99

What are the other traits of a good leader or a good manager? What is your leadership philosophy?

Leading by example is one of the best ways to be a leader. As I've gotten into leadership positions over time, I've found that to be the most natural way to try to lead. I'm not the most extroverted person— definitely more of an introverted person. I try to do my thing and not worry so much about the people with whom I'm working seeing what I'm doing. It's also important, as a manager, to provide people on a team with what they need to succeed. As I've been put into management positions, my approach is to feel that I'm working for the team; the team isn't working for me. My job is to give the people that I'm working with what they need to succeed in whatever it is we're working on, but also beyond that in their careers, and, longer-term, as people. I try to work for them and not the other way around.

What is a common error that leaders commit and what do you think they should do instead?

I've seen leaders be a little bit too careful with information and not sharing information readily. That can be demoralizing to teams. It's important to be as communicative as possible with all members of a team. People don't appreciate being kept in the dark. If that happens regularly, it can bring a team down and be demotivating. There are valid reasons why people in leadership positions can only give out so much information. But I've seen leaders and managers that have done that way too much. It's very important to give as much communication to your team as you can and let them know what's going on to the greatest extent that you can. It empowers people once they have a better idea of what the goals of an organization are and they see how you are planning to get there.

In drawing your own insight from outside resources, what do you prefer—podcasts or books?

I enjoy both. I listen to podcasts as much as I can, for sure. Having said that, I am a huge book person. I buy way too many books and eBooks. I'm kind of at the point where I can't find books to buy because I'm constantly at the bookstore looking for new things and always trying to make sure I'm staying on top of the latest technologies. I find that books, even though they're not as real-time as blog posts or the things you would find online, have a full narrative of start to finish. I get to start from the beginning of the book and then feel that I've accomplished something once I'm done.

When eBooks first became a thing, I thought they were the holy grail. I thought, "Oh this is so great; I can stop buying all these books and spend less money and have everything on my computer." But, then, over time, I realized I do prefer print books. I like the fact that they're formatted and people have put a lot of thought and effort into making them look good and giving them a real flow. For most books, especially ones that I'm into, I buy both—print and eBook if it's available. When I have time to sit down and read, I'll pull up the print book and then, especially if it's a technical or programming book of some kind, I will have it on my computer to try to follow along with the code.

What are three books that have had a lasting impact on your work?

One would be *Clean Code: A Handbook of Agile Software Craftsmanship* by Robert C. Martin. It's a well-known book that many software developers have read. My background isn't in software or computer science. I was actually a physicist before starting my career as a software developer; my background training is in physics. So I didn't come to software as a software engineer, I came to it more as a scientist. Clean Code made an impact on me in understanding that there's a lot more to programming than just writing code. It's a prevalent idea that code is read much more frequently than it's written. That book was the first one that exposed me to the idea that you're writing code for yourself and other developers, not so much for whatever the application is you're developing. You have to balance both things. It made a strong impact on me and it is still completely relevant to this day.

Another one is more recent. It's called *The Problem With Software: Why Smart Engineers Write Bad Code* by Adam Barr, and it's also made a strong impact on me. It's about the experiences that we, as software engineers, all have. Barr writes about the difficulty with software and why it's hard, and the ways to deal with the complexity of making software. It's a little bit less technical than Clean Code and more anecdotal on why writing software is hard.

The last one is more specific to my role as an Android developer. Most of my experience in the past five years has been in Android development. There's a book named *Kotlin in Action* by Dmitry Jemerov and Svetlana Isakova, from Manning. The Manning books are fantastic. Kotlin in Action was one of the first books available for learning how to program in Kotlin. But I mention it because it's such a well-written book. I think one of the best technical books I've ever read. The two authors are from JetBrains, the company that created the Kotlin language. It definitely assumes that you're a developer and that you are probably coming from a Java background. It's probably not a book I would read if I were starting from scratch as a developer on Android.

Having gone through that book, I felt that I suddenly knew how to program in Kotlin; not all technical books give you that feeling. With some, you feel that when you're done, well, you've learned a little bit about the topic. But this book covers almost everything in the Kotlin language and it was unbelievably efficient. It's just an amazing book and I love it so much. I'd recommend it to any experienced Android developer who's looking to pick up Kotlin for sure.

JOE'S RECOMMENDATIONS

Can't Hurt Me: Master Your Mind and Defy the Odds | David Goggins

The Meaning of Happiness: The Quest for Freedom of the Spirit in Modern Psychology and the Wisdom of the East | Alan Watts

12 Rules for Life: An Antidote to Chaos | Jordan B. Peterson

ISRAEL FERRER CAMACHO

" *Communication and collaboration.* "

🐦 @rallat

srael Ferrer Camacho was born in Barcelona and studied Computer Science at Lasalle University Barcelona.

The last year of university, he dropped out to co-found Bubiloop. com with Luis Moreno, where he was in charge of technology. At the same time he and other tech enthusiasts started the GTUG in Barcelona, the Google Technology User Group, which later was renamed to GDG. In 2012, he moved to San Francisco where he started to work for Lookout, a mobile security company, working as an engineer in the security team.

From 2014 to 2018, he worked at Twitter as an engineer and contributed in a wide variety of projects in the Fabric team, Twitter for Android and Periscope. In 2018, he moved to Tokyo to work for Mercari as an Android engineer leading the project to scale a five-year-old codebase which would allow for faster development. Currently, he is working as a Software Engineer for Dropbox in New York City, US.

What are you reading or listening to these days?

I listen to a lot of podcasts about politics, economics and history. I can recommend several. The *New York Times The Daily* podcast with Michael Barbaro is in my favorites podcast to listen every morning. *The NPR Politics* podcast is really good, but really any NPR podcast about any topic is always a pleasure and really valuable to listen. One of my favorite podcasts about history is called *Stuff You Missed in History Class*; the podcast does research about history and not only from the U.S. For example, one episode was about the Spanish dictator Franco. I learned more in that podcast than I had learned about it in school. Right now, I am temporarily living in Japan, so I'm trying to pick up the language by listening to Japanese podcasts *News in Slow Japanese*.

Some of the most influential books that changed me as an engineer were *Clean Code: A Handbook of Agile Software Craftsmanship* by Robert C. Martin, *Effective Java* by Joshua Bloch, *How to Win Friends & Influence People* by Dale Carnegie, *The Growth Mindset Coach: A Teacher's Month-by-Month Handbook for Empowering Students to Achieve* by Annie Brock and Heather Hundley, and *Nonviolent Communication: A Language of Life* by Marshall B. Rosenberg. As you can see, those aren't only technical and that is because when you work in a tech company, you are never working alone and more skills other than technical ones are important.

❝ *The thing I really care about is to continuously learn and improve as a person. I am always thinking about what that means and how I can quantify that improvement and keep learning.* ❞

You've relocated from Spain to the United States to Japan. What were these transitions like?

I'm from Spain, and I lived there for 27 years. Before I left Spain, I started a company as a co-founder with Luis Moreno, @carthesian on Twitter. We were building a modern app store back in 2009. At that time, the App Store was terrible. You needed an expert to help you find the best app. Mostly, you were downloading apps that didn't work well. We were trying to fix that problem, by recommending the best apps for the type of user profile and location. At the same time, that experience led Luis and me to meet people in Silicon Valley, through those people and after we shut down our company, I landed a job in San Francisco at Lookout.

The work culture in San Francisco was totally different from what I was used to. I had worked for a Spanish supermarket chain called Caprabo. It's like Wal-Mart. I worked in the IT department. In that company, technology was a tool to get things done, but it wasn't the core business of the company. The tech culture there was nonexistent.

When I moved to San Francisco, I started to understand how to develop solutions and communicate effectively. I found that people in Silicon Valley communicated directly. It was shocking for me. At the same time, I was learning a lot. It was exciting to have so many mentors. I'm where I am today because of my mentors. I would especially like to mention Lien Mamitsuka and Ty Smith, with whom I worked together at Twitter in the Fabric team, and it was one of the teams where I learned more than ever. What makes Silicon Valley so interesting for our field is that there is a high density of really talented and knowledgeable people, not only engineers but designers and product managers too. Many product managers and designers can code, which makes collaboration easier and products better. Without a doubt, by being there and being able to work with the professionals there, I felt I was learning and growing every day and becoming better at my job.

Fabric was a new team at Twitter, built on the top of the Crashlytic team, which was a recently acquired company. I still remember like it was yesterday my first 1:1 with my Engineering Manager, and he asked, "What do you need to be effective and happy on the team?" I didn't understand the question. I thought, "Wait, what? You want me to be happy?" It's a really different approach to management than what I was used to.

The manager's response was to frame his role as the coach of a team. They are the people trying to help everyone work together and give us the necessary resources so we can build products faster and better. That really changed my perspective on leadership, and my manager quickly became a true mentor. I am who I am because of what I learned from my mentors and, in retrospect, my time at Twitter was the period when I learned more knowledge as an engineer and team player.

Twitter's culture allows people changing teams, which keeps talented people challenged and happy. If you're a high-performing engineer, your manager is likely to let you work on whatever product you're most interested in. After Shipping the Fabric SDK, I joined Twitter for Android, which is the first time I've worked in such a gigantic codebase. It's also one of the oldest Android apps that is still around. We faced challenges there in terms of scale and the amount of legacy code.

The problem with the infamously named "legacy code" is that it makes the team slower, and it makes it easier for an engineer to produce user defects. Moreover, it is difficult to quantify and detect early that your code quality is decreasing. That's why every company that survives after five years will 100% hit this rock bottom of not being able to build product as fast as before even if the company hires 100 engineers; the code will break 100 times faster.

I think the code has to be ready for the number of developers you put on it. The codebase needs to be done consistently, allowing everyone to work independently to avoid conflict.

I was at Twitter for Android during a turbulent time. They were going through a reorganization, and it was difficult to get anything done. I ended up moving to the Moments team based in New York. After that, I joined the Periscope team and reconnected with one of the first engineers that I worked with at Twitter, Lien. She was an Engineer Manager at that time, and one of the best engineers I ever worked with. Lien has great leadership skills. She helped me improve a lot, especially in terms of the way I communicate and how I approach collaboration.

At the end of the day, you don't build the product alone, but with a team. When there's a team involved, there are relationship problems. It's really important to be able to collaborate and communicate effectively with others.

In 2018, I moved to Japan, where I'd always wanted to live, but never found a company that hired non-Japanese speakers. A company called Mercari believed in me, despite my lack of Japanese skills. I decided to try it and see what happened. It was scary to come to Japan, but I don't want to make decisions based on fear. The worst-case scenario was a failure. In that case, I'd return to the U.S. or Europe. It is always good to have a backup plan or at least be ready for failure and how big that fail can be so you can be prepared better in case that happens. Through all of these transitions, the thing I really care about is to continuously learn and improve as a person. I am always thinking about what that means and how I can quantify that improvement and keep learning, but that is another story.

Of all the interview paradigms, what do you think is the best way to interview software engineers?

It's difficult to objectively know whether an engineer is good or not. Therefore, the team needs to optimize the process to minimize false positives and investing a fair amount of time for each candidate process. Nowadays, in the industry, there are a few standard ways to determine if a candidate is talented: the whiteboard algorithm or a tech assignment with a real domain-specific problem. In my opinion, the whiteboard algorithm interview will produce many false negatives because it doesn't weigh the experience of the candidate. However, everyone who has worked with an experienced engineer knows that they are key players that help to avoid making the same mistakes, to be able to scale systems or ship robust products. Personally, I prefer a hybrid model of interviews that have domain-specific problems, behavioral questions and an algorithmic question that don't require knowing an obscure or specific technique.

How can companies navigate this problem?

After a few years of experience, you realize that the top performers are also really good at building relationships and helping the team get things done. With my current team, we have a tech assignment that I know is very time-consuming for the candidate. We conduct on-site interviews, too. One of those is a conversation with the hiring manager that doesn't involve coding. One is a code review, in which we ask the candidates questions, especially about how to scale assignments. The answer to these kinds of questions can only come with experience. After you work on the same app for many years, you realize how bad your early code was, and you learn to scale it. It's important to talk with the candidates about how they envision the future of their code.

During the coding interview, we provide a laptop, and we do whiteboard work, too. We don't expect perfect syntax or for them to finish the code in any way. We're looking to see how the person breaks down the problem. The problems we use for the interview aren't extremely complex. We ask the candidate to parse some data, transform it, and then with optimal performance. It's basically an input, a function, and an output.

What's your view on companies that do interviews based on computer science theory, mathematics, algebra, and data structures?

I think those interviews are a really cost-effective way to know if the candidate is smart. If you fail, it doesn't mean you aren't a good engineer. It just means you didn't prepare for that type of interview. You have to be mentally ready, and you have to have the knowledge relevant to those questions fresh because in 45 minutes there is no time for doubts. The more interviews you do, the better you get at it.

I think it's somewhat dehumanizing. Companies that interview this way are treating people like nothing more than a brain. They put the brain in a high-pressure situation and see how the brain handles it. They do it because they can. They have so many people applying every day that they can afford to miss talented people who might not want to go through that process. The companies doing this are the big four. They have similar minds. I don't like it.

It seems to skew the process in favor of junior developers. Senior developers working at a high level of abstraction might not perform as well as someone fresh out of university who's been focusing on data structures and algorithms. I think this is especially true when you are working on something like Android. If you are working in the back end, you have those types of problems more often. Not everything is so complex.

How does leadership fit in? What makes a good leader?

I used to think everything was about data, but at the end of the day, we're humans. What I mean by that is that during my career, the best-performing managers have all been very sympathetic and caring humans, but at the same time, really sharp engineering managers that constantly provide feedback and collaborate with their reporters. The way they collaborate is by helping their reports by giving them the tools and unblocking them rather than the old fashioned top-down management style.

Is a good leader made or born?

Mostly, you can train yourself to do anything. Your genes and experience can give you advantages, but I believe everyone can develop leadership skills. The only time I think that's not true is if your motivation comes from wanting to be more powerful. I don't think that kind of mindset makes for a good leader.

How do we make leadership more of a servant position, rather than a power position?

I always say you're only a manager because you have this knowledge. You need to help the team, or you won't be useful to them. When the team fails, it's the manager's fault. Hopefully, companies are measuring their managers. Often, you'll see 90% of the company leave suddenly. In those cases, the problem may be management.

I think the key is to have a culture in which the manager gives and receives feedback and uses the feedback to improve. Then, the manager's manager should measure the satisfaction of the engineers. There should be strong metrics for leadership skills in an organization. It doesn't mean we all have to be friends, but we need to have professional relationships that let us improve and work together.

How can a developer make the leap into a leadership position?

I'm asking myself that question right now. I've been reading books, trying to learn the best way. If you have a good mentor, they can help guide you through that process. If your manager is a good role model, consider asking whether he or she will help you put together a road map to take on a management role.

It's culturally dependent, too. I really like the book *Radical Candor: Be a Kick-Ass Boss Without Losing Your Humanity* by Kim Scott, but the problem with being too candid is that some cultures perceive it as aggression.

Is Japanese culture an example?

Yes. I don't think the strategies in *Radical Candor* are relevant in Japanese culture. There's a great book called *The Culture Map: Breaking Through the Invisible Boundaries of Global Business* by Erin

Meyer that explains with real cases how different cultures approach engineering work, and how leadership is understood in those cultures.

Israel, you mentioned that you follow some mentors on Twitter. Who are they, and how do you check them out and see how their philosophy fits?

My favorite Twitter mentors for leadership @kimballscott author of Radical Candor. Another favorite one Lara Hogan @lara_hogan, and Marco Rogers @polotek, Tracy Chuo @triketora and Tracy Miranda @tracymiranda

What's something you wish you'd known when you started out in the industry?

In the beginning, I wanted to see everything and show that I didn't need help. In reality, the most important thing is to ask questions and ask for help. Some people jump into management when they realize they don't want to be a developer forever. Is management the logical exit path? If you're in a culture that only values quantity and speed, you may not want to stay in that position. It's important to find the right environment that allows you to have a healthy balance.

I'm 35 now, and I just don't want to open a new watermelon. I just want to stay in a good company with a good team of people where we can all collaborate and build better products together. Once you find that sweet spot where you have enough income and you have a good company culture, you want to stay there and try to progress as much as you can, career-wise.

How can a company cultivate an environment where people want to stay?

Engineers value different things. I want to be in a place that's solving a unique problem but one that's broad enough to help others in the community. I want a company that allows me to use my time to learn. I would like to be in a company that values more than just my output.

What do you think is broken in our industry? How would you fix it?

We've discussed interviews. I think that system is broken, but I don't think there's an easy way to fix it. Do you want to make it cost-effective, or to ensure that all the candidates are talented? There are a few movable variables, but there's no perfect process. The system of accreditation may need changing, too. I have 90% of the credits for a degree in computer science, but I started my own company instead of finishing the degree. Because I didn't finish, I've had problems with immigration in both the U.S. and Japan. Having the degree opens the doors for immigration.

As well, I think the computer science degree taught in universities is too scientific. The curriculum isn't necessarily relevant to the workplace. After entering the workforce, I felt there was a huge gap of knowledge between what I had learned and what I actually needed to do as a software developer in a company.

A software engineering degree may equip you better for software development than a computer science degree. A computer science degree gives you a broad knowledge. You can't navigate Qualcomm doing CPUs and GPUs right, you know how to do them all. I actually built a CPU in college. It was fun. You can learn that going to Qualcomm, but then you can learn that going to some electronics company, too, like by building hardware, software, etherware, and front-end, too. A computer science degree teaches you a broad knowledge, but I don't think it helps you to get a specific job.

Performance reviews are another area of our industry that troubles me. If it's difficult to hire people and be sure that you're hiring the right candidate, of course, it's difficult to review the performance of your employees. At the end of the day, it seems subjective. That's not great because it leaves room for bias. Performance reviews need to be more objective and more based on metrics, and those metrics need to be totally objective.

How can we do performance reviews more objectively?

Companies need to define their engineering values, and those values should be publicly visible and level-based. If you are level one, this is what we expect from you. Level two, this is what we're going to expect from you. Some of them will be about communication and style and leadership. Those are less objective, but those should not be very important until you become a principal. Performance reviews should be based on level-appropriate metric measurements.

How do you stay productive?

I sleep well, and I start my day by focusing on what I want to get out of it. Before going to the office, I check my tasks for the day and ensure that I know what I'm going to achieve. At the end of every day, I write down what I wanted to do and what I actually did. I set goals and check in occasionally. At the end of the year, I review everything and consider my five-year plan.

What is your five-year plan?

I'm 35 now, and I wonder whether I'll still be a developer when I'm 40. I'm starting to realize that I care about coding, and I've decided to care more about themes and people. I don't think I'm ready, but I want to move towards helping people to get better. When I find the right place, I'll likely try to become a manager, or I'll lead my own company.

What's an across-the-board drain on productivity you've observed?

The lack of a process consumes a lot of time. I've seen this across countries and companies. There's a lot of chaos at the start of each project. A standardized process for project implementation would save a lot of time that's now wasted. I think questions open doors to knowledge. We need to ask whether we can be doing better.

Is there any sport that you do regularly that helps you maintain sanity?

I really enjoy yoga. It really helps with all the classic pains. When I was working at Twitter, we had a yoga class for free. It was magical. I would do yoga for an hour and go back and code, and I had seemingly endless energy to code.

What final advice can you give to someone new to this industry?

Something that made me a better engineer is developing my critical thinking. It's important to know why you do something. Being analytical is the key to being a good engineer. I'm in a phase in which I'm interested in people and things. We're on the shoulders of giants. Learning all of these things allows you to understand what you're doing now to fix the machine, including the process. The deeper we go into the knowledge, the better work we'll do.

I'm interested in assumptions. When I came to Japan, I had a set of assumptions and found that they weren't shared. In order to work with people, you need to share a common foundation, right? It turns out, that's not obvious. We come from different backgrounds and sets of experiences. When someone new joins our team, it's important to share how we communicate, code review, and build code, for example. I think people often miss this step.

ISRAEL'S RECOMMENDATIONS

Radical Candor: Be a Kick-Ass Boss Without Losing Your Humanity
| Kim Scott

The Mythical Man-Month: Essays on Software Engineering |
Frederick P. Brooks, Jr.

Mindset: The New Psychology of Success Paperback |
Carol S. Dweck

.

RAY
WENDERLICH

“ *Always keep learning.* **”**

🐦 @RayFromVA   in /in/raywenderlich   f /raywenderlich

Ray is part of a great team—the raywenderlich.com team, a group of over 300 developers and editors from across the world. He and the rest of the team are passionate both about making apps and teaching others the techniques to make them. When Ray's not programming, he's probably playing video games, role playing games, or board games.

Ray, we would love to hear more about your story. How do you move from writing articles as an indie developer into founding a company with over 200 elite developers and editors? Was there any common pattern along your way in this process?

Before I started as an indie iOS developer, I was working at Electronic Arts on the back-end tools for a game called Warhammer Online. I absolutely loved the job and the people there. But the thing was: I had always wanted to start my own business. And when I got married to my wife Vicki in 2010, I realized if I ever wanted to start my own business, now was the time—before any major responsibilities (like kids) might make it a lot more difficult!

So I decided to quit my job and become an indie iOS developer. I spent a couple of weeks reading books and learning, then started making my own apps. I did the programming, and Vicki did the art. At first, we weren't earning much money through our apps, but after about a year we were earning enough to pay our bills. While I was creating apps, I was writing tutorials on what I was learning on my website, raywenderlich.com. I didn't think much of it at the time— it was something I was doing just for fun. The tutorials became popular, and eventually became too much work to do on my own. So I recruited a team of awesome authors, and we wrote tutorials together and became known as the Tutorial Team.

After a while, someone on the Tutorial Team suggested we write a book together. We did, and the book was very popular—so the next year we wrote another. We continued doing this, and eventually the books did so well that Vicki and I decided to focus on the web site full time. Since then, the site and the team have continued to grow, and we are now a team of 200 authors and editors from around the world who team up and create high-quality tutorials, books, and video courses, currently focused on iOS, Android, Unity, and Server Side Swift.

How does your team create an article or tutorial that provides value to the potential readers?

It definitely takes a lot of care to craft a great tutorial. The goal is to make the tutorial fun and easy to understand, and for the instructions to 100% work. The way I see it is developers are busy people with a very limited amount of learning time. If a busy developer trusts you with their limited time, you don't want to let them down!

In order to reach this high-quality standard every time, we have a guide of tips and tricks we've learned over the years creating tutorials, that all of our tutorial authors follow. For example, we have a rule called, "Build and run, build and run." This means each instruction section should end with a command for the reader to build and run so they can check their work as they go, just like you would normally while programming. That prevents you from a terrible situation where you follow along pages and pages of a tutorial, only to realize you typed a line wrong somewhere, and have no clue where!

In addition, every tutorial on our site goes through three rounds of editing: a tech edit, an English language edit, and a final check by a senior member of our team. That way, we can be sure that every tutorial that goes out is amazing!

We see a rampant term in our industry: ageism. Elders seem to move into management positions or disappear from technical careers. Is there any life after 40? How can we keep ourselves updated and staying technical as we age?

I think part of this is natural. As you become more senior in your field, you also become more experienced and knowledgeable, and those are desirable traits for a leader to have. That's why there is often pressure for developers to progress from an individual contributor to a team lead to a manager and onwards.

For some people, that's great and a valid career path. I think the challenge, though, is sometimes developers feel like this is the only way they can progress in their career. However, that's not true: There is definitely tremendous value in super-experienced individual contributors, and having developers on your team who have been through the "school of hard knocks" for many years, in many technologies, is incredibly valuable. If your company doesn't recognize that, find another that does.

I think the first step is you need to decide what is best for you personally: Do you want to advance to management positions, or are you happier staying as an individual contributor? And then stay firm with your choice, even if you may get pressure in the opposite direction. If you live your life according to your values, you'll be happier for it.

For those entering the industry for the first time, there are very strong opinions of how to conduct interviews: whiteboarding, homework, pair programming. Which system do you find ineffective?

At Razeware, we use the following interview process for all positions (whether technical or not). This is optimized for speed of hiring, and it works well with a small team (we're only 15 full-time people) in a remote environment (we're 100% remote).

First, we use resume screening. I look through the resumes and weed out anyone I think isn't a good fit for the job. I try to give folks the benefit of the doubt at this point and keep a wide net at this stage.

Next, we do a video interview. I send them a short seven-minute video about our company, the job, and the interview process. This allows me to give more people a chance than I would if I were to schedule interviews with each person at this stage.

We then provide a challenge. At the end of the video, I give them a short challenge that should be able to be completed in a half hour or less, and it is related to something they will do on the job. Once they are past this stage, we do a half-hour interview. This interview is mostly focused on culture and big-picture fit at this point. To better test their skills, we do a short paid contracting job. This is usually an eight-hour task that can be completed on evenings or weekends, and we pay hourly for the time—that way people are compensated even if we don't offer the job. The job mimics real-world tasks they would do if they take the job, so is an excellent indicator to us if they'll be successful here once they take the job—and shows them if they like the work!

Then, a final 1.5-hour interview for the top 1–3 candidates. We have a final interview where we go into much more detail on the person and their background. We send the offer to the best candidate at the end.

I prefer this method of interviewing because it closely mimics how our company works: we all work independently, remotely, and (mostly) asynchronously. We've had good success with it so far!

What would you recommend to an already experienced developer to keep progressing in the career?

Always keep learning. As an experienced developer, it's sometimes tempting to settle into a rhythm and do things you're already very familiar with. After all, who doesn't like that feeling of expertise! But I think you'll grow even further if you push yourself to always be learning something new—even if you have to go back to being a beginner again! Learn a new language, a new platform, a new architecture, how to be an effective manager—whatever you're passionate about! Not only will this help your career, but I think you'll find it a lot of fun, too.

You are mostly managing a team of international people. Some people might be interested in transitioning from a technical position into a managerial one. How can they reach this milestone; what would you recommend them?

The best way to become a leader is to demonstrate leadership— even if you aren't in a leadership position already. For example, a few years back, someone applied to our tutorial team in an entry-level position: as a tech editor for videos. He always gave excellent feedback, he was prompt and responsive, an excellent communicator, and went above and beyond in helping the video courses he worked on stay on track and be as excellent as possible. Essentially, he was leading from within. He did so well that we promoted him to a final pass editor—that senior editor we have who does the final review on all of our tutorials. Again, he demonstrated his strong ability to meet deadlines, communicate well with his team, and went above and beyond to keep his projects running smoothly—and even helped out with areas outside of his responsibility! So we promoted him again, and I'm happy to say he is now our iOS team lead—Richard Critz—and is one of the best leaders I know.

So if you want to become a leader, be a leader now—in whatever role you already have. Take on extra responsibility, and show people you know how to get things done. If you have good leaders in your company, your efforts will be noticed and rewarded.

What is the biggest mistake you see junior developers making over and over again in their work? Why do you think they keep making this mistake?

As someone running a tutorial site, I see too many junior developers getting stuck in "tutorial purgatory." They just read tutorial after tutorial, but are a bit afraid to go off and build something on their own. Tutorials are an incredibly helpful way to learn quickly, but every once in a while, it pays to take a break from tutorials, and try implementing what you've learned on your own. It may be hard at first, but that is how you learn.

By doing this, you'll solidify the knowledge that you've learned in the tutorials through practical experience. Then you can come back to some more tutorials to learn even more, but now that you have some solid experience, the concepts will make even more sense. The tutorials and practice combination is a virtuous cycle.

What is the biggest obstacle, technical or personal, that you have had to overcome to get where you are today? How did you get past that obstacle?

By far, my biggest challenge so far has been identity. Throughout my life, my identity had always been as a software developer. That's what I did and enjoyed doing. And I had this idea that managers were always "the people who did nothing," while the developers did the "real work." But as my company grew, I found myself doing less and less software development, and more and more management. So when I looked in the mirror expecting to see a software developer, and instead saw a manager, there was this mental dissonance that made me feel quite badly about myself. I faced a choice: I could either change my actions (stop being a manager and get back to programming), or I could change my identity (and think of myself as a manager/leader/entrepreneur). I obviously decided on the latter. And although it seems easy to just make that mental switch, it was still a struggle for me—and took many years to change the way I thought about myself. Luckily, it was mostly a matter of time for me, and I'm very happy with my current role!

What is your leadership philosophy? That is, what core principles and beliefs guide you when you are in a position of leadership or mentoring others?

Follow the Golden Rule. Care about your people and treat them the way you would like to be treated. If you do that, everything else works itself out. The most important part of any company is your team, so nurture them with care.

What are the best apps or tools that you just can't live without? This could be in your personal or professional life.

For project management, we use Trello, which is a lightweight tool that can be easily used to manage multi-stage group projects. We use it to manage the process by which we create tutorials, books, and videos.

For documentation, we make heavy use of Confluence, which is a wiki-like tool by the creators of Jira. As our company grows, it is important to have a central place to store links to all the information we create. This way, we can have a "one-stop shop" for all the information we have as a company.

For project plans, we designate a person who takes the lead and creates a proposal in Google Docs, then sends it to the rest of the team for asynchronous comments and review.

For my personal notes, I use Evernote, which is a tool to write notes and sync them across multiple devices, quite heavily. For example, I have kept notes on every video chat I've had for the past 10 years in Evernote, which is incredibly helpful when I forget a conversation I had a few months ago. I also use it for TODOs and other notes I need to keep for future reference.

Although we prefer asynchronous communication as a remote team, sometimes we need to talk to each other instantly, and we use Slack for that.

> ❝ *It's critical to give yourself permission to take breaks when necessary to recharge your batteries—again this isn't weakness, but is normal and essential.* ❞

What is something you have learned "the hard way" in your career, that you wish you'd known 10 years ago?

Know your limits. Jobs can be demanding—especially for developers and leaders. There are times you'll need to burn the midnight oil, but it's essential to be aware of your own limits, and to understand what you can get done each day/week, in a sustainable way.

When you are an organized and responsible person at work, people will notice that you can get things done, and next thing you know they'll throw more and more work at you. As a person who gets things done, you might have a temptation to keep saying yes, and keep working harder, doing more and more.

But part of being dependable is to understand your limits, and sometimes you may need to push back—even to your boss—and say, "I'd love to do this, but right now my plate is full. Can you help me prioritize these tasks so I can focus on what's most important, or is there anyone else who can help with this?" This isn't a sign of weakness; it's actually a sign of strength, and you'll gain even more respect for it.

In addition, it's critical to give yourself permission to take breaks when necessary to recharge your batteries—again this isn't weakness, but is normal and essential. Remember a career, or a business, is a marathon and not a sprint. It's more important to have the energy to keep going day after day, than overdoing it and burning out. Burning out is real—I've been there many times. It took me a while to learn and accept my limits, and I hope you can find that perfect work/life balance in your life faster than I did.

RAY'S RECOMMENDATIONS

Toastmaster's International organization | toastmasters.org

"Identity" RWDevCon Inspiration Talk by Vicki Wenderlich |
raywenderlich.com/1855-rwdevcon-inspiration-talk-identity-by-
vicki-wenderlich

CATE HUSTON

> **"** *Inclusion: A noun,*
> *not a verb.* **"**

🐦@catehstn   cate.blog   WhereTheHellIsCate.com

Cate is an Engineering Director at DuckDuckGo and an Advisor at Automattic, where she led the mobile, Jetpack, and Developer Experience teams. Cate admins the New-(ish) Manager Slack and writes regularly for Quartz. You can find her on Twitter at @catehstn and at cate.blog.

Cate has lived and worked in the UK, Australia, Canada, China, Colombia and the United States, as Director of Mobile Engineering at Ride, an engineer at Google, an Extreme Blue intern at IBM, and a ski instructor. Cate built Show & Hide (available on iTunes), and speaks internationally on mobile development and tech culture. Her writing has been published on sites as varied as Be Leaderly, Lifehacker, The Daily Beast, The Eloquent Woman and Model View Culture. She is an advisor at Glowforge. You can also find her at WhereTheHellIsCate.com.

You recently wrote a post on your blog *Accidentally in Code*, "Answer These 10 Questions to Understand if You Are a Good Manager." What makes a person a good manager? Can a good leader be made or must it come naturally?

I definitely think good leaders are made. What we think of as "natural" leadership is often really charisma, which again, can be learned—the book *The Charisma Myth: How Anyone Can Master the Art and Science of Personal Magnetism* by Olivia Fox Cabane is a good start. The biggest things I look for in a leader are self-awareness and humility. These two characteristics open people up to admitting and learning from their own mistakes, which makes them very coachable—the effort you expend on coachable people is always multiplied. Humility means you have these conversations with the person, not their ego. It's much more effective and much less exhausting.

How do you keep a team productive, happy and consistently delivering?

These things go together. Developers like to ship, and not shipping will create a level of angst that no amount of perks or team-building exercises will compensate for.

In general, I like to orient and align teams around delivering continual user value. This is about, first, understanding our users and how we best serve them. And, second, being focused on sustainable delivery so that we deliver the most value to our users over the medium term.

In this model, we align the success of individuals with the success of the team; when a successful person is contributing to the team—we talk about "making the whole team better," although the details of this vary per person—and a successful team is delivering user value, continuously, paying close attention to metrics of user success and using that to inform the priorities and tactics.

> **❝** *I think a successful career is one where you feel you're operating from a place of strength in an environment where you feel valued.* **❞**

How do you define "a successful career"? Are there any strategic shortcuts or optimizations people can make to get there faster?

I think a successful career is one where you feel you're operating from a place of strength in an environment where you feel valued. I think the best optimization is to be a decent human being and show up for other people. This doesn't always pay off in the short term, but it does in the long term in the form of trust, people looking out for you, wanting to work with you, and forgiving you for your mistakes—we all make them!

What do you wish someone had told you when you first started software development that you had to learn the hard way?

The industry really is that sexist. To be fair, people probably did tell me this. I guess some things we do have to learn the hard way.

Seriously, or less darkly, probably the thing that would have been most helpful to understand is how to talk about work in a way that makes the impact clear. I spent a lot of time just working hard and hoping people would notice, or doing things that I felt were so clearly important they didn't need to be justified or explained. Something I work a lot on now is making impact clear at every level—for both individuals and teams—especially the things that it's easy to ignore. If someone does a great job at onboarding, that's impactful. If we're able to roll out a huge change with minimal drama, that's impactful.

Although it's not an easy problem to solve, how can people start making a difference in tackling the gender bias you reference that seems to be an ever-present issue in this industry?

Sometimes I joke that men don't have a word for "sponsorship" because they just call it "going to work." The reality is that nothing will change until the balance of power changes. We need to be looking for people who are unlike us, and seeing how we can help them move up, have more impact, and—bluntly—have more power. Power to influence hiring processes, promotion processes, compensation.

I'm not here for an industry wherein white women can fail up at the same rate as white men and where we adopt the same toxic behaviors. I'm here for building environments in which a broader spectrum of people can be successful. This is a lot of work—there are many axes of diversity, and none of us can be an expert on all of them—but it starts by being clear about what that work is, and what is holding us back from it. The biggest thing that stops us making progress is that people expect the work of inclusion to be comfortable. It's not. Confronting our biases and the structural inequity that has worked for and against us is brutal—and often upsetting. Sitting with the emotions of discomfort and defensiveness, doing the learning, and then showing up and doing the work is the thing. Inclusion is not a noun—it's a verb.

Are there any other current industry trends you think are just plain wrong?

Success porn. The "think pieces" and talks of "We did this and we are so awesome." On a structural level, it conflates correlation and causation—what was brilliance, what was luck? It also re-enforces problematic dynamics around who is allowed to take risks and why. On a personal level, I don't trust what I might learn from someone who won't admit their mistakes.

What would you suggest is a better alternative to this trend?

One of the questions I've started asking with new teams is, "What's your failure mode?"—and admitting mine in return. We all have them, and talking openly about what it looks like when we start to struggle, and why, puts that conversation on the table so we can at least support each other, and even better, get ahead of it.

I also like retrospectives. Within our teams, we should be able to have a level of honesty. Perhaps we can't have quite that level when we talk about what we do in public, but I think we can always admit some places we've fallen short and the ways we have tried to be better.

You read quite a lot about the industry and share your reviews publicly. Which three books have had the greatest impact on your life, and would you recommend them to anyone in particular?

First, *Leadership and Self-Deception: Getting Out of the Box* by The Arbinger Institute. I read this book for the first time nearly ten years ago, and it's really been formative for my leadership style, and how I approach conflict.

The next two go hand-in-hand. First, *Women Don't Ask: The High Cost of Avoiding Negotiation—and Positive Strategies for Change* by Linda Babcock and Sara Laschever. And *Whistling Vivaldi: How Stereotypes Affect Us and What We Can Do* by Claude M. Steele. I read widely on topics relating to diversity and inclusion. These two were very key for me in my approach to inclusion and how I have personally navigated the tech industry. *Whistling Vivaldi* is the best book on stereotype threat—the way we respond to being stereotyped, which is a byproduct of marginalization. Women Don't Ask is very helpful about how this plays out specifically in terms of negotiation, for example, women tend to be expected to advocate for others, but penalized for asking for ourselves.

Finally, *Good Strategy Bad Strategy: The Difference and Why It Matters* by Richard Rumelt. This is a recent addition as I moved into managing larger pieces and having more influence, strategy—defining it, communicating it—has been more and more part of my job. Personally, I have a hard time with a lot of floaty concepts like "vision," and this book presented strategy in a way that was much more relatable as an engineer. It helped me understand the depth required for good strategy, the kind of work that I was already doing that is strategy work, and how to better communicate it to bring others along with me.

In setting yourself up for your own work, how do you start your day off with a bang? Do you have any secret morning routines that set you up for success?

I aim to avoid bangs at the start of my day—or really most times of day! A good night's sleep, a pot of tea, breakfast and some time to myself before I log into work are my morning needs. So much of my job is based on what other people expect or need from me, that starting my day with something for me makes a big difference—whether it's going for a walk and breakfast, hitting the gym, reading a chapter of a book or writing a blog post.

How do you stay highly productive in your own work for long stretches of time?

Generally, the better I feel physically and emotionally the better the work I do. I stay active—I sit on an exercise ball, try taking a walk at lunchtime, also good for experiencing daylight in the winter, and work out regularly. I've worked with the same coach for nearly three years now, and also have a professional network—mainly on Slack as I am one of the moderators for an engineering management Slack, and Twitter. I also think there's really nothing better for productivity than regular breaks; it's not uncommon for me to work or travel on a weekend, but I take them off and fully disconnect as much as I can. I aim to take a week each quarter off and completely disconnect. I also only have work Slack on my phone when I'm traveling!

On a day-to-day level, I try and balance my work between things that give me an immediate sense of accomplishment and longer-term work. Each week, I put up some weekly notes for my team, sharing what I've been doing. It helps me take a step back and see not just the details of what I did, but where I was able to have more impact. I also do regular reviews over longer periods—monthly, quarterly, and annually—which is where you really see change and progress over time.

CATE'S RECOMMENDATIONS

The Manager's Path: A Guide for Tech Leaders Navigating Growth and Change | Camille Fournier

Good Strategy Bad Strategy: The Difference and Why It Matters | Richard Rumelt

Burnout: The Secret to Unlocking the Stress Cycle | Emily Nagoski Ph.D. and Amelia Nagoski, DMA

ANSWER THESE 10 QUESTIONS TO UNDERSTAND IF YOU'RE A GOOD MANAGER

Self-Guided Success Metrics for Managers

CATE HUSTON

Something I struggled with as a new manager was finding a sense of accomplishment, and as I've moved on to manage managers, I've seen this become a challenge for them, too. It's hard to find the right success metrics upon which to judge our work because our output is to make the team better, and so hopefully we give credit generously to them.

Without success metrics beyond the team's improvement, though, it can be easy to feel like you're just riding a wave of good people doing good work without contributing anything yourself.

Some managers deal with this feeling by seeing their success metric as being available to their teams 24/7 (unsustainable), or by counting lines of code (which would be like editors focusing on the number of words they wrote themselves—absurd). Some embrace the performance of management without understanding the underlying motivations. They "perform good manager" in one-on-one meetings, team stand-up meetings, and feedback cycles, but it doesn't really make them feel accomplished, and it's hard to put a finger on why.

To that end, I've compiled a list of signs that I look for in managers on my teams that suggest they're doing a good job.

Can you take a week off?

A rough one to start with if you lean toward constant availability as your metric, but there's nothing like a week off (or more!) to show which of your activities has the most impact. When you come back, pay attention to what you find. What's surprising to you? What comes up in your one-on-one meetings? What did people miss? What did they not need you for?

If your team is in a tough spot, and you don't feel you can really disconnect, try designating one trusted person to check in with each day. Ideally, you should be able to leave some way to contact you in an emergency and then disconnect—confident that if you were truly necessary you would know (and be relieved to find you're not).

Can problems be handled without you?

On both the engineering groups I've led at Automattic, we have infrastructure teams dedicated to building and releasing the software. Recently one of our team leads was away when a problem arose that required an unplanned release. His team, which was relatively new to working together, found some gaps in our documentation, got wildly creative, fixed it, pushed a new version, and put up a detailed account of what had gone wrong, with next steps. At some point both he—and I—checked in to see if there were anything we could do, but the team had everything handled.

This is huge—you'll never get away from using constant availability as your metric if every emergency must come to you. Ensuring that everyone on the team feels a sense of responsibility and ownership, and having a clear Directly Responsible Individual (DRI) is key.

Does your team deliver consistently?

Delivery is a trailing indicator for a healthy team, but it is an indicator. Healthy teams ship, consistently, and keep shipping over time. We all have projects that become unexpectedly complex, and every individual one may have a reasonable explanation, but if you look at the overall picture, is the team delivering more often than not?

Do people tell you what they think?

One thing that we all have to get used to in leadership is people being less candid with us. We need to make ourselves available explicitly to people who don't want to presume to seek us out (these are important people to listen to; otherwise you just hear the loudest voices). Yes, there are still people who lean toward speaking their minds, but if we can create space and listen, we can get others to be open with us, too.

It's also important to note how people give you critical feedback. Do they wait until it's something they are really frustrated by? Or is it an ongoing conversation? Will people tell you what they are worried or insecure about? Will they share what they notice is going on around you?

I was talking to one of my peers (who used to be a lead on my team) about a situation recently, and she said, "Cate, I would never let you do anything that stupid." I laughed, of course, but I was also deeply grateful to know that there are people around who will call me on bad decisions.

Do people on the team treat each other well?

Effective teams are inclusive teams. Fundamentally, I believe that inclusion is the right thing to do. However if we consider problems of exclusion—racism, sexism, ageism—they come from the idea that some people can do better if they push others down, and, of course, they start with the most marginalized amongst us.

As a leader, it's on you to cultivate a respectful environment on your team, and to make it clear that you will not tolerate discriminatory words or behavior. This is the minimum. Beyond that, you can set some values around reward and advancement that make it clear that success on your team is something that happens interdependently, not as a competition.

Is the team self-improving?

Self-improving teams critique and iterate and change things as a part of their process. They're not afraid to discuss what worked and what didn't, make suggestions, and try changes knowing that some of the changes they make will fail.

These teams get better over time with less and less intervention from you. It can be really hard to get teams reflecting on what went right and wrong with a project, because this process is scary (and the first few times might be quite rough). But getting to a place where these "post-mortems" are a matter, of course, is the outcome of a self-improving team.

Can you give people who report to you meaningful, in-depth feedback?

The way I think about feedback is this: Feedback is someone's work reflected back to them, in a way that helps them take pride in their accomplishments and makes actionable the places where they can improve.

This means having enough insight into their work, accomplishments, and struggles to be able to do that. A lot of that feedback happens as we go, but at most every six months I make a point to get some (qualitative or quantitative) feedback from team members that I can use to put together a bigger picture of how someone is doing. Think hand-mirror in one-on-one meetings, full-length mirror in a feedback round.

What kind of things can you delegate?

Do you feel like you can hand off pieces of work or problems to people on your team? Are those projects getting bigger over time?

Maybe you started by giving people tasks, but over time, you want to be able to give them broader problems to own. This allows you to take on more from your boss.

If you manage managers and you don't have people you can hand stuff off to, you will drown. It's just not possible to operate effectively at that scale without the shock absorption of people being able to take things off your plate and handle them. If you don't have it, you will need to build it, because it will only get worse over time.

Who is taking on bigger roles?

Two years after I joined Automattic, it's gratifying to look at who on the mobile team I led is now a tech lead, or a team lead, or generally taking on things with larger scope. As the team grows, there's more opportunity—and more need—for people to step up. Delegation flows down: pushing things onto the managers forces them to push things onto people on their teams, and this is how we grow new leaders on the team.

As much as we might adore everyone on our team, and want to keep them together, having a strong team means that sometimes people's best path for success lies outside of it. It's our job as managers to help them toward it, and to help our peers when they need a skill set that someone on our team can best provide. It's a sign of success when people from our teams go to other teams and take on more responsibility there. It can also be a sign of success when people leave and take on bigger roles elsewhere.

Hopefully, this is something you can talk about together, but the success metric is: How have you helped them? What feedback, what projects, what responsibilities have you given them? How have you used your insight into their capabilities to help them find their next role inside your organization? If it's more indirect, how has the way you've run the team contributed to creating opportunities for a broader set of people?

Can you take on work outside of your immediate scope?

Having our own teams in order, and strong support within them, makes it possible for us to provide more support to those above and around us.

What could you take on that would most help your boss? Your peers? What scope of things could you take on? Can that get bigger over time?

When I joined Automattic, one of the things the mobile team really wanted was for mobile to have a bigger role in the organization. One way that we achieved that was for me to take a bigger role in the organization, to do more to support other teams, to spread our practices and get invited into more conversations.

Do your peers value your perspective and come to you for advice?

Every organization has its own unique set of quirks, and the people who best understand the stress under which we operate are our peers. If we have a functional environment, and we're not competing with each other, who respects who within a peer group says a lot. Pay attention to the topics people seem to value your opinion on. It shows what they notice—which are often the things we most take for granted.

CREDIT

A version of this article was first published on Quartz at Work (November 1, 2018). The original article can be found here: qz.com/work/1447711/how-to-tell-if-youre-a-good-manager/

CYRIL MOTTIER

❝ *Be human.* ❞

🐦@cyrilmottier   github.com/cyrilmottier   in /in/cyrilmottier

C yril is an avid lover of mobile platforms and a multi-skilled engineer. He is actively involved in the Android community and shares his passion writing blog posts, helping others on social networks, creating open source libraries and giving talks. His motto: "Do less, but do it insanely great."

Which do you prefer: podcasts or books?

When it comes to software engineering, I have to confess that I do prefer the good old books. Books' main advantages are that they are generally more polished and in-depth. At the same time, podcasts are generally better when you want to have an overview of a subject or just want to know about the latest trends or great tools.

What are some books that have had a lasting impact on how you do your work?

Of all of the engineering books I have read, none of them are dedicated specifically to Android. They are generally more focused on global concepts that apply to software design in general. My top two? *Effective Java* by Joshua Bloch; I consider this book as a must-read when you start developing in Java. It gives so much of the dos and don'ts in Java and helps new developers write Java code that is clear, correct, robust, future-proof and maintainable. *Java Concurrency in Practice* by Brian Goetz is another great choice; concurrency is definitely hard. Concurrency issues are generally difficult to reproduce and understand. And the very first day you think you get it, you will actually discover the day after you are still off-track. I haven't read this book for a very long time but I remember learning a lot with it.

I'm not sure I learned all of this thanks to a book in particular, but I remember spending a large amount of time reading about design patterns at the very beginning of my career. I would definitely encourage people to understand why/how they can solve design/architectural problems, and there are a lot of great resources to help you do that.

In terms of insight from an individual in the community, what is something you wish someone had told you at the start of your software development career that you had to learn the hard way instead?

I think it would be to never ever be afraid of deep-diving into the source code! Books and documentation are handy, but the one and only source of truth is the source code. Most of the things I have learned in school are actually based on the knowledge of my teachers. Sometimes they were telling me to read books and look at the documentation, but I never had the simple advice of looking at the source code (when available of course). I learned it the hard way because it's always difficult to understand how a project is structured and organized. But, at the end, I learned something very important: The only source of truth for any library, tool, platform, etc. is its source code.

You are one of the most experienced Android developers. At the start of your career, you developed several libraries that were extensively used, covering some holes that the Android SDK was not serving yet (GreenDroid, Polaris). In what ways do you find the mobile development world has changed since you began your career?

It's changed a lot, of course. Android development in 2009 is radically different from Android development in 2019. I actually started developing on Android with a pre-1.0 early look version. There are several aspects that changed, specifically.

First of all, regarding tooling, we have switched from an Eclipse, Ant-powered, dependencies-less world to an Android Studio, Gradle-powered, dependencies-aware world. Put simply, we now have a robust and extensible dependency-management system. For instance, at the time I released GreenDroid, there was no AAR file format. The only possibility to include dependencies was to add JARs directly into the project. At that time, I had to create a script to copy/paste resources to the appropriate directories in the project. On the tooling side, Android Studio and all of the included developer tools helped improve productivity a lot.

Secondly, Google released a lot of libraries helping developers create stunning user experiences and focus more on creating great products. I released GreenDroid—Android Support Library equivalent—and Polaris—Google Maps SDK equivalent—because none of these Google libraries existed or were nice to use at that time. Google did awesome working on that part; it's nice to see third-party libraries are now generally focusing on very particular subjects that are not related to Android or Google.

Finally, the frsamework is now not as important as it used to be. A lot of the work that has been done in the past few years is to ensure none of the new features are tied to a particular platform version. While it wasn't easy at the beginning because the platform wasn't mature enough, this new paradigm has several advantages—mainly, it decouples platform updates from library updates improving the "time to production."

What about the mobile development world has frustratingly not changed in your time in the industry?

There are always issues we're not happy about. In the mobile development world, there is still one frustrating thing that hasn't changed and has actually gotten worse: the build time. I've seen build time up to two minutes for a less than 10MB IPA/APK. It's scary.

Similarly, I'm always frustrated to see a lot of apps continue to be slow and janky. Because devices are getting better and better, we could imagine everything that would create a jank 10 years ago would be completely unnoticeable today, but that's not the case. Indeed, at the same time, there are more and more pixels to render on screen, applications do more and more, etc. All of this gives me the impression apps are not "more useful" or more "user friendly" than they used to be. They basically provide the same level of service but in a more graphical way.

Do you currently see any missteps or shortcomings in the software development world that are not being dealt with properly?

There are two things I would point out. First, mobile development is getting harder and harder because the frameworks and libraries evolve. For instance, you have to deal with retro-compatibility, dependency versioning, more and more system services, etc. I'm always wondering how a beginner can really understand how to kickstart a new project. Second, as platforms evolve, some of the decisions that were made cannot be discussed or changed. For instance, the fact that way too much stuff happens in the UI thread— especially animations—on Android that needs to be tackled.

Are there any other current industry trends that you think are just plain wrong?

To be honest, I don't think any of the current or past industry trends are "plain wrong." I've never seen things as black or white; they are always shades of gray. It's rather a matter of weighing the pros and cons. That being said, there are some trends that, to my mind, gather a lot more cons than pros. Everything that tends to enlarge the distance between the machine and the developer, for example. I clearly understand that's the trend, in general, to relieve the developer from the burden of having to write low-level code. But I've seen several approaches considering, for instance, the web as the only viable option. This has given us some tools like "Electron" (115MB for a "Hello world," runtime/libraries duplication per app, etc.) and tools built on top of it: text editors, messaging clients, IDEs or command-line terminals.

Another thing I am not a fan of—but this is less and less true thanks to server-side rendering—are heavy web applications requiring long loading times. To my mind, it breaks the central idea of the web which is everything can be accessed instantly.

What would you suggest is a better alternative to this trend?

Use a modern language that can scale to large projects and stop adding layers and layers of runtimes and indirections; for instance, I expect my text editor to be written in a language that compiles to native.

What else would you recommend to the freshly graduated student to do in order to boost his or her career?

First, I'd say attend conferences because you can learn a lot there. They should also read source code to go deep into the internals and learn from the past. They'll have better success if they are passionate: computer science is very demanding and living it with passion is the best way not to live it as a pain. Finally, keep experimenting; the best way to learn and evolve is to keep coding.

> 66 *Lead by example to show your team the path they need to take. Be transparent and honest. Trust people. Finally, be human—listen to people, communicate, be emotional.* 99

At Captain Train, you played the role of Head of Mobile and Web. What are the traits of a good leader? How do you successfully lead a team?

Being the Head of Mobile and Web at Captain Train was really challenging. I don't think there is a finite list of traits to being a good leader. I really consider it depends on the person. I would sum up my personal point of view with a few key ideas. First, lead by example to show your team the path they need to take. Next, be transparent and honest. You also need to trust people. If you expect them to trust you, you need to trust them first. And, finally, be human—listen to people, communicate, be emotional.

For your own work, how do you start your day off with a bang? Do you have any secret morning routines that set you up for success?

Some people like the evening, some like the morning, and some others like neither! In a more serious way, I've read some studies about this and it looks like it's something you can decide or change. Personally, I'm a morning person. I just love mornings because, to my mind, it's the moment by moment in a day to enjoy nature, like the awesome light when the sun rises up, the freshness of the air, the peacefulness of the flora and fauna, etc. It's really a moment in which you can enjoy calm and quietness both outside and at work.

I don't think I have a secret routine and to be honest I don't like routine as it's boring. In general, I wake up pretty early though and always take this time to do something that is not related to work: go out for a run, read something, get to the bakery to prepare a nice breakfast, etc. Having those kinds of peaceful moments in the morning is the best way to start a successful day.

How do you stay highly productive for long stretches of time?

I think the easiest way to stay highly productive is to find a job that acts both as a job and a passion. If you match both, you have your ideal job. In a more practical way, I don't follow methodologies at all when it comes to productivity for long stretches of time. I spend a lot of time ensuring I'm productive such as tweaking my dev environment, learning shortcuts, installing or developing tools, etc.

Lastly, tell us a little about your Twitter handle, where you describe yourself as a "devsigner." What does this mean to you exactly? Do you believe there is a role in IT that covers both development and design?

Not sure there's a role for that. My personal point of view is that I don't consider technology is useful when taken alone. Technology is a tool that can be used to fix problems users have. Because of that I have never considered development and UI/UX design independently. Both of them are needed to solve issues. I think I noticed this pretty rapidly and even though my school background is mainly about development, I rapidly self-taught myself with design in general.

CYRIL'S RECOMMENDATIONS

Effective Java | Joshua Block

Game Engine Black Book: Wolfenstein 3D | Fabien Sanglard

The Design of Everyday Things | Don Norman

HUYEN TUE DAO

❝ *Don't be afraid to ask questions.* **❞**

🐦 @queencodemonkey   randomlytyping.com

Huyen is an Android developer and Google Developer Expert for Android and Kotlin. She currently works on the Trello Android app at Atlassian and is also co-producer of the "Android Dialogs" YouTube channel. Huyen lives in Denver, CO, though is often found in the Washington D.C. metro area. When not up late programming, she is often found up late gaming (video, mobile, board, card—anything).

What do you wish someone had told you when you started software development that you had to learn the hard way instead?

Don't be afraid to ask questions. When I first got out of school I was so preoccupied with getting a job and looking capable. I felt pressure to know everything off the bat. Looking back, that perspective seems silly. How can anyone expect you to know everything about a new job? As a senior developer, I would never expect that of someone. A lot of people feel pressured to be the smartest person in the room and never to be wrong. That kind of pressure may cause someone not to ask questions out of fear that it will affect how others view that person. That was definitely true for me. I'd always try to figure out the answer on my own, or I faked it until I made it.

Honestly, I missed out a lot by not asking questions. Nowadays, I'd encourage people to do their best and never be afraid to ask questions. If there's something you don't understand, ask the question, and don't be afraid of not knowing. Now that I'm more senior and working with other people, what really excites me is when someone asks great questions which make me think. Even better than always having the right answer is asking interesting questions. I wish I'd learned that earlier.

> ❝ *I'm really disappointed at still seeing job listings looking for 'rockstar' engineers. To me, this just perpetuates the unfair and unrealistic pressure to be the smartest person in the room, to always be right.* ❞

What's a negative trend in the industry, and how would you fix it?

I'm really disappointed at still seeing job listings looking for "rockstar" engineers. To me, this just perpetuates the unfair and unrealistic pressure to be the smartest person in the room, to always be right. I think that is actually quite limiting. I would rather see the industry emphasize the ability to grow and to learn from mistakes. I would rather see the industry emphasize passion for technology and willingness to change and adapt.

You work at Trello, one of the strongest advocates for remote work. Is remote work the future of the work paradigm?

For 90% of my career, I've worked remotely. My experience working in an office was very much like that movie *Office Space*, and very uninspiring. My bosses were in another state, about 300 miles away. In fact, no one on my team worked in that office. I felt completely disconnected and eventually made the decision to just work from home. While I regret that I haven't had a great in-person, collaborative office experience, I now prefer working remotely.

Remote work, at times, felt isolating. But eventually I learned how to work remotely better. A selling point of the second company that I went to work for was that they would hire talented engineers from anywhere. At the same time, they did the work to make sure that we engineers collaborated both with each other and with clients. There was definitely some pain in the process, because it's not as if once you hire remote workers that you are done and everything works perfectly.

I believe that, as an industry, we need to be open to hiring brilliant and hard-working people everywhere. I believe that remote work is the future. However, it requires a lot of investment, understanding, and effort.

Certain things are more challenging for a remote worker, especially interaction with others. Remote workers need to be conscious of how much and how well they communicate in order to solve problems. You have to communicate more openly and immediately. You have to learn how to connect with your teammates and know how to bridge those gaps when you don't see each other every day. I've always been shy and reserved. This was definitely a hurdle for me early in my career, especially as a remote worker. But ultimately I think remote work has forced me to get out of my shell.

How would you advise companies looking to implement a remote-work policy?

Be very pragmatic and set boundaries. Some companies might be intimidated by remote work because it feels like a world without rules. But that's not true. For example, at Trello, we adhere to a workday based on Eastern Standard Time. Tools like video chat allow us to reach out to each other, whatever time zone we're in.

Early on, when we didn't have as many remote workers, we'd hold company meetings in one small room. Everyone would crowd around a small speaker, and the remote workers would dial in. It wasn't great. The audio was awful on both sides. Remote workers calling in couldn't hear the conversations happening in the room.

To ameliorate this problem, we had everyone, regardless of whether they were in the office or not, call in from a personal computer. That way, everyone had the same level of engagement and communication. This small change had a big effect on our work culture.

When going remote, set boundaries and enforce them. Make it possible for people to work asynchronously and synchronously. Remember that little things matter.

You have a YouTube channel, Android Dialogs, where you interview prominent personalities in the software development world, particularly in the Android ecosystem. How did you get involved in this?

At my first job out of university, I made friends with a great developer, and when we went to a conference together, he introduced me to a lot of people. I started networking a lot and discovered this entire world of blogs and public speaking. I was inspired to enter this world, and, as I did, I felt my career take off.

Separately I've been a big podcast fan ever since I got my first iPod. Anyone can pick up a microphone and create a show, and I have always had a desire to do the same and to connect with other people.

Around the time I got into the developer community, there was the Fragmented podcast and Android Developers Backstage (ADB). I love this kind of content, but I tend to listen or pay attention for short spans of time. I had the idea to create similar content but in smaller pieces.

There are so many celebrities in the tech world. There are also a lot of people doing amazing work that isn't recognized or well-known. I wanted to create a platform to give a voice to people in both groups.

At this time, I had moved to Colorado and made friends with Android developer Chiu-ki Chan. This was just before Google I/O 2015. I asked Chiu-ki what she thought of a five- to seven-minute podcast based on interviewing engineers. She liked the idea, and she volunteered herself and her video camera. So instead of a podcast, we started a YouTube channel.

We interviewed several people from the Android community at the I/O meeting. I like to think about our channel as bragging on all the amazing people in our community and sharing the Android community with the broader engineering world.

Since you're a fan of podcasts, what are some podcasts that you'd recommend?

My favorite podcasts are Android-centric. For sure, the *Fragmented* podcast with Donn Felker and Kaushik Gopal, and *Android Developers Backstage* are two of them. ADB, in particular, I love because often the Google engineers who appear as guests bring a sense of history and context. You learn so much about the bumps in the road, the cool experiences they had, and the rewrites they had to do. Hearing that people you admire have experienced challenges that are similar to yours is so helpful and inspiring.

As well, I love listening to podcasts that talk about Android from a consumer perspective. I want to see what's out there. What are people excited about? What are people looking forward to? How do people feel about the new Samsung phone? I like to know what people that aren't developers are excited about. Often as a developer, your perspective is shaped by your day job. It's always good to hear what people who have a different take on technology have to say.

Do you follow any particular routines that set you up for success when doing your own work?

As engineers, it's easy to sit in front of your computer and just work and work and work and never see the sun. I spent many years doing just this. Now, I like to start the day by doing some things for myself: exercise in the morning and then a cup of coffee. As engineers, we get so wrapped up in our programming that it's easy to forget about ourselves. There is a stereotype of the sedentary engineer but it is easy to slip into this stereotype. It's important to take care of our bodies and minds.

In general, I'd recommend thinking about what excites you about your day. Then sit down, catch up on emails, and most importantly catch up on what my teammates are doing before actually crunching on code. If someone has an idea, I can give some feedback. If someone is having a problem, I can try to help. It helps to get out of my own headspace. Especially as a remote worker, when you don't have the water cooler to stand around, interacting with your team is important. It's often these conversations, whether it's a serious conversation or just a social one, that energize me for the day.

How do you deal with the pace of change in the industry?

As an engineer, you have to be very comfortable with changing technology. Change is a good thing, but it's often not easy to deal with. Everybody feels behind at some point. You have to give yourself permission not to know everything. As well, I believe building a strong community and having a long-lasting career go hand in hand.

HUYEN'S RECOMMENDATIONS

The Mythical Man-Month: Essays on Software Engineering | Frederick P. Brooks, Jr.

WikiWikiWeb online developer community | wiki.c2.com

MARCIN KRZYZANOWSKI

❝ If it feels good for you, do it. ❞

🐦 @krzyzanowskim   blog.krzyzanowskim.com
speakerdeck.com/krzyzanowskim   github.com/krzyzanowskim

M arcin is an eclectic developer with years of experience in mobile and desktop applications, as well in enterprise solutions. He is a 10x developer who likes to learn new things with a pragmatic approach to the art of programming. Occasionally, he speaks at conferences and shares knowledge. Active in open-source software development communities, he has published a wide range of iOS/macOS libraries and tools, such as CryptoSwift, ObjectivePGP and the amazing Online Swift Playground, capable of running Swift code interactively from a Web Browser. He's currently working on SwiftStudio.app, an indepedent third-party IDE for Swift.

You are an incredibly proficient open-source producer—maintainer of CryptoSwift, among others. From your experience, is it possible to make a living out of open-source software?

I think it's very hard or even impossible. Lately, I saw a diagram showing that even the most popular open-source projects don't receive enough money to provide a living for an author or team. There are a couple reasons why you cannot make a living out of open source or why it's very hard.

The initial thought behind open-source was to share the code, of course, everything being free. Over time, the big companies started to use the code and turn that into their revenue without paying back to the community. That helped build backend stack at Amazon. Many of the big companies are built on the shoulders of open-source projects.

I can speak of CryptoSwift, which happens to be a quite popular library. After publishing CryptoSwift, it started getting GitHub stars; however, a star is not a sign of popularity of an app or tool because the star doesn't mean that the people actually use it. Then I saw that GitHub gives us stats about the frequency of visits; daily, it's thousands of downloads, now. At the same time, I saw the third-party analytics report that there are millions of installations in applications that use the CryptoSwift library. Also, a few people told me they use the library. I was surprised when, at first, somebody told me they knew and used my library. This indicates that all this kind of feedback is not necessarily transferred back to the authors.

And if the feedback is not going back to the creator, then the money isn't going back as well. I tried to get some donations. I have a donation link. Well, over five years, it's got a total of like $50.

There were two companies that needed the functionality we provided and wanted to sponsor the feature implementation. I implemented that and merged it back to the open-source codebase, so everyone profited from it, and I got some money for my work. But that only happened twice.

Mostly you have to have another job to pay your bills and use open-source as your side project, which is valuable, but it's hard to focus on that full time. Open-source work can also give you visibility and opportunities when you are searching for a gig, or companies are looking for new employees; they see that you are an author and can read the public comments on your work.

The thing is for instance OpenPGP is hard; nobody really understands old technology and so it's hard to build such a tool by yourself. I spent a few months building this library and I thought, okay, now I will sell it. By now, I sold a few licenses. I know that some of the companies just use the free version that is available on GitHub.

And I also got, and this one is significant, some funds to keep the project up and alive for a year. It was a few years back. My work was crucial for proper functioning of a company's product. This is the sponsorship of living from the open-source I would like to see more often.

If you rely on the open-source product—say, the "webpack," which is extremely popular in JavaScript or other free tools to build the code—and you cannot contribute back by coding, it's fair to pay for it. There's a greater chance that the product will not disappear next year, which will also affect you.

Sometimes, publishing the open-source can help you be better known and will affect your visibility. I've heard several times from different people, "I know you wrote this, so you're probably familiar with the subject, so we may be interested in you helping us build something else."

I worked on the open-source projects because I was interested in the subject. I was learning and getting some level of expertise. I could help companies or people to build solutions based on my knowledge.

And here's a funny story: I once found, on one of these freelance-employment websites, a job offer to add CryptoSwift into a company's app. Somebody wanted to use CryptoSwift and I applied... Well, my offer was too high for them.

It seems to be one of the problems in these platforms that, because they're open to the entire world and we live in a time of globalization, there might be people from countries who are cheaper to employ. If companies are purely basing value on price, that isn't great for developers trying to make a living.

Yes, definitely. I've never looked at this website again. Turns out you can be rejected for a job which uses your work.

In using resources yourself, are there any books that have had an impact on you or your career?

I don't have a lot of specific titles. Currently, I'm listening to more audiobooks, especially autobiographies. I like learning about history, what happened, how things were built, how things were before, how people interacted with each other and what was the outcome. Everyone had something interesting in their lives. I also read a lot of reportages, which gives me a history lesson and some insights —how people work, how the world works. That's the most interesting part for me—how other parts of the world work beyond my backyard.

I'm very interested in the people outside of my expertise. I want to be open-minded about how people live and be respectful of them. And this also affects my work because it means I can design or build products for everyone.

Always in the back of my mind, I think things are not the universal truth just because I'm doing them that way. Other people do things another way, and they have valid reasons to work it a different way; I should at least listen to them or try to understand. This applies to the programming style—how I write code—because I think everyone is different.

I don't believe there is one universal truth on how to write code. Of course, we have some guidelines but if you read someone's code base, you think, Oh, it's shit... because I didn't write it. I try not to do this.

Even when you take your codebase from four years ago, right? You think, "Did I write this?"

My goal is to be respectful and try to embrace that. I may not agree with something, and I may discuss that, but I try to not be binary about it, thinking it is wrong because somebody else did it differently. It's not wrong. Everyone had their reason behind the solution and constructs. I don't necessarily have to pursue my idealistic point of view because there are reasons to do things differently and maybe I'm wrong after all.

You are a person who works from home. What is your take on this trend?

The biggest disadvantage of working remotely in Europe is the time-zone variance. Most IT tech remote jobs are in the United States. Living in the same timezone makes getting work done easier. The U.S. is a big country; you don't have to live exactly in the Silicon Valley, for example, where the costs of living are high and not everyone wants to be. A lot of people are just moving out to other cities just to have a space to live and they work remotely.

Of course, a lot of people work remotely in Europe and then we work in our timezones. But it depends on the company.

The trend is to have more and more remote work. Google, for example, published a reporting tool that stated remote work is the future. But Google itself is not very famous for hiring remote workers. So something must change to make that big switch on a global scale. People have to trust more that remote setup is feasible in the same way a regular office is.

Many offices now have an open-concept. The majority of people dislike the open space. So why force people to go to the open space and not let them work remotely? It also offers flexibility in working setups. For instance, I show up in the morning at my desk and stay until 5 PM, so I'm virtually sitting next to my teammates. I'm just at a different location, but I'm there, working.

I also worked in the setup where the hours are more vague. It's not that strict. I worked but the hours were not that important. So it depends on how the company is organized. I prefer to organize my own life. I'm aware of when I am the most focused. I know the hours when my productivity is the best, and I can build or schedule my day around that knowledge. So it lets me be the most productive for the project.

I have a family, and I have some duties as well. Working remotely allows me to be happier in family life. I have time to spend with my kids. I have time to do my parent obligations, and I have time for doing my job. It's best for everyone. And I don't have to commute. I still talk to my colleagues; I'm just a click away from seeing each other and discussing things. Today's technology allows us to work remotely.

Company organization is important, too. You may feel out of the loop when you're remote if you're the only person working remotely, and everyone else is sitting in the same room. But if you're organized in a way that the business has to be discussed on Slack or on a call, you don't feel out of the loop because you see what everyone else sees.

Are there any particular practices that help you work remotely successfully?

My life has changed over time, so my rituals have changed as well. I start my day by walking my kids to school. Then I'm back and my colleagues have already started work, but I'm not ready to start. I'm doing breakfast and minor housework, which gives me the energy and the feeling that I already did something with my day. Chores are out of my head and I can focus on my work. Then I sit and evaluate how much time I need for tasks. It depends. But I know I will work until 3 PM. This is my time to work and no one bothers me. This is important.

Otherwise, especially if you work remotely, it's very easy to get distracted. It's important to set boundaries. My family understands that it is my working time. And after the work I just switch my mind and do all the other stuff in my life. And, later on, I'm back to work in the evening—like every programmer probably.

So I have the session during the day, then the break, and then back in the evening, because during the break I usually think about the problems I didn't solve yet. And in the evening, I just solve it. If I don't have an urgent task to finish I carve out time for learning the new technologies, mostly in the evening. I read some books or blog posts or watch the videos or build something just to keep up in the tech world.

How else do you set yourself up to be productive?

In my case, I like to change the environment; this is why I also like to work remotely because I can work in different places. I have a setup at home where I have a desk and a computer, but I also use a laptop, and I can go to a cafe or just a different place for one, two days to change the environment. I find it very refreshing if the scenery around me is just different, otherwise, it's easy to get in the trap that you just sit in one room and just get bored or lose focus. I can meet some other people on the way, so that will help with my mental state as well.

Another tip is not to overwork yourself; it's very easy to burnout. We need to manage the burnout because when the burnout comes, our productivity goes down and it's not good for me or a company.

The fix for the burnout is, of course, change something. I change the scenery, but changing even the project or something that is not related to your job can help.

Preventing burnout is why I have these side projects; I have a lot of side projects and not all of them are published, but I experiment a lot. It helps me keep my sanity.

You've mentioned that it's hard to keep up with new technologies; how do you stay current on new trends?

I have a strong phobia: fear of missing out. With so much going on, I don't have time to keep up with everything. I wish I could, but it's not possible; everything is too complex to keep up on top of everything. I try to just avoid some information; I know there's a technology but it's okay not to be an expert in this. I know there's Kotlin, and I don't know Kotlin, and I'm okay with that because I never need it.

If I would have a project or urge to use Kotlin, I would probably need a week or two to start using it. Of course, I will not be an expert from the first day, but it's enough to get along with a new language. So then I would just allocate some resources to learn the technology and start using it. If I want to learn something, I just find time for it. Either it is in the evening or try to find a problem to solve in that technology because learning by using is the most effective way of learning I can find. I have a problem with reading the programming books from cover to cover. After a few pages I want to experiment with the material because reading is not enough. I can read, but I have to experiment.

In all your years of software development, is there something you wish someone had told you that you had to learn the hard way instead?

How to estimate the cost or time of a project. I was once fired because I didn't estimate a project well. In the early days, I didn't know that underestimating or overestimating is okay. I felt guilty. My first big problem was underestimating big, and it failed. I felt very bad but I shouldn't have.

I should have accepted that. My colleague might estimate differently and can decide that the task will take two times more or less, and it's okay. We can work on that.

When it comes to estimating, have you developed any techniques that help you?

I keep repeating in my head that I tend to underestimate so I try to just make the numbers bigger. I don't have a reliable technique. When I work with a team, we usually have some techniques such as we take cards on and everyone puts a number and, eventually we agree on some value. This is very valuable. But being on your own is harder to estimate. Over time, I have more experience, and I'm more predictable with these estimates. That said experience would be the best tool to have the most accurate estimates. The less experienced the developer is, it will give the least accurate estimation because they are related to each other.

Beyond remote work, what is a current industry trend that you think is problematic?

I would say it's our habit of abstractive everything. We build abstraction over abstraction, and everything is so complicated that nobody can see how things work. Ten years ago, a developer could handle the development environment by themselves. The knowledge of the programmer was enough to set up the build, configure the environment and start working. But now, you need to set up all the machinery behind the tests, behind the build system, behind the dockers, the virtualization. It's complicated.

The solution people find is to build another abstraction over that. For instance, we had a Docker, which was fairly new technology and easy to follow. But it was not enough. We needed a Kubernetes. And nobody understood how the Kubernetes worked. A Kubernetes is not needed for the developer. It's needed for the cluster, it's needed on the server. If a developer today wants to build a website built on Node.js or similar, they will need a Docker container, and the developer will probably be asked to set up the Kubernetes just to deploy it to one of the cloud providers.

Building abstraction is particularly visible in the JavaScript world in all these frameworks on top of the frameworks, on top of the frameworks, and nobody any longer understands what's going on under the hood. It happens in programming languages as well; C++ has become so complicated at this point that it's very hard to start with it. It happens also with Swift. The new features are getting harder and harder to understand. I think this is the root of the problems we have. We do not know how it works anymore and we just do a patchwork. We don't fix the real problem—we just add something to cover the real problem.

Is there a way to fix this problem?

Do not abstract early; start with simple tasks that solve your problem and then eventually abstract it. So if all you need is a Docker container, just stick with it. You don't need a Kubernetes. The cloud provider shouldn't force us to use all this machinery just to deploy an application. And as programmers, we shouldn't start with the abstraction. We should start with the working solution and then abstract it.

> **❝** *I don't think everyone should transition to management because not everyone feels interested in doing it or is capable of doing it.* **❞**

For someone interested in helping solve these kinds of problems, do you see a need for people to transition into management?

I don't think there is a need for a transition into management at all. The software industry has no promotion opportunities for programmers who want to remain in an engineering position. You start as a junior programmer and you become a senior programmer in two, three years. And then there is the ceiling.

If you want to get promoted at work you have to go into management because the company has nothing more to offer to you. It should not be like that. Not everyone has a predisposition and ability to be a manager or not everyone is interested in doing it. It's a different kind of work. If the company has a choice, I definitely recommend creating a promotion path for software engineers that is not related to management.

It's okay to be quasi-manager - a leader of the team. But strictly taking a management position is so different that we should not be forced to go into that direction. If you feel it's good for you, go ahead; you will learn a lot of new stuff, but if you don't feel it just don't go there because you will be a bad manager.

I'm an educated manager, but I don't feel that I want to work as a manager—at least now. I find myself better suited in a technical position or a smaller team, like a leader but not necessarily a manager. If you decide to be a manager, the best way is to learn from the other managers. School won't give you the knowledge you need. Of course, you need at least basic academic knowledge, mostly about how people work, how teams work. But day-to-day work is different and comes with a lot of stress.

I really would love to live in a world where we don't have to go to the management position and we have more steps other than junior software developer to senior software developer. It is limiting for us.

MARCIN'S RECOMMENDATIONS

Swift Unwrapped podcast with JP Simard and Jesse Squires |
spec.fm/podcasts/swift-unwrapped

Point-Free Swift video series | pointfree.co

Wise Guy: Lessons from a Life | Guy Kawasaki

The Emperor: Downfall of an Autocrat | Ryszard Kapuscinski

MIKE NAKHIMOVICH

“Separate the job from the person.”

🐦 @friendlyMikhail

Mike is a Google Developer Expert in Android and Kotlin, and he is heavily focused on making performant apps by leveraging functional reactive architectures. He started his Android career 6+ years ago working on logistics software, particularly with physical barcode scanners. Since then, Mike has done a stint at NY's premier Android shop, TouchLab, chased the equity dream at a few startups, helped fight the good fight at the *New York Times* and spend some days as the Android Lead at Nike. He is currently working as a Staff Engineer at Dropbox. Mike is also a co-founder of FriendlyRobot.nyc where he helps NY startups turn their dreams into Android realities. In his free time, he enjoys writing and speaking about overly complicated concepts at conferences and area meetups, writing for tech blogs and maintaining his open-source libraries which include NYT Store, TinyDancer and Apollo-Android.

You have been the Team Lead at the *New York Times* first and, currently, at Dropbox. What are the traits of a good leader? Can a good leader emerge from a "non-leader"?

Good leaders strive to become the worst engineer on their team. Overall, I want everyone to work with me to be better than me. I achieve this by teaching others everything I know. Team members can then build on my experience and achieve things I could only dream of. As a follow-up, my criteria for hiring someone: "Would I be ok with this person being my boss one day?" I wholeheartedly believe that every member of my current or previous team would make a phenomenal staff engineer or director.

How does one realize if leadership is the best path for themselves? How can one best transition your career into becoming a leader?

You just have to try it. It's okay to suck at being a leader—or anything. Failure at something is not a reflection of who you are as a person. There are jobs in which I have succeeded and others not so much. I learned in both instances. No questionnaire will predict whether being a leader will make you happy. As far as advice, pay attention to those individuals who are doing it now. There's a nice Mark Twain quote that says, "When I was a boy of 14, my father was so ignorant I could hardly stand to have the old man around. But when I got to be 21, I was astonished at how much the old man had learned in seven years."

66 *My favorite coworkers were ones who asked for help when they needed it and offered it when they saw that they can make my day better.* 99

As a leader, what do you value most in a team?

Kindness, understanding, and the ability to separate a job from a person that does it. I value those people who bring out the best in me by making work a pleasant environment. My favorite coworkers were ones who asked for help when they needed it and offered it when they saw that they can make my day better.

How do you consistently keep a team of software developers happy and highly productive?

Constant improvement. I help those around me refine their skills while improving weaknesses. For some, it's coding. For others, it's growing into a more senior role. Others may want to work on soft skills toward being a better citizen in the community. When my team succeeds, I succeed.

What is a piece of guidance you wish you had gotten when you started software development that you had to learn the hard way instead?

I wish I'd known that no one will be great forever. This took me years to learn that the folks on my first team were not dumb, old or lazy. They were just burnt out. I wish I spent more time learning how to be an effective engineer at times when you can no longer spend all weekends learning the latest technology. As I enter the second decade of my career, I find myself needing to plan when and where to use my brainpower and to know when I can delegate something to someone younger with a lot more energy.

In a field with a fast pace, such as software development, how do you keep learning? Are there any "secret" or lesser-known sources that you like to rely on to stay current?

Network! Folks who live in the woods have a tough time keeping up with the latest fashion.

It's like that for tech, too. I am a member of Slack communities, attend meetups, read *r/AndroidDev* everyday, subscribe to multiple tech newsletters and try to host gatherings of industry leaders when conferences are in New York. Additionally, I did consulting in addition to my standard job through my company Friendly Robot LLC. By moonlighting, I gave myself an opportunity to learn and practice techniques in new codebases—while getting paid!

What is a programmer trait that is undervalued, and why should it be taken more seriously?

I would say technical writing. My favorite mentor is one who is also able to articulately explain why his goals are aligned with others. A lot of what we do as an industry is about communication. I don't think enough time or energy is spent on our writing abilities.

Who are your mentors or people who inspire you to become a better developer and professional?

First, Jake Wharton, an active open-source GitHub member. He inspires me not only because of how much he does but how he does it. He helps developers everywhere and in any way he can. André Staltz is another inspiration. He is a great mind and was responsible for writing a blog post —"The Introduction to Reactive Programming You've Been Missing"—that finally got reactive programming to click for me. Lisa Wray is someone I'm in awe of for both her technical ability and her ability to boil down big ideas into something easy to understand; few people delight a crowd as well as she can. And, most importantly, my wife Leigh Scherrer; she switched careers three years ago to become a software engineer and has not-so-slowly been catching up to me. The race is on.

In drawing inspiration or motivation from other sources, do you prefer podcasts or books?

I prefer books and rarely listen to podcasts. Even though I have lived in the United States for 25 years, I still have trouble learning through an audio medium. Books allow me to go at my own pace. If I have trouble with a word or a term that I have not seen before, I can look it up or slow down and reread. I find it much easier to learn when I can do it at my own pace.

What are the three books that have had a lasting impact on how you do your work?

First, *Clean Code: A Handbook of Agile Software Craftsmanship* by Robert C. Martin. This book showed me the difference between writing code and being a software craftsman. *Effective Java* by Joshua Bloch is another because it was like learning all the secrets of someone's career in well-organized individual points. And, finally, *The Pragmatic Programmer: From Journeyman to Master* by Andrew Hunt and David Thomas; while many tech books deal with a particular stack, this one goes into how to deal with bosses, estimates and all the other things that I feel separate junior and senior developers.

In terms of other industry trends, what is a trend that you think is just plain wrong?

Particularly on the Android platform, there has been a movement towards "easier" libraries. The reason I put "easier" in quotes is that I am seeing a trend in which tools and libraries are becoming less robust rather than easier to use. As an industry, we should do a better job not labeling things as overly complicated when all it takes is learning what decisions were made the way they were. Dependency injection is a good example; it is a concept that may not be simple to grasp but that does not make the use of dependency injection libraries not worth it.

What are your must-have industry tools or apps you use daily that you'd recommend?

Confession: I don't use Git from the command line. My first tool suggestion is IntelliJ; JetBrains did such a great job with the Git integration within IDEA & Android Studio that I have never had to learn what Git commands do what. I'd highly recommend taking advantage of the version control integration that Android Studio has. Another is Google Play Music—I'm a deadhead (a Grateful Dead fan). There are 100+ albums of Grateful Dead music that I usually have on my headphones while coding.

For your work, how do you start your day off with a bang? Do you have any secret morning routines that set you up for success?

My alarm goes off at 7 AM. I start by catching up on the internet reading from the bed. First is *Google News* for overnight events; I enjoy starting with something that is more articles than small blurbs. Next, I spend ten minutes on an Android Slack channel where I can look at conversations that took place in parts of the world that are up while I am not. Twitter is next; I am very selective about who I follow and stick to tech only. Twitter also gives me a channel for communicating with folks from all over the world. Next is a shower and I'm off on the 8:24 AM train to New York City. My commute is split 60/40 train and walking. I am at my desk by 9:15 AM, usually, where I review pull requests and eat breakfast. I'm currently weaning myself off of croissants toward healthy breakfasts of nuts and veggies.

Finally, how do you stay highly productive in your work, for long periods?

I don't, actually. It's why I always make sure to work in a team. Even when I started a company, I did it with a co-founder. Life is about peaks and valleys; no one can go 100% all the time. It's also one of the reasons why we try to rotate engineers from doing bug fixes to doing long features to prevent burnout. If I have big projects at work, then I don't do consulting/speaking/writing. If I want to focus more on personal growth, I make sure to not take on anything big at work during that time. It is all about finding the balance that works for you.

MIKE'S RECOMMENDATIONS

Clean Code: A Handbook of Agile Software Craftsmanship | Robert C. Martin

Effective Java | Joshua Bloch

The Pragmatic Programmer: From Journeyman to Master | Andrew Hunt and David Thomas

DANNY
PREUSSLER

" *It's okay to say no.* **"**

@PreusslerBerlin github.com/dpreussler M @dpreussler
in /in/danny-preussler-557a3b79

anny is a mobile developer by heart. He lives and works in Berlin, the city he loves as much as Android. Danny signed the Software Craftsmanship manifesto as a strong believer in the value of life long learning. He dreams in clean code and could speak about unit testing all night. That's also his favorite topic when speaking or writing about Android. Danny was in charge Android for eBay's classifieds business in Germany before moving to Groupon to build a team there bringing mobile to life for merchants. Even before Android came along he programmed for mobile phones and every device that could run some kind of Java. Currently he is using his learnings about media streaming at Viacom for the music app Soundcloud. His first computer was a Robotron KC87 and he still loves technology. In fact so much he has a magnet and an NFC implant.

You've been advocating for better testing in Test-Driven Development, or TDD. How would you define "better" testing?

I've been looking into testing for quite some time now. I actually gave my first public presentation to a tech audience about ten years ago at a Blackberry developers conference. Even back then, I was focused on Unit Testing. I've learned a lot since then.

I see developers caring more about testing nowadays, which is something I really like. Especially with Android, testing wasn't a priority in the early days. Now, developers have testing in mind, but it's still not as important as it should be. When corners are cut, testing is the first thing that is skipped. But skipping testing is a bad practice.

We all look to heroes like Kent Beck, Martin Fowler, and Uncle Bob, who've contributed a lot of great quotes about testing. Martin Fowler said something to the effect of, "Refactoring without testing is like changing shit." I couldn't agree more.

You might think you can write high-quality code without testing, but once the software is out, and probably even before, things will break. This is where I believe testing is beneficial.

Tests are about so much more than testing functionality. They are documentation. They are something that the next developer can utilize. Testing is the one thing that enables effective code.

You know, I tried a lot of things in testing but, at some point, I felt there was something missing and something is still wrong. My tests were still flaky. Doing TDD solved these problems for me. In other words, I found the best way to do testing—for myself.

It sounds like you think the best way to approach testing is on an individualized basis. Is there anything developers often underestimate when we are developing our tests?

In terms of quality, I think we are not putting enough effort into the tests themselves. We learn all these rules, like not to repeat ourselves, right? Often, developers ignore this when it comes to testing. But tests should be as clean as production code. The same rules apply! Make your tests easy to change! If you change functionality, the changes in your tests should be small, as well. But very often, the reality is duplication everywhere. It's at that point when people start to hate testing. However, the real problem may be that the developers didn't apply the same principles to testing that they applied to their code.

That's an interesting perspective. I'd like to know more about how you've developed your point of view. What are some books that have had a lasting impact on how you do work?

There are several books that have made a significant impact on me. The first is *Effective Modern C++: 42 Specific Ways to Improve Your Use of C++11 and C++14* by Scott Meyers. I started my career as a C++ developer, and this book kick-started everything for me. It's still the best-written and most engaging IT book I've ever read.

Then there is *Clean Code: A Handbook of Agile Software Craftsmanship* by Robert C. Martin; it changed the way I program. It's the one book I recommend to every single developer out there.

Finally, one called *Rocket Surgery Made Easy: The Do-It-Yourself Guide to Finding and Fixing Usability Problems* by Steve Krug. It's about how all of us can easily set up user-testing. Having a big UX lab isn't necessary. Most usability bugs you find by just giving your software to someone to try. You could even take a competitor's app or website, the perfect prototype for what you probably want to build. Test those with your users. These are some examples from the book.

I'm sure we've all been impacted by resources that have become standards in the field, even if we haven't encountered those resources directly. What about your direct experience? What have you invested in, whether that investment was material, immaterial, or an investment of time, that has provided you the highest investment in terms of revenue your career?

I could mention *Clean Code* again, as I spent just a few euros on the book and it made a huge impact.

But I've also invested time in free activities that paid off in a big way. A few years ago, I started attending a software craftsmanship meetup. I met developers that had a completely different mindset. It was all about learning and coding together and getting out of our comfort zones.

I still go to one of their conferences per year. I highly recommend joining these conversations. Pairing up with someone working in a new language or on a different topic from your own is definitely worth doing.

> **❝** Don't over-engineer. I've done that... I learned to be more pragmatic and build what's needed without trying to build a spaceship. **❞**

We all have a lot to learn from each other. What is something you wish someone had told you when you started developing that you had to learn the hard way?

Don't over-engineer. I've done that. Like splitting everything into tiny modules, trying to build this one perfect system that fits everywhere. Later, I realized I had missed one point and we always will. I learned to be more pragmatic and build what's needed without trying to build a spaceship. Often, what you need later will be different than what you imagine now.

Here's another important lesson: It's okay to say no. If you know that you can't make a deadline or can't build a feature, say no. Raise your voice. I think a lot of developers don't do this. I've been in situations where everybody sat together knowing that we wouldn't make the product in time, but no one said a word. This is especially something that especially happens to junior developers.

Finally, I've learned that it's okay to fail. I mean, it happens. Learn from your failures.

Sometimes there is a collision between people who are focused on products and developers. Developers need to see the technical sides like complexity. They know timelines might not be achievable. As a software engineer, how would you face these problems? How would you let another person know that something couldn't be done or needed to be done another way? In other words, how exactly would you say no?

I'm very direct. When I need to say no, I say no and tell my reasons. If necessary, I will explain why I think something isn't possible.

That's important, if I leave just a bit of doubt, the response might be, "Yeah, but come on, give it a try." In general, I think we need to be firm when we say no. Often, saying no is an opportunity for discussion. Maybe your colleague has a different opinion for different reasons, for example.

I like when everyone puts what they have on the table. You may start with disparate opinions, and after discussing, both parties might end up somewhere new, whether or not they agree with each other. This is exactly what we need to do in this kind of situation. Is the "no" "no," or has one person missed the point? Maybe one side just understood something wrong or maybe the other person didn't know how complicated the situation was. It's important to talk things through and uncover these assumptions.

I agree. Transparency is important in these conversations.

Sometimes I feel that people in different roles speak different languages. For example, many developers don't like to talk to stakeholders because they feel the stakeholders don't speak the developer's language. The stakeholder might not understand what the developer wants to say. This is a problem.

But also, trying to understand the other's position is important. Developers don't always ask why we are doing something. In response to a job ticket, a junior developer might follow the description without asking what the point is. What is the task we are trying to achieve? Frequently, there is a better, maybe simpler way to respond. I think the more we discuss a project, the more specifically we can identify our goals. In the end, a timeline that seemed unachievable may be achieved by using different strategies.

In our industry, it seems a common aim for developers to jump up to the corporate ladder and become managers. What are your thoughts about this?

Yes, but I have a feeling things are changing here. There are still many developers out there who want to become managers. But many veteran developers are still coding and teaching. I hope that developers will stay in development but regularly dedicate a portion of their time to sharing their knowledge. They might not be coding all day. They become mentors.

I can use myself as an example. At some point, after I became a manager, I went back to development, full-time development, and went back and forth ever since.

Uncle Bob keeps saying that every five years the numbers of developers worldwide doubles. Think about the number of junior developers out there who need instruction from those of us who came before them. We may need fewer managers but more mentors.

Since you know what it's like to be both the developer and the manager, what would you tell a software developer who wants to transition to a management role?

First, I would ask why he or she wants to become a manager. Is there a desire to manage, or does it just seem like management is the next step on the career path? Are they following a perceived trend, or is it really what they want?

When considering a move to management, one question you have to ask yourself is how much you can still code, and how much do you want to code? Many developers who make the leap into management want to keep coding. On the one hand, it's great to have managers with current knowledge. On the other hand, it's difficult to play multiple roles.

Companies are finding different ways to deal with this. In the last ten years, I've seen the emergence of leadership roles for engineers like Team Lead, Architect, and other principal roles, and then there are management roles focused on managing people. In some cases, this organizational style means your boss might be paid less than you. I think this is really a game-changer.

Also, once you become a manager, two problems arise. First, it's harder to find a new job because the industry needs fewer managers than developers. Second, as a manager, by the time you're looking for a new job, your technical skills might be outdated. Who's going to hire a manager with outdated knowledge? It's important to keep these things in mind.

How do you keep yourself learning new things and staying up-to-date on every new framework technology?

I follow Android Weekly and Kotlin Weekly. Platforms like Medium send you recommendations based on what you read. Those recommendations often help expand my interests or knowledge base. But in the end, it's all about talking to people. Go to meetups. Go to conferences. It's not so much about the content you'll see. It's more about informal information sharing. I was introduced to Kotlin in this way, and one week after hearing about it, I started using it. You can't overestimate the importance of these experiences.

Another way I learn about a new topic is to talk about or blog about it! Because there's always that moment when you have to dig into the topic and you'll find out at least one thing that you didn't know before.

There is this Chinese saying, right? If you want to learn something, teach.

Yeah. It's totally true.

You've spoken at many conferences. How would you recommend someone gets started speaking at conferences?

I'd recommend starting with a meetup because it's a smaller audience. Start with an audience of ten people and work your way up. In front of a smaller group, you can be very technical. In the end, speaking at a technical conference or a technical meetup is just sharing what you know, right? It's easy to forget this. This is the one tip I would give people who are nervous to speak to a group: You're probably the person who knows the most about your topic. Talk about what you know.

Many conferences include a short format, like "lightning talks." It's much easier to do a 20-minute talk than to deliver a full hour. Start small, and ask people for feedback. Then, do it again. The second time will always be better than the first. You learn from the mistakes and from feedback, and you improve. Don't give up after the first time. Even if your first public speaking experience went well, try to give the same talk again.

Let's talk about your daily routine. How do you set yourself up for success? How do you keep working through the day?

I don't really have a morning routine. But I think the best moments are those when I'm starting with something active like going running. I live by the water, so in the summer, I like to start my day with taking the kayak out for an hour. I feel much more relaxed when I start my day with something active. I use my bike to commute to work, whether it's five minutes or 45 minutes. Exercise gives me the energy for the day I would say. Then comes the coffee, afterwards.

What's your best advice to a person starting a career in software development?

Here's an important lesson: Every developer will face a situation in which a fixed deadline requires the scope and quality of a project to flex. When you're asked to compromise quality for time, here's my advice: Don't make something quick and dirty. A temporary workaround will live much longer than you might think.

What are your views on remote work?

In my last job, I became a fan of remote work. In general, I think it's here to stay. It's the future of work. We have to learn to adapt to it because it's easy to get remote work wrong. Many people who work remotely find increased happiness. They are much happier if they can work from home, for example. They may also notice a productivity boost.

But remote work also can lead to a productivity drop for a team. For example, if everybody is sitting in one office and one person is working remotely, or if the majority of the team is in the office and a few developers are remote, the productivity will likely not increase. Often, the problem is that the workflow isn't set up to be remote-friendly.

You have to adapt a lot of your daily routines and tools to be remote-friendly. I think you only learn that if most of your developers are remote. For example, if you're trying remote work, it's best if everyone works at least one day from home a week, if only to understand the experience. There are many things like this that you need to adapt to make work remote-friendly.

In general, I love remote working. I can go to different cities and work from a café or home office, or at a conference, and I feel very productive. I like having this freedom. This is something that long-term I want to do more, but there are a lot of things that you have to get right with the team to make that possible.

How can a company implement a good remote-work policy? What are the first aspects that they should care about?

In general, a company that wants to implement remote work needs to assess whether the tools it currently uses will work in a remote setting. I think all remote teams have something like Slack, which allows everybody to communicate. A company going remote should move all discussions into this kind of tool because talking in meeting rooms leaves the remote workers out. In the end, it's all about documenting your decisions and making sure everyone has the same information.

As well, try to make remote work a nice atmosphere. I try to build this when I build a team. It's hard, but possible. For example, if you have two offices, set up a camera with a constant stream of the office so remote workers feel connected.

A company going to remote work should anticipate a lot of video conference meetups. This means using tools, and of course, tools break. You can easily waste 15 minutes trying to fix your video conferencing. Be prepared for this. Have a backup plan. Okay, Skype doesn't work today; let's all go to Hangout. The best tools aren't necessarily fancy. You can draw on a whiteboard in front of the camera. Use what tools work best for your situation.

A primary challenge is to adapt to an asynchronous way of working. We are used to synchronous communication. It gets much harder with remote work. With remote work, colleagues may be in different time zones. Answers may come six hours after questions. The whole idea of remote work is to get the best talent, and the best talent may not be local.

At some point, to accommodate time zone differences, you'll have very early or late meetings. Keep your meetings to a minimum. At one company that I worked for, we had a daily developer call held in the evening when the people in New York were waking up. We also had a daily morning meeting. So only part of the development team was there. Sometimes this was five minutes, and sometimes it was an hour but it was the most effective meeting we had. Be really pragmatic about this.

In the end, remember that even remote workers should meet face-to-face. You have to come together, not only to discuss things easily, but also to feel connected. Go out and have fun together, right? I think this is really, really important. Often, companies choose remote work because it's cheaper. Bringing people together is an additional cost that's needed to create a team feeling. Having trust between team members is so important. Face-to-face meetings help build that trust.

Many companies choose to work remotely because it's cheaper. I think a company's motivation to go remote should be a move to a global workforce. What do you think?

I totally agree. There are two things that remote work provides: The remote worker gets happiness and freedom. The company gets the best talent pool in the world. The moment we open all jobs and resources globally, we can compete for the best talent.

Is there a tool you use for remote work that is maybe not that well-known and you would like to share?

I'm a big fan of Screenhero. It may have been integrated to Slack now. I'm not sure whether Screenhero is still 0.8. It was the first tool to allow for remote pairing, which was really, really awesome.

To do pair coding right?

Exactly. With Screenhero, you could share one screen but use two mouse cursors. I think a lot of those things are integrated right into Slack so that you can draw on the other person's screen. This is super important for sharing things.

Finally, how do you stay focused through an entire day of distractions?

A lot of developers want to be in this flow, this highly concentrated mode where they don't do anything but code without interruptions. In reality, working like this is very draining. I prefer a more relaxed environment. I like to ask questions and listen to music while working.

Which brings me back to TDD. Small and continuous test cycles allow developers to build in time for distractions and interruptions.

That reminds me of another tip I'd give to a junior designer: When you have a list of things you need to do, start with the ones that are quickly done, even if they are the ones that you don't like to do. This way, you can accomplish a volume of your TODO list quickly and spend more time on the one thing that takes three or five hours. Following this system, you're not stressed at the end of the day because you didn't do all these small tasks. This has really helped me.

DANNY'S RECOMMENDATIONS

Clean Code: A Handbook of Agile Software Craftsmanship | Robert C. Martin

Effective C++: 55 Specific Ways to Improve Your Programs and Designs | Scott Meyers

MARK ALLISON

**" The secret is
hard work. "**

🐦 @MarkIAllison   blog.stylingandroid.com   github.com/StylingAndroid

Mark is a GDE for Android and software engineer with over 30 years' experience. He is passionate about providing the user with the best possible experience. He has developed both server and client side, most commonly Android on the client side, but also for iOS, HTML5, Symbian, and J2ME. Mark started writing a technical blog (blog.stylingandroid.com) in 2011, which focuses on Android UI/UX topics, but often covers more general Android development techniques. It is recognized as the longest running technical Android blog and, aside from a six-week period where contractual issues prevented him from posting, Mark has published a new article every week since 2011. In 2014, Mark started Styling Android Limited, which provides freelance software development and consultancy services. When not being geeky, Mark likes to unwind by hurling abuse at football referees, specifically those who are unkind to his beloved Watford FC with whom he holds a season ticket. Mark also loves single malt whisky. Buy him one and you'll have a friend for life!

You've been both an employee and a business owner. What are the most significant differences in how you approach your work as an employee versus an owner?

As a business owner, I find I view some things in a much more detached manner. For example, when negotiating new contracts, the head has to rule the heart and do what makes sense from a business perspective. On one occasion, I was in a position where I had two separate offers on the table for different roles, and had to choose between them. However, only one of the parties involved had actually sent me a contract, the other had promised a contract but never sent it. In that case, it reached a point where I was forced to make a decision that was based on what was right for my business and ignored my personal feelings of which one I would prefer to do.

I also view the company finances as completely separate from my own. I am an employee of the company and it is in my own best interest if the company is in a healthy financial state so that I still get paid even if the company is not in a contract for a period of time.

What would you say to someone interested in transitioning from employee to business owner?

While I love running my own business, it may not be for everyone. Discipline is required both in the financials and in doing the admin or bookkeeping tasks. Although I have an accountant who takes care of much of the tax and accounting-related issues, there is still work that I need to do.

Is there anything you miss from working at a larger, more traditional company?

Not really, but it really is a personal thing. While it is easy to say things like I miss paid vacation and getting paid if I'm sick, I don't really see that as an issue because I run my business so that I still get those benefits as an employee of my own company.

Now that you manage your own busy business, how important is networking to finding work or advancing your company?

Most of my contracts arise through word-of-mouth. I rarely go through third-party agents unless the company I'm contracting for requires it. In four and a half years, only one of my contracts has been via a third-party agent, the remainder has been direct. For the one that was via an agent, the agent was instructed to hire me by the company I would actually be working for, and I didn't find the role through the agent. So networking is hugely important when I'm on the lookout for new contracts. I have also had some luck with some Android Slack channels where I have been able to put feelers out and have private conversations with people who are hiring.

What are some tricks for successful networking?

If I'm perfectly honest, being known within the industry for my blog is incredibly useful. I have a reasonably good following on Twitter mainly because of my blog and that is really valuable when it comes to putting the word out that I'm on the lookout for a new contract position.

Your blog, *Styling Android*, is remarkable in that it publishes a new article every week. That is an impressive pace! What is the secret to consistently publishing such quality content on such a regular basis?

Be a really hard taskmaster—on yourself! It's nothing more secretive than hard work. When I first started writing my blog, I published content on an ad-hoc basis. I would write content as the ideas occurred to me, and then hit "publish" as soon as it was complete. However, quite early on, I recall reading somewhere that to grow traffic to a blog, it was important to keep a steady flow of new content. Having a somewhat compulsive nature—as I'm sure many software developers do—I decided to apply this by posting new content every week, and settled at 10 AM. UK time on Fridays. There have been many occasions over the years where I cursed myself for deciding upon such an aggressive timescale but, apart from a six-week spell in which I was unable to post for contractual reasons, I have never missed a week. Even when I have vacation scheduled, I get posts prepared for while I'm away so that I can still meet my weekly post schedule.

How do you choose what content to focus on for your site?

I try to find content that I feel either hasn't been covered elsewhere in any depth, or that I feel I can provide a different view on. On occasion, I find some cool APIs or tools of which I wasn't previously aware, and simple enthusiasm for something interesting does the rest! For the vast majority of articles, I write the supporting code first, and then the article text really describes what I learned in writing the code. If there are any pitfalls, they tend to get flushed out while I am trying to get the code working, and then they become important aspects of the article.

I always feel that a clear narrative is required. Much as a fiction story has a beginning, a middle and an end, I feel that the same is true of a technical article. At the start, there is a problem that we identify, then we go through how to solve that problem, and finally we look at how effective the solution was. I have a number of posts that never saw the light of day because that clear narrative was simply not obvious to me once I had some working code.

As a consumer of content, which do you prefer: podcasts or books?

I always find the written word has more value to me than the spoken word, so it would have to be books. One of the reasons that I prefer books is that it can be much easier to find what you're after if you need to return to a specific piece of subject matter a while later. A book often has a table of contents and/or an index that can help find relevant material later on. While some podcasts do provide a list of contents, books tend to do this much better.

What are the three resources that have had a lasting impact on how you do your work?

For Android, Mark Murphy's books are always the ones I recommend. *The Busy Coder's Guide to Android Development* is a great book for both beginners and experienced Android developers because it is so wide-ranging in its subject matter—plus, it is regularly updated so remains current. It's the book I always recommend if anyone asks me how to get started in Android, and I have even gifted subscriptions to it to a couple of people. An honorable mention has to go to Reto Meier and Ian Lake's *Professional Android*. This is another great Android book but Mark Murphy gets the nod from me because it's kept extremely current.

For more general development topics, Robert Martin's "Clean" series are helpful: *Clean Architecture: A Craftsman's Guide to Software Structure and Design*, *Clean Code: A Handbook of Agile Software Craftsmanship* and *The Clean Coder: A Code of Conduct for Professional Programmers*. These books are really great for understanding of the organization of your code, and architecture can make life so much easier not just in the short term, but for the future you who may have to maintain the code you write now!

In terms of writing good Android code, Joshua Bloch's *Effective Java* should be in every Android developer's library. Even if your project is 100% Kotlin, much of what is covered is still very relevant in a Kotlin world.

What is something you wish someone had told you back when you started software development, that you had to learn the hard way instead?

Never be afraid to discuss a problem with someone else. It doesn't matter how experienced or inexperienced you are, often if you are stuck on a particular problem, explaining it to someone else can help you to understand the problem better. Rubber-ducking can be an extremely effective debugging strategy!

Are there any current industry trends that you think are just plain wrong?

Over-reliance on specific tools can be a really bad thing. It's not the tools themselves that are the problem, but more the attitudes of developers regarding to how and where to use those tools that is the issue. This is by no means a new thing, so I'm not really highlighting a "current" trend as such, but more of a mindset problem that some developers have.

In current terms, RxJava tends to be rather over-used. Please don't misunderstand my point, I do not dislike RxJava. What I dislike is how some developers see it as the solution to every problem. I have seen code where an Observable has been used to replace a for-loop. This achieved nothing other than making the code less efficient and more difficult to understand. It is the classic example of if the only tool you ever use is a hammer, then you automatically view every problem as a nail.

As I have said, this is by no means a recent problem, or a problem specific to RxJava. Back in my time as a backend Java developer, I can remember very similar attitudes from some developers with regard to Spring Framework. On one occasion I was discussing with another developer how we might go about implementing a specific backend and while we were still scoping out the problem domain, he started typing away. When I asked what he was doing, he stated that he was setting up a Spring Framework project ready for when we had decided upon the best approach. When I questioned if it was sensible to start choosing tools before we even understood the problem, I simply got a blank look.

What would you suggest is a better alternative to this trend?

Always understand your problem domain before you decide on the appropriate tools. Always remember that a screw does not stay fixed to a piece of wood if it is hammered in rather than being screwed in with a screwdriver!

In working on your projects, how do you start your day off with a bang? Do you have any secret morning routines that set you up for success?

Every morning before I start work, I go for a long walk of around four miles / 6.5 kilometers. It's a great way to clean and organize your mind before starting work for the day. I often find that I do my best work in the morning after my walk because I have had a chance to think about how to solve the problems I'm facing. The simple fact that I'm far away from my keyboard keeps this as a time for thinking. It's also good exercise, which is important when much of my day will be sedentary.

How do you stay highly productive for long stretches of time?

I try not to work for long interrupted stretches. I always take an hour for lunch because it helps my productivity when I switch off then come back to things. If I find myself stuck on a problem, often it can help to step away from it for a while and come back.

Sometimes viewing a problem from a fresh perspective can give the necessary breakthrough.

> **"** *Every manager knows that they'll get the best out of developers if they're working on the things that they enjoy, and it provides developers with the best opportunity to do their best work.* **"**

Overall, what advice would you give to a new software developer who wants to have a satisfying career—not just a successful career?

As obvious as it sounds, find something that you enjoy doing. If going to work each day feels like a chore, then you're never going to have a satisfying career, and you're less likely to even have a successful career if your heart isn't in it. If there's a specific area that you really enjoy, then make sure that the people you work with know that, and encourage you to work on the things that you enjoy. Every manager knows that they'll get the best out of developers if they're working on the things that they enjoy, and it provides developers with the best opportunity to do their best work. So it's a win-win situation.

MARK'S RECOMMENDATIONS

The Busy Coder's Guide to Android Development | Mark L. Murphy

Clean Architecture: A Craftsman's Guide to Software Structure and Design | Robert C. Martin

Professional Android | Reto Meier and Ian Lake

THE FIRST FIVE YEARS

When Someone Says You Should Start a Blog

MARK ALLISON

"You should write a blog, you know."

D arren Steele uttered those words to me while out on a Christmas party back in December 2010, and on the 28th of March 2011, the first post to *Styling Android* was published. On the eve of the fifth anniversary of that first post it seemed a good time to reflect on those five years and to tell a little of the story behind *Styling Android*.

My initial reaction to Darren's suggestion was "I wouldn't know where to start writing a blog," yet the seed was planted and slowly germinated over my Christmas break. I approached my manager, Martin Smith, who was not only extremely receptive and supportive of the idea, but was kind enough to allow me to write those early blog posts on company time!

So I set about exploring the technical side of running a blog—I was no stranger to Linux sysadmin and was confident enough to install an Apache webserver running a WordPress instance backed by a MySql database on my home server. I wanted to self-host because I had tried third-party mail hosting solutions and always had problems because I couldn't configure things as I wanted so I still run my own mail server. I therefore wanted full control of my WordPress instance and self-hosting seemed the best option. In those early days, it was hosted on a Linux box in my home office and all of the traffic was coming through my home broadband connection.

My early posts were a little erratic in terms of regularity until I read a tip that one of the keys to building traffic to a blog was to post new content regularly. So I opted to aim to publish one post per week in order to achieve that, and soon settled upon Friday at 10 a.m. (UK time) to publish each week. The reasons for deciding upon that specific time have long since faded from my memory, but it has remained thus ever since.

Deciding upon a regular posting regime provided me with the structure I needed to actually motivate myself into trying to look for subjects to write about and get the posts written. With the exception of an unexpected six week break (more on that later), I have not missed a weekly posting since then—even for public holidays and even when I'm away on my holidays or at conferences (although very occasionally I have moved the time or day slightly).

However often you post, it's important to find a great editor. I couldn't possibly look back on the first five years of Styling Android without acknowledging the contribution of Sebastiano Poggi. Regular readers will know that over the years I have become extremely adept at including typos in my posts. When I'm organized enough to send posts over to Seb for proofreading, his keen eye and deep understanding of Android improve my posts enormously. When you read one of my posts which contain lots of errors and typos then it is probably a safe assumption that I did not send it to Seb for proof-reading before publication and I can only apologize that I wasn't better organized.

One of the early high points came in September 2011 when I published a post on ViewPager and got tweeted by the official @ AndroidDev twitter account. Sadly my poor server couldn't cope with the load and the MySql instance expired in the heat! While I got a huge spike in traffic the spike was less than it could have been so I decided that was the time to migrate to a dedicated server that wasn't sat behind my home broadband.

That was the first of a few server migrations which have occurred since. Over time the hardware / dedicated host machine has changed a few times, and I'm getting pretty adept at migrating things (hopefully the migrations are unnoticeable these days), and there are a few other changes as well such as the change from Apache web server to nginx (which also means HTTP2 support), all content served over https, etc. This all happens on top of the actual writing but such is the cost of self-hosting!

Another early high point happened slightly later in 2011 when I was approached by Lucio Maciel to speak at AndroidConf in Rio De Janeiro in November 2011. I actually received the email from Lucio when I was on a family outing with my father and two nieces at a UK theme park. It was a somewhat surreal moment to be queueing for a roller coaster and receive an email inviting me to speak at a conference in Brazil. But that proved to be the start of my conference speaking.

I am incredibly fortunate that I have been invited to speak at a number of developer conferences and attended dev events around the world since then. Sadly, I'm only able to go to a relatively small number of those that I get invited to. However, I have met a huge number of amazing and inspiring people (far too numerous to list them all). One person that I first met at Droidcon Spain in 2012 was Wiebe Elsinga. We have since become very good friends and it is one of the things that keeps me motivated to continue writing the blog that many friendships simply would not have happened without it.

It's not all been highs, though. One of the low points was when I felt I had to suspend posting for six weeks. At the time I was working for a small, independent software company who were acquired by a large U.S. multinational company (I won't name them because there's no need, but it's a global brand, although not one that's usually associated with Android). As part of the acquisition all of the employees were required to sign new contracts. The contract gave the new company the right to claim ownership of anything I produced irrespective of whether it was produced on company time or my own time.

There followed a few weeks of negotiation where I attempted to get some exclusion built in to the contract which would protect my ownership of any and all Styling Android content produced while bound by that contract, and while those negotiations were ongoing I felt that I had no option but to suspend posting until something was resolved in order to remove any possible claims over the ownership of any content published during that time.

I will stress that the company in question at no time claimed any such ownership of my content and most likely never would have—it was simply that the contract gave it the right to claim ownership. I felt uncomfortable with that and reluctantly made the decision to suspend my posting. The negotiations reached a point where it was obvious that there was no solution which satisfied both parties, and I had little option but to resign, move to a new job, and then I could resume posting.

At the same time as this, Droidcon London was approaching and I was scheduled to speak. For exactly the same reasons (ownership of my presentation materials) this was thrown in to doubt by the ongoing contract negotiations. I was in regular contact with Shivam Gadhia (who was my liaison on the Droidcon London organizing committee) and I know that my problems caused Shiv some problems of his own—it was touch and go whether I would actually be able to speak that year. As it turned out, I managed to send my resignation at 10 p.m. on the deadline day—two hours later and I wouldn't have been able to speak at Droidcon that year. Talk about cutting it fine!

One of my great fears when I first started blogging was of running out of ideas to write about. At times, my creative cup runneth over and I have posts written and ready for publication many weeks in advance but sometimes posts have been completed very close to publication time! In fact, I began writing this post in January 2016 but finished it in less than 15 minutes before publication in

March—which shows just how erratic things can be. While there have been occasions where I've come close to announcing "there won't be a post this week," I've always managed to find something to write about—and you will, too.

Here's to the next five years.

CREDIT

A version of this article was first published on *Styling Android* (March 25, 2016). The original article can be found here: /blog. stylingandroid.com/the-first-five-years/

ACKNOWLEDGEMENTS

A book is never a single-person journey. There are so many folks and friends that have supported me through this project.

First of all, my eternal gratitude goes to our clan of mentors. I would have never dreamed to gather such a gang of brilliant folks for this project. Each of them has an amazing story to tell, and after having this virtual conversation with them you will surely acquire knowledge that will stick with you during your career. They are the main ingredient of this book.

Thanks to Chris Belanger, Manda Frederick and Nicole Hardina who served as editors for this book; Tiffani Randolph for her marketing and promotion efforts; and Vicki Wenderlich and Luke Freeman for their cover design work. It has been several months of collaborating and working together. I have learned so much from you, and it was delightful to do this together. Thanks, Ray Wenderlich for believing in this initially crazy idea and agreeing to be a part of it.

A special thank you to our beta readers who generously provided feedback and editorial support: Annette Marlette, Márton Braun, Ray Wenderlich, Mark Powell, Katie Collins, Vincent Ngo, Scott McAlister, Joe Howard, Richard Critz, Victoria Gonda, Chris Belanger, Tiffani Randolph, Arthur Garza, and Ben MacKinnon.

Thanks to all my colleagues that have supported this through informal conversations, barricaded behind a cafe. Nick Skelton, Marius Budin, Xavier Jurado, César Valiente, Iñaki Villar. You listened and proposed ideas, and many of them were incorporated into this book. My gratitude for sharing your feedback.

Thanks to the GDE program, who actively supported *Living by the Code*. Thanks to Benjamin and Alina for your input and faith on the project. Thanks, David for having supported during all these years my efforts as a GDE. I am so glad to have had you as mentors as well. Thanks to all the folks that have created and worked with me on content over the years. You are the best school of knowledge I could have hoped for.

I could not have thought of a better foreword for the book than the one written by Dan Kim.

Last but not least, thank you Le Vu Nhu Quynh for your eternal patience with me. You supported me through months of ups and downs in this project. You make this world shine.

It is not possible to write each individual name on this section. That doesn't detract from all the support I had. Big thanks to all of you who made this project possible. An author is only a small gear of this fantastic machinery.

Printed in Great Britain
by Amazon

78962203R00294